INSTRUCTIONAL CLASSROOM MANAGEMENT

A Proactive Approach to Behavior Management

SECOND EDITION

Craig B. Darch
Auburn University

Edward J. Kame'enui
University of Oregon

PEARSON

Merrill
Prentice Hall

Upper Saddle River, New Jersey
Columbus, Ohio

Library of Congress Cataloging-in-Publication Data

Darch, Craig B.
  Instructional classroom management : a proactive approach to behavior management /
Craig B. Darch, Edward J. Kame'enui.—2nd ed.
    p. cm.
  Edward J. Kame'enui listed first on prev. ed.
  Includes bibliographical references and index.
  ISBN 0-13-013993-9 (pbk.)
    1. Classroom management. 2. Behavior modification. 3. School discipline. I. Kame'enui,
Edward J. II. Title.

LB3013.K32 2004
371.102'4–dc21

200204446

Vice President and Executive Publisher: Jeffery W. Johnston
Acquisitions Editor: Allyson P. Sharp
Editorial Assistant: Penny Burleson
Production Editor: Linda Hillis Bayma
Production Coordination and Text Design: Carlisle Publishers Services
Design Coordinator: Diane C. Lorenzo
Photo Coordinator: Cynthia Cassidy
Cover Designer: Thomas Borah
Cover Image: Corbis
Production Manager: Laura Messerly
Director of Marketing: Ann Castel Davis
Marketing Manager: Amy June
Marketing Coordinator: Tyra Poole

This book was set in Garamond by Carlisle Communications, Ltd. It was printed and bound by R.R. Donnelley & Sons Company. The cover was printed by Phoenix Color Corp.

Previous edition © 1995 by Addison Wesley Longman.

Photo Credits: Scott Cunningham/Merrill, pp. 2, 25, 44, 89, 126, 165, 170, 196, 201; Mary Kate Denny/Getty Images Inc.–Stone, p. 117; Laima Druskis/PH College, p. 218; Larry Hamill/Merrill, p. 178; Eugene Gordon/PH College, pp. 102, 152; David Mager/Pearson Learning, p. 182; Anthony Magnacca/Merrill, pp. 18, 29, 49, 56, 65, 70, 80, 113, 135, 174, 205, 211, 226, 230, 242; Karen Mancinelli/Pearson Learning, p. 104; Merrill, p. 110; Linda Peterson/Merrill, p. 143; Barbara Schwartz/Merrill, p. 11; Anne Vega/Merrill, pp. 8, 14, 39, 133; Tom Watson/Merrill, p. 156; David Young-Wolff/PhotoEdit, p. 192.

Pearson Education Ltd.
Pearson Education Singapore Pte. Ltd.
Pearson Education Canada, Ltd.
Pearson Education—Japan

Pearson Education Australia Pty. Limited
Pearson Education North Asia Ltd.
Pearson Educación de Mexico, S.A. de C.V.
Pearson Education Malaysia Pte. Ltd.

10 9 8 7 6 5 4 3 2 1
ISBN: 0-13-013993-9

Preface

The second edition of *Instructional Classroom Management: A Proactive Approach to Behavior Management* continues to be about managing behavior from an instructional point of view. We are convinced more than ever that effective management strategies for all ages and ability levels must begin with an educational analysis of the problem, followed by a solution grounded in instructional principles. We discuss that students can best be taught academic, behavioral, and social skills through the use of research-based instructional procedures and intervention strategies. The design and philosophy of our approach helps teachers proactively manage their school and instructional environments.

The second edition was developed for classroom teachers, school administrators, school counselors and psychologists, and professionals charged with the responsibility of guiding educational programs for students. It is comprehensive in scope, presenting a proactive management system designed to decrease student behavior problems in schools. In addition, we provide a full range of strategies for teaching and correcting disruptive behavior once it occurs. The conceptual framework of the text and the intervention strategies presented are based on current research in the field. This edition integrates current research into a management plan that is effective for an entire school year. This plan includes assessment and instruction that allow the teacher to develop teaching plans to proactively reduce the occurrence of disruptive behavior in the classroom and the school. In addition, we have developed a more comprehensive list of reinforcement strategies to use with students of all ages and ability levels.

Dr. George Sugai of the University of Oregon and his colleagues have contributed two chapters to our text. First, Chapter 7 is about teaching students social skills. Sugai and his colleagues present a plan for teachers to both assess students' social skills and teach critical social skills. The techniques discussed in this chapter are research-based and organized so that teachers can effectively implement them with students in need of social skills instruction. In addition, Sugai and his colleagues have contributed Chapter 10 on school-wide discipline and instructional classroom management. This research-based school-wide discipline system is a proactive instructional approach organized around a 180-day plan that can be effectively implemented at the classroom and school level.

A NOTE TO THE READER AND INSTRUCTOR

In this edition, we have upgraded and expanded the pedagogical features to aid instruction and learning.

- We have increased the number of instructional examples in the text to provide the reader with a range of examples of teachers managing classroom behavior. These examples illustrate our research-based guidelines and philosophy for instructional classroom management and reflect the broad range of problems teachers face in classrooms today.
- Each chapter begins with an overview outlining critical concepts.
- Each chapter ends with a brief, succinct summary.
- We have included activities for students to translate research into practice. These activities were designed to enhance the understanding of the concepts discussed in the chapters. For example, students are asked to observe in classrooms to determine the type of management strategies teachers use with disruptive students.

ACKNOWLEDGMENTS

The second edition again represents a collaborative effort extending from Eugene, Oregon, to Auburn, Alabama. As with any project, we had the assistance of colleagues, friends, and family. The ideas central to this edition of *Instructional Classroom Management* came from several of our colleagues, particularly Zig Engelmann, Douglas Carnine, and Geoff Colvin. Their research in instructional design and classroom management is reflected in each of the chapters in our text. We are grateful to Dr. George Sugai and his colleagues Shanna Hagan-Burke and Teri Lewis-Palmer for contributing chapters on social skills instruction and school-wide discipline. Their participation has strengthened this edition of *Instructional Classroom Management*.

We would also like to acknowledge colleagues who continue to influence our thinking about classroom management: Hill Walker, Deborah Simmons, Phil Browning, and Ron Eaves. We extend sincere appreciation and thanks to the following reviewers: Andrew Brulle, Wheaton College; Edwin Helmstetter, Washington State University; Colleen Randel, The University of Texas at Tyler; Brenda Scheuermann, Southwest Texas State University; and Mary Ann Waldon, Texas Southern University. We thank our editors at Prentice Hall for their support of this edition of our text. We are especially appreciative of Katie Tate, University of Oregon, who provided us with valuable assistance in the preparation of the manuscript.

Finally, our deepest gratitude goes to our families: Brenda, Bree, and Ani Kame'enui and Gabriele and Eric Darch. Brenda Kame'enui has served as our personal editor for this edition. We could not have completed this book without her help.

Discover the Companion Website Accompanying This Book

THE PRENTICE HALL COMPANION WEBSITE: A VIRTUAL LEARNING ENVIRONMENT

Technology is a constantly growing and changing aspect of our field that is creating a need for content and resources. To address this emerging need, Prentice Hall has developed an online learning environment for students and professors alike— Companion Websites—to support our textbooks.

In creating a Companion Website, our goal is to build on and enhance what the textbook already offers. For this reason, the content for each user-friendly website is organized by topic and provides the professor and student with a variety of meaningful resources. Common features of a Companion Website include:

For the Professor—

Every Companion Website integrates **Syllabus Manager**™, an online syllabus creation and management utility.

- **Syllabus Manager**™ provides you, the instructor, with an easy, step-by-step process to create and revise syllabi, with direct links into Companion Website and other online content without having to learn HTML.
- Students may logon to your syllabus during any study session. All they need to know is the web address for the Companion Website and the password you've assigned to your syllabus.
- After you have created a syllabus using **Syllabus Manager**™, students may enter the syllabus for their course section from any point in the Companion Website.
- Clicking on a date, the student is shown the list of activities for the assignment. The activities for each assignment are linked directly to actual content, saving time for students.

- Adding assignments consists of clicking on the desired due date, then filling in the details of the assignment—name of the assignment, instructions, and whether it is a one-time or repeating assignment.
- In addition, links to other activities can be created easily. If the activity is online, a URL can be entered in the space provided, and it will be linked automatically in the final syllabus.
- Your completed syllabus is hosted on our servers, allowing convenient updates from any computer on the Internet. Changes you make to your syllabus are immediately available to your students at their next logon.

For the Student—

- **Overview and General Information**—General information about the topic and how it will be covered in the website.
- **Web Links**—A variety of websites related to topic areas.
- **Content Methods and Strategies**—Resources that help to put theories into practice in the special education classroom.
- **Reflective Questions and Case-Based Activities**—Put concepts into action, participate in activities, examine strategies, and more.
- **National and State Laws**—An online guide to how federal and state laws affect your special education classroom.
- **Behavior Management**—An online guide to help you manage behaviors in the special education classroom.
- **Message Board**—Virtual bulletin board to post and respond to questions and comments from a national audience.

To take advantage of these and other resources, please visit the *Instructional Classroom Management: A Proactive Approach to Behavior Management,* Second Edition, Companion Website at

www.prenhall.com/darch

Brief Contents

Contents

Chapter 6   **Using Reinforcement to Increase Student Motivation   126**

Chapter 7   **Social Skills Instruction in the Classroom   152**

Chapter 8   **Punishment: A Transition Tool Only   174**

Chapter 9   **Managing Persistent Behavior Problems: Strategies and Examples   196**

NOTE: Every effort has been made to provide accurate and current Internet information in this book. However, the Internet and information posted on it are constantly changing, and it is inevitable that some of the Internet addresses listed in this textbook will change.

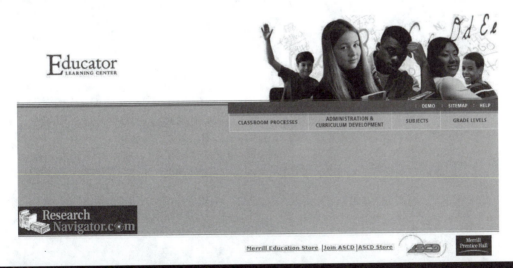

Chapter

1

Classroom Management and the Context of Instruction

OVERVIEW

- Management and the Context of Instruction
- Orientation of the Text
- Thinking About Behavior Management
  Can't Versus Won't Problems
- Assumptions About Instructional Management
  Organizing Principles About the Learner
  Organizing Principles About the Teacher
- Summary

In this text, we offer an approach to classroom and behavior management that is different, but not altogether unfamiliar. In fact, the procedures may look so familiar they don't appear different from the typical classroom practice of behavior management. However, the approach we describe is greatly different conceptually, theoretically, and philosophically, because it is concerned with instruction and based on the instructional requirements for managing and organizing behavior. While the general requirements of instruction are obviously familiar to practitioners, what may be most challenging is the subtle, yet enormous shift in how to think about instruction in the context of managing children's social and academic behavior.

According to literary folklore, Mark Twain once remarked, "The difference between the almost right word and the right word is really a large matter—'tis the difference between the lightning bug and the lightning." The difference between behavior management (or a strict behavioral approach to classroom management) and instructional management is also a large matter, not unlike the difference between the lightning bug and the lightning. Just as a one-word change between *lightning bug* and *lightning* appears subtle and insignificant but represents a significant change in meaning, the semantic difference between behavior management and instructional management is a subtle but significant change in thinking about instruction, children's behavior, teaching, and the context of instruction itself. The difference is perhaps best captured in the words *reactive* and *proactive*.

In this text, we argue that the primary difference between an instructional approach to classroom management and all other approaches (*all* other approaches; not some, or a few, but all) is that an instructional approach is proactive. This means that *before* an action or problem occurs, *the teacher teaches carefully and strategically all that is required so that students have the information necessary to perform or behave appropriately*. More importantly, the teacher's systematic teaching sets up numerous opportunities for reinforcing what's been taught and communicating to students how well they are doing as reflective and problem-solving citizens of a school (Simmons et al., 2002).

"Teaching carefully and strategically" all that is required for students to perform or behave appropriately sounds like what most teachers do on a daily basis. However,

3

the shift in a teacher's focus and thinking on a day-to-day basis is profound and necessary if instructional management is to be successful.

The basic assumption of the instructional classroom management (ICM) approach we propose in this text is that teachers must first teach students how to behave in every circumstance for which appropriate behavior is expected by the teacher and school officials. This may appear to be a tall order, but it's not; in fact, it represents exactly what we expect of ourselves as teachers—to teach. More importantly, the opportunity to create new ways of behaving is initiated by the teacher, who takes advantage of those opportunities to reinforce newly taught behaviors, actions, and events.

In contrast to a proactive instructional approach to classroom management are behavioral, psychological, and social approaches, all of which are basically reactive. In reactive approaches, the teacher intervenes after an inappropriate action occurs— after a child shouts out an answer, or after students come into the classroom in a noisy and disruptive manner, or after students are caught cheating on homework. The list is indeed endless. In short, the teacher simply "acts back" and fails to prepare the learner to successfully demonstrate skills taught before "appropriate behavior" is demanded by the environment. Although an instructional approach is concerned with teaching and not simply reacting to problems, it is difficult to fully appreciate how different this approach is from traditional approaches to classroom management.

Many requirements of effective classroom management are obvious and are known intuitively and experientially by teachers and school administrators. For example, we know the importance of (a) developing and setting rules on the first day of school; (b) establishing acceptable limits of social behavior in the classroom, playground, and cafeteria; (c) praising acceptable behavior while providing explicit and sometimes immediate consequences for unacceptable behavior; (d) providing consistent consequences for unacceptable behaviors every time they surface; (e) maintaining clear and consistent expectations of student behavior throughout the entire school year; and (f) creating and nurturing a positive, engaging, and safe classroom environment that encourages students to take academic risks and doesn't punish them for making mistakes.

However, what is not so obvious is that these procedures known intuitively by teachers and school administrators are more than simply classroom and behavior management procedures. They are first and foremost, *instructional procedures*. When teachers manage (i.e., handle, direct, govern, control, *The Random House Dictionary of The English Language*) social behavior, they assume students have been taught or know instinctively how to act (or not act), react, move, respond, acknowledge, gesture, and in general, behave. If students don't *know* (i.e., the information is not clear, and students are uncertain) how to behave, then they must be taught how to meet the expectations the environment is placing on them. In the absence of this information and teaching, the "management" of human beings who don't know how to behave is, at best, chaotic. Therefore, the process of managing social behavior is more than a matter of managing student behavior within a social context through delivery or withdrawal of praise (reinforcers) and reprimands (punishers).

For all practical purposes, classroom management is the management of instruction. But this way of thinking about classroom management is often lost or ignored in the research, even when it is made by those who have studied classroom management in a substantial and serious way. For example, in interviews with classroom teachers, Brophy and his colleagues (cited in Wong, Kauffman, & Lloyd, 1991) found that "teachers rated by their principals as more effective in dealing with chronic behavior problems reported using interventions that *teach* students how to behave. That is, they said they usually tried to teach misbehaving students something about how to behave appropriately, not just assert their authority or control over students" (p. 109, emphasis added). Clearly, the role of teaching is profoundly important in classroom and behavior management approaches. However, what's missing from the genre of classroom management approaches is an approach that has instruction as its centerpiece and foundation. Instruction is the anchoring concept in instructional classroom management.

MANAGEMENT AND THE CONTEXT OF INSTRUCTION

The process of classroom management always takes place within the context of instruction—a context in which information is always changing hands or being clarified and exchanged between the teacher and students, between student and student, and between teachers and administrators or parents. In this context the teacher designs and sends a message to a student about what is acceptable and unacceptable behavior or performance. The message could be something straightforward and simple, such as, "Thanks for parking your bike at the bicycle rack," or the message could be general and abstract, such as, "You are expected to use respectful language at all times in school." If the message is reasonably clear, the student receives the message and interprets it based on his or her experience, disposition, background knowledge, prior learning history, and the immediate social context. In short, the student attempts to assign meaning to the message. In the process of instruction, the teacher is responsible for sending clear, unambiguous messages to students, not only about unfamiliar academic concepts such as those in science (e.g., learning about friction and machines), reading (e.g., discerning the theme of Jack London's "To Build a Fire"), math (e.g., finding prime numbers), and social studies (e.g., learning why groups of people moved from place to place), but also about "familiar" concepts of acceptable social behavior in the school environment (e.g., "You are expected to use respectful language at all times in school"). The substance of these messages, as well as their clarity, frequency, and intensity, comprises the *process of instruction*. The teacher must design communication of these messages in ways that increase the probability students will receive clear and unambiguous signals about how to behave, both socially and academically (Bernstein, 1998).

ORIENTATION OF THE TEXT

Our orientation in this text is on the instructional process for managing behavior and not simply on the management process for merely reinforcing (increasing), shaping (gradually increasing), or punishing (decreasing) behavior. We do not consider classroom management a set of conditions and activities separate from instruction. When teachers manage, they also teach or communicate information to students about how to behave or perform (or how not to behave or perform). By thinking about classroom management and classroom instruction as significant parts of the same process, teaching is likely to be clearer, more focused and balanced, more sustaining, and more enriching for both teachers and students over the course of a school year.

The approach we offer in this text assumes the teacher first teaches students, thoroughly and carefully, how to behave or perform. In essence, the teacher provides all necessary information to students about what is appropriate in both the school and classroom settings. Although managing and controlling student behavior is part of the instructional management process, our primary emphasis is on instruction, not management. At first glance, this difference may seem small, and perhaps trivial, but it is not. As noted earlier, the differences between behavior management and instructional management are profound.

THINKING ABOUT BEHAVIOR MANAGEMENT

One profound difference is how so-called "behavior" or management problems are conceptualized or considered (Kame'enui & Simmons, 1997; Sugai, Kame'enui, Horner, Simmons, & Coyne, in press). Specifically, Colvin and Sugai (1988) argue that educators (i.e., administrators, teachers, teacher trainers) often approach instructional problems differently from social behavior problems. For example, when a student makes a persistent error on a complex reading comprehension skill such as identifying the main idea in a passage, we engage in a range of instructional strategies. We might prompt the student to scan and reread a particular passage in the story, or we might engage in a facilitative questioning procedure (Carnine, Silbert, & Kame'enui, 1997) to assist the reader to think through the various propositions in the passage. Following this teacher assistance, we might provide more practice and review for the student on a range of passages. If the errors persist, then additional remedial steps are taken to diagnose the problem and rearrange the teaching presentation and schedule of instruction to allow the student to succeed.

All of these steps are taken to ensure the child will succeed, because the teacher has conceptualized the student's error as an academic learning problem and not a management one. In contrast, when a social behavior problem occurs, we frequently respond in a very different way. When a student breaks a classroom rule, such as calling out an answer without raising a hand, the instinctive response is to "punish" the rule breaker by using a verbal reprimand (e.g., "You need to raise your hand; you know the rules!"). In some cases, we might even ask the student to leave the room (e.g., "How many times have I told you to raise your hand? I think it's time for you to sit out in the hall and think about how to behave the right way."). The underlying assumption of these approaches is that negative consequences are likely to change the child's behavior in the future (e.g., removing the student from the classroom will cause him or her to behave appropriately in the future). The approach is clearly reactive, not proactive. In many cases, when one negative consequence doesn't work (e.g., verbal reprimand), the teacher increases the level of negative consequences (e.g., exclusionary time out, detention) (Sugai, 1992; Sugai et al., in press).

Of course, the responses to any kind of perceived misbehavior vary considerably from teacher to teacher. For example, one teacher may choose to ignore the in-

TABLE 1.1   A Comparison of Approaches to Academic and Social Problems

Frequency of Effort	Procedures for Academic Problem	Procedures for Social Problem
Infrequent	Assume student is trying to make a correct response.	Assume student is not trying to make a correct response.
	Assume error was accidental. Provide assistance (model-lead-test).	Assume error was deliberate. Provide negative consequence.
	Provide practice. Assume student had learned skills and will perform correctly in the future.	Practice not required. Assume student will make right choice and behave appropriately in future.
Frequent (Chronic)	Assume student has learned the wrong way.	Assume student refuses to cooperate.
	Assume student has been taught (inadvertently) the wrong way.	Assume student knows what is right and has been told often.
	Diagnose the problem.	Provide more negative consequences.
	Identify misrule.	Withdraw student from normal context.
	Adjust presentation. Focus on rule. Provide feedback. Provide more practice and review.	Maintain student removal from normal context.
	Assume student has been taught skill and will perform correctly in future.	Assume student has "learned" lesson and will behave appropriately in future.

Source: From "Proactive Strategies for Managing Social Behavior Problems: An Instructional Approach," by G.T. Colvin and G.M. Sugai, 1988, *Education and Treatment of Children, 11*(4), 341–348. Reprinted with permission.

appropriate behavior, while another praises a behavior that is incompatible with the misbehavior (e.g., praise a student who raises a hand), and still another teacher acknowledges the behavior with a long, stern, nonverbal glare at the bewildered violator. Though the responses are different in their physical action (e.g., verbal praise, glare), they are the same in at least four important ways. The responses are all (a) reactive (i.e., the teacher acts only after the behavior occurs), (b) predicated on the assumption that the learner already knows (i.e., understands clearly and with certainty) how to respond appropriately, (c) predicated on the assuption that the learner is capable of responding appropriately, and (d) confident that the negative consequence will increase the probability the inappropriate behavior will decrease in the future.

The differences between the approach to academic problems and the approach to social problems as described by Colvin and Sugai (1988) are summarized in Table 1.1.

Can't Versus Won't Problems

The basic difference between an instructional approach to an academic error and a noninstructional approach to a social error is how one thinks about it. When a learner makes an academic error (e.g., learner can't name the 13th President of the United States), we usually think about it as a *can't* problem; that is, we assume the learner simply doesn't know the answer and, therefore, can't respond correctly (Kame'enui & Simmons, 1997). We make the reasonable assumption that it's impossible for the learner to come up with the answer from out of the blue, just as it is impossible for the learner to walk through a concrete wall. The assumption is

It is important teachers understand the motivation behind a student's behavior in the classroom.

reasonable, and we give it no second thought. The primary solution to the learner's lack of knowledge is to tell him or her the answer, or to develop a teaching strategy or problem-solving sequence to communicate the skills needed to answer the question previously deemed unanswerable by the student.

On the other hand, if a learner misbehaves, we usually assume the problem is a *won't* problem; that is, the learner knows how to behave or knows the correct response but chooses not to behave or respond appropriately. Teachers may be familiar with a student who says, "No, I won't do it. I *can* do it, but I won't!"

Understanding the difference between a can't problem and a won't problem is important, because a misdiagnosis can cause serious management and learning problems in the short run and the long run. If we treat a can't problem as a won't problem, we end up unfairly punishing the learner and losing trust necessary for effective instruction. In contrast, if we incorrectly treat a won't problem as a can't problem, we end up inappropriately reinforcing the learner's prior history of deception and agitation. Moreover, we lose the authority necessary to effective instructional management, and the student avoids responsibility for his or her learning and performance.

By approaching social behavior errors or problems from an instructional point of view, we guard against the misdiagnosis of both can't and won't types of problems, because we engage in a set of decision rules that examines a child's misbehavior within an instructional context. By viewing potential behavior problems as instructional problems, the teacher knows what skills have been taught, reviewed, and mastered, just as a teacher knows what specific reading or mathematics skills or operations have been taught, reviewed, and mastered. A teacher wouldn't require a child, for example, to work multidigit subtraction problems involving renaming if the teacher knew the student had not mastered the prerequisite skills (e.g., knowledge of basic facts, numeral identification, the concepts of more than and less than) (Kame'enui & Simmons, 1997). By knowing what has been taught, what needs to be taught, and what the learner already knows, the teacher avoids the pitfalls of both *can't* and *won't* problems.

Schwartz and Lacey (1982) argue that, "How we understand an event can have a dramatic impact on what we do about it" (p. 2). Certainly how we *think we understand* a problem influences how we act on that problem. As noted earlier, if we understand a problem to be a *can't* problem, we are likely to act differently than if we think of the same problem as a *won't* problem. Moreover, Alderman and Nix (1997) suggest that understanding the causes will increase appreciation of the complexities of behavior, and "when greater understanding of problems is achieved, the problem looks different" (p. 92). For example, teachers who attribute a student's behavior to genetic or medical causes might consider environmentally based behavioral interventions ineffective. According to Alderman and Nix (1997), teachers are more likely to choose negative, punitive (e.g., verbal reprimands) strategies to control behavior in the absence of information about the causes of learning and behavior problems. Teachers who have information on causes focus more on positive, instructional interventions (Alderman & Nix, 1997).

To appreciate the instructional approach to classroom management, consider the problem of lying. Lying is not generally considered an instructional problem (Kame'enui & Simmons, 1997) but is often viewed as a devious social misbehavior, akin to a fundamental character flaw. The problem of lying is a tricky one to "manage" for at least three reasons. First, it generally represents a low-frequency behavior. Second, it is difficult to discern where truth ends and lying actually begins. Finally, we respond to lying only after a child has lied. Not surprisingly, children typically lie to avoid punishment or gain attention.

To punish a child for lying is to make at least one very clear assumption: The child knows how to tell the truth. Interestingly and not surprisingly, this assumption is rarely ever tested. A child who lies may simply not know how to tell the truth in much the same way a child who misreads the word *paint* does not know how to read the *ai* vowel combination in the middle of a word. In other words, what is perceived, accepted, and treated as a *won't* problem (i.e., not telling the truth) may actually be a *can't* problem (i.e., not knowing how to tell the truth). No matter how much a child wants to tell the truth, truth telling may not be something the child knows how to do.

Kame'enui and Simmons (1997) provide a beginning teaching sequence to teach the skill of telling the truth. The teaching sequence consists of the teacher requiring a learner to perform some rather obvious and unchallenging tasks, such as picking up a pencil on a desk or walking to a spot in the classroom and returning to the teacher. The teacher frames the teaching sequence by telling the learner that she will be asked to perform some silly actions and report the actions by telling "exactly what she did." After performing a request (e.g., picking up a green pencil and returning it to the teacher), the teacher asks the child to state exactly what she did. The child states, "I walked over to your desk and picked up the green pencil and brought it to you." After the child describes exactly what she did, the teacher responds with a rule: "When you tell someone exactly what you did, you are telling the truth. You just told me exactly what you did, so you told me the truth."

Although the "truth telling" teaching sequence is incomplete and represents only the beginning of an instructional strategy for this significant problem, it demonstrates that how we respond to a management problem depends in part on how we come to understand the problem.

ASSUMPTIONS ABOUT INSTRUCTIONAL MANAGEMENT

As we noted, the actions we take as teachers depend in large part on how we choose to understand a problem, whether it's a problem of lying or decoding single syllable words. The knowledge of teaching—subject matter, pedagogy, instructional procedures—that a teacher brings to the classroom is certainly important to being an effective teacher. However, what a teacher believes about his or her ability to affect how children learn, behave, and perform is also important.

We propose a set of ongoing principles we consider critical to an instructional approach to classroom management. We characterize these as ongoing principles because they represent the principles or premises on which an instructional approach to classroom management is built. These principles provide the teacher a foundation for managing children within the broader context of instruction. By holding to the principles, we believe teachers will identify behavior problems in ways that translate into instructional solutions.

What is important is not only the principles themselves, but also the process of reflection and professional commitment implied by them—a process in which the teacher drives some pedagogical or philosophical stakes into the ground and announces, "These principles are important to me as a professional and a teacher and will serve to guide my performance as a teacher." In a sense, the principles reflect the teacher's commitment to the teaching profession and to all children, irrespective of their diverse learning and curricular needs.

The principles are developed in two areas of the teaching and schooling context that include learner and teacher (see Figure 1.1). For each context, three principles are described. Of course, more principles can be developed about each context, but for purposes of this text, we begin with these. The principles presented here are merely representative of considerations teachers should give to each context.

The first set of organizing principles is about the learner and is intended to examine how the teacher should view the learner.

Learner

Principle 1: The learner should always be treated with respect.
Principle 2: Every learner has an extraordinary capacity to learn.
Principle 3: The learner's behavior or performance is always purposeful, strategic, and intelligent.

Teacher

Principle 1: The teacher makes a profound difference in how, what, when, and why students learn.
Principle 2: Teaching involves creating as many opportunities as possible for successful learning.
Principle 3: Effective teaching enhances what the learner already knows and enables the learner to do things that could not be done before.

FIGURE 1.1 Organizing principles about learners and teachers.

Organizing Principles About the Learner

Principle 1: The learner should always be treated with respect.

This principle represents a truism in education, but it is one easily forgotten when serious and chronic behavior management problems surface, or when a learner, saddled with a history of academic or social failure, continues to make little progress in school. In situations such as these, it is easy to "blame the learner," and the effort required to overcome the temptation to give up on the learner is great.

Treating the learner with respect when he or she is behaving appropriately is not a challenge. However, when the learner is disruptive, abusive, deceptive, inconsiderate, threatening, or, in the colloquialism of street culture, "in your face," then it is certainly a challenge to treat the learner with respect. Respectful treatment means, at the very minimum, not responding to inappropriate behavior by physically or verbally assaulting a student. In rare cases, students may need to be physically restrained, but even under these conditions, the restraining must be conducted in a professional manner that respects the student. Unfortunately, situations that involve verbal or physical threats are very difficult for teachers, because the "heat" of the moment typically prompts teachers to respond in a heated way, which is understandable. However, these are unusual circumstances that require unusually controlled responses from teachers.

Principle 2: Every learner has an extraordinary capacity to learn.

An instructional approach to classroom management requires that teachers hold to the principle that every learner has an extraordinary capacity to learn. As we have discussed earlier, the principle says "every learner" and does not refer to "some" learners or the "average" learner. In this case, *every* means each individual in the

When teachers create a positive learning environment, students enjoy interacting with their peers.

classroom, irrespective of accompanying social and educational labels, prior school history, or family circumstance. Simply, every individual has the capacity to learn what is being communicated in the classroom. In the absence of this principle, an instructional approach to classroom management based on clear and effective communication of information is meaningless. If information is not acquired, retained, or recalled by students, then both the content and delivery of the information must be reexamined by the teacher to ensure that all learners acquire, retain, and recall it. However, the burden to communicate the information clearly and effectively in this case is placed on the teacher, not the student. In short, the teacher makes every effort to explore the instructional remedies available within his or her province, and in doing so, refrains from blaming the learner for failure to learn.

This principle may resemble other slogans about children frequently cited in educational circles. However, holding to this principle is not easy and will require an instructional tenacity that thinks about student performance in a different way. It requires framing problems in terms of instruction and not in terms of a learner's ability, learning style, motivation, or learning history. As Kame'enui and Simmons (1997) note, "To assume that a problem is inherent in the learner leaves the teacher without any influence, because the problem is framed as being outside of the teacher's province of control (i.e., in the learner's head)" (p. 13).

Principle 3: The learner's behavior or performance is always purposeful, strategic, and intelligent.

It seems a basic predisposition of human beings is to feel valued. As such, human beings engage in activities and events that are likely to be rewarding to them in both the short and long term. However, one of the oddities of human behavior is that we often repeatedly engage in behaviors that do not appear to be rewarding and valued. This is particularly true of children who have significant histories of academic and social failure. For example, a child who has failed repeatedly, like the child who has succeeded repeatedly, learns from the experience and understands, in a shrewd and perceptive way, the circumstances of his or her own failure and what works best in a particular context. If a behavior or a series of behaviors that leads to some kind of punishment is repeated by a learner, it is safe to assume the consequences of the behavior are valued or are reinforcing for the learner in some way. A specific example is a child who does something very foolish, such as hitting a teacher. While this behavior appears to be stupid, it is for the learner purposeful, strategic, and intelligent, because in the long run, the learner fundamentally changes how the environment will respond. In this case, the learner finds that the teacher places fewer academic and social demands on her, avoids potentially troublesome situations, and simply leaves her alone. What initially appeared "stupid" might be viewed as purposeful and intelligent by the learner.

By viewing the learner's behavior as purposeful, strategic, and intelligent, we position ourselves in a way that is reflective and allows for problem solving, because it broadens the context in which responses to a child's behavior are considered. By viewing a response as intelligent, instead of stupid, we are prompted to problem solve by considering ways in which the inappropriate response best serves the learner in a particular situation. We must determine how best to respond to the perceived unintelligent behavior in an equally purposeful, strategic, and intelligent manner.

Organizing Principles About the Teacher

The principles described in this section relate to how teachers view their profession, their role as significant forces in the lives of children, and themselves.

Principle 1: The teacher makes a profound difference in how, what, when, and why students learn.

Most people are able to identify by name a teacher who made a profound difference in their schooling experience. This difference, however, can be profoundly good or profoundly bad. More than a decade ago, Ernest Boyer (1990), as United States Commissioner of Education, noted that, "The harsh truth is that teaching in this nation is imperiled. There are poor teachers, to be sure, and one bad teacher is more dangerous than one bad surgeon, because a surgeon can only hurt one person at a time. But good teachers outnumber the bad . . . " (p. 3).

Not surprisingly, what makes a teacher "good" or "bad" is constantly debated, even though some characteristics of good teachers (or bad teachers, for that matter) are intuitive and straightforward. Interestingly, the research on teachers' perceptions of their ability to make a difference in children's learning suggest that what teachers believe about their role and ability to bring about change influences how and what they teach. For example, Smylie (1988) notes "Teachers' perceptions of their own ability to affect student learning have been associated with their choice of classroom management and instructional strategies" (p. 6). Teachers are more likely to change their behavior to improve their classroom practice if they believe they are instrumental in student learning. In order for teachers to feel instrumental in their students' learning, they must be certain of their practices, and they must hold a high sense of "personal teaching efficacy"; that is, they must believe they have the capacity to directly affect a student's performance. If teachers feel competent and confident in their teaching tools and instructional strategies, they are likely to make a profound and positive difference in how, what, when, and why students learn.

A teacher's sense of efficacy is a powerful variable related to student outcomes such as achievement (Ross, 1998), motivation (Midgley, Feldlaufer, & Eccles, 1989), and self-esteem (Anderson, Greene, & Loewen, 1988). Teachers who feel efficacious are open to new ideas and are more willing to utilize new teaching and management methods to better meet the needs of students. Efficacy also influences teacher persistence when things don't go smoothly and increases resilience in the face of setbacks. The "Nonreciprocal Laws of Expectations" state that negative expectations yield negative results. The corollary of this law suggests that positive expectations yield positive results. If teachers believe they can make a difference in children's school performance, then they very likely will.

In addition to teachers' beliefs, the recent research on staff development suggests several other conditions necessary to bring about significant and sustained educational improvements. These include, for example, (a) the importance of strong support for teachers from both principals and superintendents (Berman & McLaughlin, 1978), (b) collegial support (Little, 1982), and (c) strong instructional leadership at the school and classroom level. While support of teachers at every level of the

An active teacher creates many successful learning opportunities for students.

school process is important, substantial convergence of the research continues to support one clear and simple fact: Teachers engaged in the process of teaching do make a difference (Whitehurst, 2002). Similarly, not teaching also makes a difference. If we were to dispense with the teaching of beginning reading or of mathematics altogether, would there be any question as to the outcomes for students?

Principle 2: Teaching involves creating as many opportunities as possible for successful learning.

Most models of school learning include as an important component the opportunities schools provide for learning. The logic to these models is straightforward, that the quantity and quality of learning opportunities is directly related to successful student performance in school. For example, Carroll's (1963) economic model of the school learning process argues that "the learner will succeed in learning a given task to the extent that he spends the amount of time that he *needs* to learn the task" (p. 725).

The principle we propose acknowledges that the process of teaching involves creating opportunities for successful learning. Of course, these opportunities go beyond the typical teaching schedule in which specific blocks of time are allotted for basic subject matter (e.g., reading, mathematics, social studies). An instructional approach to classroom management requires teachers to maximize both the "scheduled" and "unscheduled" opportunities for learning. More importantly, however, this principle requires a different way of thinking about managing and organizing instruction. For example, consider a definition of *positive reinforcement,* which Wolery, Bailey, and Sugai (1988) define as "the contingent presentation of a stimulus following a response that results in an increase in the future occurrence of the response" (p. 235).

Definitions of positive reinforcement from a behavioral perspective on classroom management won't vary greatly. Positive reinforcement generally has two essential but limiting features. First, the power of a reinforcer can only be determined by what happens to a child's response in the *future*. Second, the teacher's response always *follows* the student's response. These two features are noteworthy because they bring into perspective the limitations of a behavioral approach, and at the same time, the advantages of an instructional approach to classroom management. If we are concerned with increasing the likelihood a response will occur again in the future, then the more opportunities we create to influence the learner's behavior, the more likely the target behavior will occur. Instructional classroom management requires the creation of as many opportunities as possible for successful learning.

The other feature of a behavioral approach is that reinforcement always follows the learner's response, which suggests the learner must "emit" a response in order for reinforcement to take place. In short, reinforcement is reactive, not proactive. An instructional approach to positive reinforcement (a) first teaches students what should be reinforced; (b) increases the opportunities to practice what was taught, which also involves reinforcement; and (c) primes the context for reinforcement through a set of "preteaching" or "precorrection" and "framing" instructional procedures. These procedures and the analysis of reinforcement will be discussed further in Chapter 6. By understanding the requirements and dynamics of reinforcement, we can appreciate the power of instruction and how reinforcement enhances successful learning.

Principle 3: Effective teaching enhances what the learner already knows and enables the learner to do things that could not be done before.

This principle is borrowed from Kame'enui and Simmons (1997) who recognize "the often unacknowledged and unspoken power and influence a teacher holds in the teaching context" (p. 10). The principle clearly underscores the importance of the schooling process and is predicated on the simple proposition that schools are designed to take a learner from a state of "unknowing" or partial knowing to a state of full and complete "knowing" (Carroll, 1963; Simmons et al., 2002). This analysis is admittedly an oversimplification of the complexities inherent in the processes of teaching, learning, and schooling. However, to understand the full measure of the complexities requires applying some "simplifying assumptions" (Carroll, 1963, p. 724).

In a simple but poignant way, Principle 3 captures the potential excitement and power of what successful teaching is all about, the simple notion that one can come to know something entirely new that was not known before. Or one can come to know something more fully that was known before in only a partial way. This new state of knowing is limitless and includes the full range of human experience and knowledge—from reading simple words (e.g., *sat, am, bit*) to understanding the complexities of words such as *contronym, eonomine,* and *hendiadys;* from naming a pair of pliers as a tool to identifying pliers as a first-class lever; from knowing nothing of Shakespeare's play *King Lear,* to explaining its significance as a tragedy; from identifying an event, to understanding its significance in terms of probability theory. The list is endless.

SUMMARY

In this chapter, we presented a rationale for what we characterize as an Instructional Classroom Management (ICM) approach. We argue that when teachers manage behavior, they also teach. Behavior management procedures are by their very nature instructional procedures, because management always takes place in the context of instruction. We recognize this shift in thinking about management as instruction is not easy. It will require teachers to examine the assumptions they make about the learner, the context of instruction, and the significant role they play in the daily lives of children.

REFERENCES

Alderman, G., & Nix, M. (1997). Teachers' intervention preferences related to explanations for behavior problems, severity of the problem, and teacher experience. *Behavioral Disorders, 22,* 87–95.

Anderson, R., Greene, M., & Loewen, P. (1988). Relationships among teachers' and students' thinking skills, sense of efficacy, and student achievement. *Alberta Journal of Educational Research, 34,* 148–165.

Berman, P., & McLaughlin, M. (1978). *Federal programs supporting educational change (vol. 3): Factors affecting implementation and continuation* (Report No. R-1589/7-HEW). Santa Monica, CA: The Rand Corporation.

Bernstein, P. L. (1998). *Against the gods: The remarkable story of risk.* New York: John Wiley & Sons.

Boyer, E. (1990). Introduction: Giving dignity to the teaching profession. In D. D. Dill and Associates (Eds.), *What teachers need to know: The knowledge, skills, and values essential to good teaching* (pp. 1–10). San Francisco: Jossey-Bass.

Carnine, D. W., Silbert, J., & Kame'enui, E. J. (1997). *Direct instruction reading* (3rd ed.). Upper Saddle River, NJ: Merrill/Prentice Hall.

Carroll, J. B. (1963). A model of school learning. *Teachers College Record, 64,* 723–733.

Colvin, G. T., & Sugai, G. M. (1988). Proactive strategies for managing social behavior problems: An instructional approach. *Education and Treatment of Children, 11*(4), 341–348.

Flexner, S. (Ed.). (1987). *The Random House dictionary of the English Language.* New York: Random House.

Kame'enui, E. J., & Simmons, D. C. (1997). *Designing instructional strategies: The prevention of academic learning problems.* Upper Saddle River, NJ: Merrill/Prentice Hall.

Little, J. W. (1982). Norms of collegiality and experimentation: Workplace conditions and school success. *American Educational Research Journal, 19,* 325–340.

Midgley, C., Feldlaufer, H., & Eccles, J. (1989). Change in teacher efficacy and student self- and task-related beliefs in mathematics during the transition to junior high school. *Journal of Educational Psychology, 81,* 247–258.

Ross, J. A. (1998). *Antecedents and consequences of teacher efficacy.* In J. Brophy (Ed.), Advances in research on teaching (Vol. 7, pp. 49–74). Greenwich, CT: JAI Press.

Schwartz, B., & Lacey, H. (1982). *Behaviorism, science, and human nature.* New York: Norton.

Simmons, D. C., Kame'enui, E. J., Good, R. H., Harn, B. A., Cole, C., & Braun, D. (2002). Building, implementing, and sustaining a beginning reading improvement model school by school and lessons learned. In M. Shinn, G. Stoner, & H. M. Walker (Eds.), *Interventions for academic and behavior problems II: Preventive and remedial approaches* (pp. 537–569). Bethesda, MD: National Association of School Psychologists.

Smylie, M.A. (1988). The enhancement function of staff development: Organizational and psychological antecedents to individual teacher change. *American Educational Research Journal, 25*(1), 1–30.

Sugai, G. (1992). Instructional design: Applications of teaching social behavior. *LD Forum, 17*(2), 20–23.

Sugai, G., Kame'enui, E. J., Horner, R., Simmons, D. C., & Coyne, M. C. (in press). Effective instructional and behavioral support systems: A schoolwide approach to discipline and early literacy. In T. Hehir (Ed.), *Five goals for special education in preparing today's children for tomorrow's world.* Washington, DC: Office of Special Education Programs.

Whitehurst, G. J. (2002, March). *Research on teacher preparation and professional development.* Paper presented at the White House Conference on Preparing Tomorrow's Teachers, Washington, DC.

Wolery, M., Bailey, D. B., & Sugai, G. M. (1988). *Effective teaching: Principles and procedures of applied behavior analysis with exceptional students.* Needham, MA: Allyn & Bacon.

Wong, K., Kauffman, J., & Lloyd, J. W. (1991). Choices for integration: Selecting teachers for mainstreamed students with emotional or behavioral disorders. *Intervention in School and Clinic, 27*(2), 108–115.

Understanding Student Behavior: Translating Theoretical Perspectives Into Effective Practice

OVERVIEW

- Behavioral Perspective
  What Is It? Definition, History, and Critical Features
  How Does Behavior Modification View Student Behavior?
  How Do I Use the Behavioral Perspective in My Classroom?
  Advantages and Limitations of the Behavioral Perspective

- Biophysical Perspective
  What Is It? Definition, History, and Critical Features
  How Does the Biophysical Perspective View Student Behavior?
  How Do I Use the Biophysical Perspective in My Classroom?
  Advantages and Limitations of the Biophysical Perspective

- Psychoeducational Perspective
  What Is It? Definition, History, and Critical Features
  How Does the Psychoeducational Perspective View Student Behavior?
  How Do I Use the Psychoeducational Perspective in My Classroom?
  Advantages and Limitations of the Psychoeducational Perspective

- Ecological Perspective
  What Is It? Definition, History, and Critical Features
  How Does the Ecological Perspective View Student Behavior?
  How Do I Use the Ecological Perspective in My Classroom?
  Advantages and Limitations of the Ecological Perspective

- Social Learning Perspective
  What Is It? Definition, History, and Critical Features
  How Does the Social Learning Perspective View Student Behavior?
  How Do I Use the Social Learning Perspective in My Classroom?
  Advantages and Limitations of the Social Learning Perspective

- Instructional Perspective
  What Is It? Definition, History, and Critical Features
  How Does the Instructional Perspective View Student Behavior?
  How Do I Use the Instructional Perspective in My Classroom?
  Advantages and Limitations of the Instructional Perspective

- Summary

- Chapter Activities

In this chapter we present six theoretical perspectives often used to understand the behavior of students. In addition, we present examples of classroom management approaches for each of these theoretical perspectives.

For an intervention approach to be considered logical and effective, it is essential it be grounded in sound theory. General and special education are fraught with

TABLE 2.1   Six Current Theoretical Perspectives in Education

Perspective	Focus
Behavioral	Behavior is learned under varying stimulus and consequence conditions.
Biophysical	Behavior is a function of genetics, brain chemistry, and developmental phases.
Psychoeducational	Behavior is influenced by unconscious motivations and desires.
Ecological	Behavior is a function of a student's interactions with his/her environment.
Social Learning	Behavior is influenced by a student's feelings, school, home environment, and the behavior of others.
Instructional	Behavior is learned and, therefore, taught. Academic skills and social behaviors are taught in the same way.

examples of well-intentioned classroom management interventions based on opinion or unsound research. An effective theoretical perspective on the causes for classroom problems will enable teachers to develop clear and concise explanations about causes of behavior problems, generate a series of intervention options for solving the problems, and make predictions about the future learning and behavior of the student.

We will discuss six current theoretical perspectives that provide teachers ways of thinking about behavior and learning in the classroom (Buskist & Gerbing, 1990). Each of the following perspectives is presented in Table 2.1: behavioral, biophysical, psychoeducational, ecological, social learning, and instructional. Each perspective offers a unique orientation to why students behave as they do. As you consider each, it is important to note several points. First, while each perspective has a particular focus for explaining student behavior, similarities exist between the six perspectives. Secondly, a theoretical perspective helps teachers examine their assumptions about the factors that contribute to behavior problems. A theoretical perspective should also guide development of effective management techniques. Without an organized and careful structure to analyze a student's behavior, it is difficult for a teacher to identify effective intervention options for students with learning and behavior problems.

In Figure 2.1, a teacher's theoretical perspective shapes how a teacher thinks about a student's behavior. The teacher may not understand the full range of possible causes of a behavior problem if the teacher is unable to evaluate the behavior from several theoretical perspectives. After all, as we noted in Chapter 1, how we think about a problem will dictate how we go about solving it. For example, a teacher who assumes there is a chemical basis for a problem (e.g., chemical imbalance) will understandably focus on a medical intervention for the student. Conversely, a teacher who views a problem as primarily environmental may focus instead on consequences of the behavior and provide more positive reinforcement. In our view, a teacher who is knowledgeable about different theoretical perspectives will consider a greater range of effective interventions to address the student's learning and behavior problems.

In the sections that follow, we discuss popular classroom management approaches in general and special education that are representative of six theoretical approaches. After discussing the characteristics and theoretical basis for each management approach, we describe the assumptions on which each is based. We pro-

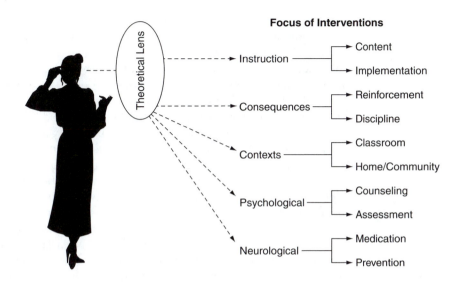

FIGURE 2.1 A teacher's perspective defines intervention options.

Focus of Interventions

Theoretical Lens

Instruction → Content, Implementation

Consequences → Reinforcement, Discipline

Contexts → Classroom, Home/Community

Psychological → Counseling, Assessment

Neurological → Medication, Prevention

vide an example of how each approach can be used to manage a problem behavior and conclude with a discussion of the advantages and limitations of each theoretical perspective.

BEHAVIORAL PERSPECTIVE

What Is It? Definition, History, and Critical Features

Teachers who use a behavioral perspective to analyze student behavior are primarily interested in how the environment affects the student's social and academic behavior. While a student's biology and neurology are not ruled out as contributing factors, the teacher's *primary* interest is to determine the relation between environmental events and the student's behavior. For example, a teacher observes that a particular student works very hard during one class, but an hour later, his behavior is disruptive. From a behavioral perspective, the teacher attempts to understand the student's behavior in the context of the two classes. The core tenet of the behavioral perspective is the belief in a link between the student's behavior and its consequences (Buskist & Gerbing, 1990).

Behavior modification is a familiar term and is one way a teacher can use the behavioral perspective to intervene with inappropriate student behavior. Behavior modification is known by various other names, such as *applied behavior analysis, behavioral analysis, behaviorism,* and *M&M therapy.* In general, the terms refer to various methods to modify student response. Behavior modification is practical application of the principles of operant conditioning, made popular by B.F. Skinner (1971), and is used widely in education.

The first use of behavior modification with children was in the 1960s, and it continued to be developed and refined in the 1970s. Application of behavior modification to some of society's most difficult problems characterized the discipline in the 1980s.

Early use of behavior modification was designed to "verify that the principles of operant conditioning that were shown to govern animal behavior also governed human behavior" (Rusch, Rose, & Greenwood, 1988, p. 35). Once this relationship was established, the practical application of behavior modification involving students identified with mental retardation and serious emotional disturbance was demonstrated.

Behavior modification is especially prevalent in special education. Baer (1988) described the important link between behavior modification and special education: "The application of behavior analysis is almost always educational, in the best and broadest sense of the word; and special education is the branch of education that most requires an applicable analysis of behavior in order to teach" (p. ix).

Teachers who adopt a behavioral perspective believe that students' learning results from an interaction between the behavior and environment. The environment includes all events, activities, and situations that precede or follow a student's behavior. Behavior is defined as any observable, measurable event or action. Conditions that occur just prior to a behavior, such as classroom organization, instructional materials, and teacher directions, are called antecedents. In short, how a teacher arranges the antecedents and consequences that follow a behavior will determine the future occurrence of that behavior. Using behavior modification, teachers are able to increase appropriate behavior or decrease inappropriate behavior either by adjusting antecedent conditions or by applying reinforcers or punishers.

In the language of behavior modification, the contingent application of consequences is of primary importance. Consequences refer to actions, events, or words that follow a behavior and are defined only by their effects on that behavior. Consequences can increase, decrease, or have no effect on a behavior.

Reinforcers are consequences (e.g., actions, events, words) that follow and strengthen the behavior of a student and increase the likelihood the behavior will occur in the future. A teacher who uses positive reinforcement will use a variety of reinforcers (e.g., verbal praise, points, M&M's candy) to increase appropriate behavior. At first, reinforcers are most effective if they are applied continuously and immediately after the behavior occurs. Such applications make the delivery of the reinforcers "contingent" on the behavior demonstrated. Specifically, reinforcement depends on the kind of behavior displayed. If an appropriate behavior is demonstrated, a reinforcer is likely to follow the behavior, while an inappropriate behavior will not be followed by a reinforcer.

Like reinforcers, punishers refer to events or actions that follow the occurrence of a behavior. However, a punisher is defined as such only if it results in decreasing the probability the behavior will occur in the future. If a teacher uses verbal praise to increase student on-task behavior but the behavior decreases instead, then in this instance, verbal praise is not a reinforcer but a punisher. What constitutes a positive reinforcer for one student may not be a positive reinforcer for another student. Punishment is also defined by its impact on a student's behavior. A consequence that decreases a behavior of one student (e.g., verbal reprimand) may have little or no effect on another.

A behavior modification program incorporates four general procedures. First, the teacher must identify the problem. For example, the teacher might determine that a student has a poor self-concept. Second, the problem must be analyzed and explained in terms of observable and measurable behaviors (Baer, 1988). The teacher defines self-concept using clear, observable, and measurable terms, such as how frequently a student smiles, volunteers answers in class, makes positive self-statements, and achieves at a high academic level.

The third general procedure of behavior modification is that the teacher systematically arranges the learning environment and applies reinforcement and punishment procedures to modify (i.e., increase or decrease) the occurrence of the behavior in question. For example, the teacher may devise a program that increases the frequency of certain behaviors that are already present. The teacher may weaken the frequency of an inappropriate behavior or teach an entirely new skill the student has never demonstrated (e.g., teach expressive language to a child who is severely disabled). Finally, the teacher records the number of times the behavior occurs to determine the effectiveness of the behavior modification program.

How Does Behavior Modification View Student Behavior?

The underlying assumption of behavior modification is that all behavior, acceptable or unacceptable, is learned. Behaviorists (i.e., practitioners who subscribe to the behavioral approach) believe that learning is determined in part by the feedback the student receives from the environment. Therefore, a child who is willful and difficult to manage in the classroom is not considered by a behaviorist to have a genetic predisposition toward disruptive behavior. Instead, the behaviorist assumes the student can be taught appropriate alternative behaviors. By applying this assumption, behaviorists believe students can be taught appropriate behavior, while inappropriate behavior can be reduced and replaced with more acceptable alternatives. Based upon these assumptions, the teacher plays a prominent role in the management of student classroom behavior.

Teachers are considered in the best position to control consequences in the classroom and teach students appropriate classroom behavior. Less direct approaches to changing student behavior, such as psychoanalytic counseling, are not considered viable options for addressing disruptive behaviors.

Duke and Meckel (1984) point out that just as the conduct of students is controlled by the principles of behavior modification, the teacher's behavior is similarly influenced. ". . . the teachers who utilize Behavior Modification may need to consider their own behavior and how it may be subject to reinforcement from classroom environment" (p. 16). A prominent feature of behavior modification programs is for the teacher to assess how his or her behavior is influenced, and perhaps controlled, by student behavior.

Even though the behavioral approach focuses on observable and measurable behavior, it does not exclude the role or diminish the importance of the neurological aspects of learning. Wolery, Bailey, and Sugai (1988) assume that learning has a neurological basis, and the developmental aspects of learning must be acknowledged when planning an instructional program. However, individuals who are designing and implementing behavior modification programs place "primary emphasis on observable behavior as well as the observable antecedents and consequences to behavior" (p. 10).

How Do I Use the Behavioral Perspective in My Classroom?

Sara, a sixth-grade student of Ms. Johnson, has a habit of calling out answers during class discussions, before the teacher has a chance to call on students. Ms. Johnson considers this a problem because she is not able to assess the knowledge of other students in the class. Students also find Sara's behavior obnoxious and perceive her as trying to dominate class discussions.

Ms. Johnson decides to implement a behavior modification program. First, she targets the class period in which Sara's disruptive behaviors are most frequent. In order to establish the rate of Sara's call-outs, she decides to count them for 3 days. When the rate of call-outs is documented and the stability of the behavior is established, Ms. Johnson develops a two-part intervention plan. She first decides to ignore Sara's answers each time she calls out, regardless of whether the answer is correct or not. The teacher is careful not to respond to Sara's frequent call-outs during social studies and refrains from giving Sara any form of attention—verbal, visual, or physical. When Sara does call out an answer, Ms. Johnson immediately selects another student who has appropriately raised his/her hand and says: "Thank you for raising your hand. I appreciate how you follow the rules during class discussion."

In addition to ignoring all call-outs, Ms. Johnson praises Sara each time she raises her hand or waits to be called on before giving an answer. When this occurs, the teacher is very specific in her praise to Sara: "Sara, thank you for raising your hand and not calling out your answer." Throughout class, Ms. Johnson continues her data collection and counts Sara's call-outs. At the end of class, the teacher records them on a graph to show frequency of call-outs before and after the intervention. Ms. Johnson notes that after implementing the ignore-and-praise strategy, Sara's call-outs increased dramatically for 2 days and then decreased significantly.

Advantages and Limitations of the Behavioral Perspective

Advantages.   Teachers must first identify the problem to be modified and use a strategy for observing and monitoring behavior in their classrooms. Behavioral programs are well suited for modifying disruptive classroom behavior, as well as modifying noncompliance and aggressive behaviors in students of all ages and ability levels. There is also evidence that behavior modification programs are effective in changing more complex academic problem behavior.

Behavior modification programs can be useful in preventing behavior and learning problems if implemented at the beginning of the school year.

Limitations.   A potential limitation of behavior modification is that the teacher uses the same program for all students in the classroom, when individual programs are more desirable. While it is possible for a teacher to have several behavior modification programs going at once, this requires careful organization and monitoring. Training in behavior modification is critical to success.

Most behavioral programs are developed in response to disruptive behavior and consider how the teacher can best apply consequences. Less emphasis is on how

As part of an effective behavior management program, a teacher must collect data on the academic performance and social behavior of the students.

problem behavior may be caused by inadequate instruction or poor organization. Teachers who use behavior modification procedures look less to the curriculum and instruction as causes of misbehavior and more to features of the environment that reinforce disruptive behavior. Consequently, some behavior modification programs are not integrated into the instructional program. The behavioral approach does not require teachers to analyze instruction to determine what fosters behavior problems. The focus of most behavioral approaches is correction rather than prevention, and our view is that prevention is far more effective.

BIOPHYSICAL PERSPECTIVE
What Is It? Definition, History, and Critical Features

Teachers who adopt a biophysical perspective look for explanations about behavior in the structure and function of the brain, in genetics, and in the physiological and neurological influences on student behavior (Alberto & Troutman, 2003). Teachers who adopt this perspective look for problems with genetic structures, brain structure, and function, and "how drugs and other chemicals affect our behavior, our thoughts, and our emotions" (Buskist & Gerbing, 1990, p. 7). When studying a student's behavior, the teacher considers the full range of biological variables and their influence on the student's behavior.

The biophysical perspective has played a prominent role in education. This is particularly true in special education, where the biophysical perspective has been used to explain and predict the behavior and learning of students with learning disabilities, mental retardation, attention deficit disorders, and behavior disorders. With the explosion of technology in the last decade, the biophysical perspective has become increasingly popular in education and psychology as a way to determine the physical factors responsible for behavior. In addition, there has been an explosion of interest in how the brain affects learning and how teachers can develop new instructional and management programs that reflect brain research (Buskist & Gerbing, 1990).

How Does the Biological Perspective View Student Behavior?

Proponents of the biophysical approach believe that all behavior problems have a physical origin. Biophysical problems that result in behavior and learning problems are (a) central nervous system dysfunctions, (b) allergies, (c) metabolic deficits, and (d) a genetic predisposition to noncompliant behavior. Even though proponents of this orientation acknowledge that environmental or instructional factors contribute to learning and behavior problems of a student, they believe the primary source of a student's problems is biophysical. The teacher will typically defer to a physician to determine the source of problem behavior.

How Do I Use the Biological Perspective in My Classroom?

Using this perspective, the teacher typically follows a two-phase intervention procedure. First, the teacher observes a student's problem behavior and attempts to determine if there is a biological or neurological basis for the behavior. If a student exhibits inattention and hyperactivity, the teacher may first attempt to modify the instructional program or the level of reinforcement. If a student demonstrates extreme inattention during instructional activities, the teacher might hypothesize the behavior has a physical cause. The teacher might recommend to the parents a complete medical evaluation by a pediatrician to determine if the student has an attention deficit disorder. In a case like the one above, a pediatrician might prescribe Ritalin to increase the student's attention and decrease hyperactivity in the classroom. The school psychologist or pediatrician would advise the teacher to look for possible side effects (e.g., headaches, stomachaches, tic disorders, lack of appetite) and to systematically observe the student's behavior while on medication.

Advantages and Limitations of the Biological Perspective

Advantages.   Research suggests that medication helps about 70% of children with attention deficit disorder become more focused and less active during classroom instruction (Neuwirth, 1994). In addition, there are many anecdotal reports of teachers and parents indicating that medication is helpful for students. The biophysical perspective may be particularly useful with students who have extreme forms of problem behavior. For example, students with seizure disorders, severe hyperactivity, or very poor attention problems benefit from medical interventions.

The biophysical perspective can be applied to students of various ages and ability levels. Teachers most concerned with problem behaviors associated with attention deficit disorder will find the biophysical perspective adaptable to their classrooms.

Limitations.   A problem with the biophysical perspective in that its primary focus is on factors outside the province of the teacher's influence. Proponents sometimes make the assumption that a student's behavior problem can be fixed by altering a child's diet to eliminate a food allergy thought to contribute to the problem, or by using a medication to help a child focus. Research suggests the use of Ritalin, for example, does not always translate into improved academic performance. Professionals and parents alike have been critical of the use of medications to manage behaviors associated with hyperactivity (e.g., attention deficit disorder) (Silver, 1995).

Many classroom factors must be considered in understanding a student's behavior. If a student's attention deficit (e.g., failing to maintain attention during science) is perceived as primarily caused by neurological or biological factors, the teacher might fail to develop classroom interventions before investigating medical interventions.

PSYCHOEDUCATIONAL PERSPECTIVE
What Is It? Definition, History, and Critical Features

The psychoeducational perspective assumes behavior problems result from unconscious motivations that direct a child's actions. Professionals who subscribe to this perspective believe behavior problems are caused by a student's motivation to fulfill specific needs "for attention, revenge, power, and assumed disability (i.e., the desire to be left alone) or any of these together" (Kaplan & Carter, 1995, p. 11). The psychoeducational perspective is an extension of Freud's (1938) psychoanalytical approach. Alfred Adler (1962) was one of the first professionals to translate Freud's ideas into a systematic and practical approach for dealing with a child's behavior problems in the home and classroom.

While the psychoeducational perspective has been on the wane for sometime, it is now regaining popularity as an approach for managing disruptive behavior in the classroom. Researchers (e.g., Jones, 1991) have discussed the use of the psychoeducational perspective with students who are seriously emotionally disturbed.

Cooperative Discipline is a psychoeducational approach to discipline and is based on the work of Alfred Adler and Rudolph Dreikurs. This approach is based largely on the premise that misbehavior should receive natural or logical consequences, and if a teacher understands a student's motive for unacceptable behavior, the teacher can design an effective plan to help the student. Training in this approach is based on a number of books by Dreikurs such as *Discipline Without Tears* (1974) and *Maintaining Sanity in the Classroom* (1982). A program entitled *Cooperative Discipline* (1990) by

Linda Albert is also based largely on the work of Dreikurs and Adler. Albert's Cooperative Discipline program will be used as a model of a psychoeducational approach.

The Cooperative Discipline model is based on two fundamental concepts. The first is that students choose their behavior. Although environmental conditions may invite a particular behavior, the student is free to choose how to behave. If the teacher assumes student behavior is based on choice, the teacher can begin to influence a student's decisions about how to behave.

The second basic concept of Cooperative Discipline is that the goal of student behavior is to satisfy a need to belong. Students choose different behaviors to feel a sense of belonging in different environments such as clubs, teams, or home. The student is usually trying to achieve one of four immediate goals: attention, power, revenge, or avoidance-of-failure. When a teacher recognizes a student's need to belong, he or she can help the student choose appropriate behaviors to achieve a special place in the classroom.

A teacher's thoughtful reaction to a student's misbehavior might be accomplished by a five-step School Action Plan, which serves as the procedural heart of Cooperative Discipline. Each step is described below.

Step 1: Pinpoint and describe the student's behavior.
The teacher cannot rely on subjective judgments that the student is lazy, for example, but must describe the problem objectively. The objective observation that "Thomas fails to hand in two or three assignments each week" focuses on what actually happens, not on how the teacher feels about what happened.

Step 2: Identify goal of misbehavior.
Once the teacher has identified the problem behavior, he or she has information to make a judgment about what the student is trying to accomplish with the misbehavior. The teacher then determines if the student is seeking attention, power, revenge, or avoidance-of-failure.

Step 3: Design specific intervention techniques.
Intervention should be based on what the student is trying to achieve with the misbehavior. For example, if the student is trying to get attention, the teacher might minimize the behavior by ignoring it or distract the student by changing the activity. If the goal of the misbehavior is to seek power, the teacher might use time-out or set a consequence, such as losing an activity.

Step 4: Select encouragement techniques to build self-esteem.
Interventions for misbehavior are viewed as stopgap measures that will not prevent future occurrence. To prevent recurrence, the teacher must plan interventions to help the student feel more capable. Specific techniques, such as asking the student to help with a lesson, may help the student connect with classmates or feel like a contributing member of the class. When the student's self-image improves, he or she has less need to misbehave to create a sense of belonging.

Step 5: Involve parents as partners.
Specific suggestions are given for increasing parental involvement and support. For example, parents can help with their child's homework or visit the school to provide emotional support. All previous steps are strengthened if teachers, students, and parents participate in the plan. Information is provided on productive parent-teacher conferences and how to develop a Home Action Plan.

Parent and teacher communication is an important aspect of instructional classroom management.

How Does the Psychoeducational Perspective View Student Behavior?

The etiology of disruptive behavior is a function of an underlying, unconscious motivation of the student. If a student has an underlying need to feel a sense of belonging in the classroom and does not have academic and social skills to achieve this, then the student will engage in disruptive behavior. The student uses this behavior to gain status that he/she does not know how to gain through socially acceptable means.

How Can I Use the Psychoeducational Perspective in My Classroom?

In a middle-school classroom, a student named Elliot frequently says hurtful things to the teacher. One day when reviewing an assignment, Elliot, who is sometimes witty, uses a sarcastic and disrespectful tone toward the teacher in reading his vocabulary definitions. The goal of this behavior is to get attention, and the rude tone is designed to anger the teacher.

Cooperative Discipline employs six guidelines for avoiding and diffusing confrontations such as this.

Guideline 1: Focus on the behavior, not the student.

Guideline 2: Take charge of negative emotions.

Guideline 3: Avoid escalating the situation.

Guideline 4: Discuss the misbehavior later.

Guideline 5: Allow the student to save face.

Guideline 6: Model nonaggressive behavior.

In this example, the teacher should inform Elliot that she will speak to him later. This avoids escalating the behavior at the time and lets the student know the behavior will be dealt with at another time. Before the conference, the teacher acknowledges to herself that the student's behavior hurt her feelings. By doing so, she takes charge of these emotions and doesn't become negative or hostile toward the student.

At the conference, the teacher describes for Elliot the behavior he exhibited. She informs him that he did the assignment correctly, but it is not acceptable to insult her. She acknowledges the student's wit and informs him it's acceptable to be funny, but it's important to understand the correct time and place to be funny. As the discussion continues, the student and teacher work out options for getting credit for the assignment. One is to redo the assignment and eliminate the disrespectful parts. Another is for the student to prepare a skit for the class that demonstrates his knowledge of the vocabulary assignment. The third option is to choose not to redo the assignment and receive a failing grade. In a reasoned and respectful way, the teacher has acknowledged the student's power and wit and has allowed him to save face. If the behavior continues, the teacher may need to try additional interventions suggested in the program for dealing with power and hurtful behaviors.

Advantages and Limitations of the Psychoeducational Perspective

Advantages.   This approach offers the teacher specific and practical suggestions on how to respond to misbehavior in both proactive and reactive ways. Suggestions are given for what the teacher might do at the moment of misbehavior and later to improve the student's self-image.

Cooperative Discipline can be used with students of all ages and performance levels and helps teachers avoid escalating troubling behavior by using guidelines to avoid and diffuse confrontations.

Limitations.   Because the focus of Cooperative Discipline is on motivations of the student, it is not designed for proactive classroom management. Cooperative Discipline does not consider the teacher's instructional program or classroom organization as a potential cause of disruptive behavior, and therefore teachers respond reactively to classroom disruption. Like many programs, Cooperative Discipline does not help the teacher organize the classroom and use instruction to shape students' success.

ECOLOGICAL PERSPECTIVE

What Is It? Definition, History, and Critical Features

According to Cullinan, Epstein, and Lloyd (1991), *ecology* refers to "the overall pattern of relationships involving an organism and its environment (ecosystem)" (p. 149). Proponents of the ecological perspective draw ideas from many professional areas such as psychology, anthropology, education, and sociology. A teacher who uses an ecological perspective to understand inappropriate behavior must first have knowledge of the ecosystems of the student and how the student is functioning in them. Examples of a student's ecosystems include classroom, peer groups, and family. This perspective theorizes that "social and environmental stress, in combination with the individual's inability to cope, lead to psychological disturbances" (Hardman, Drew, & Egan, 1999, p. 17). This perspective appeals to many teachers because it is "holistic," and blends "many of the strengths of the other perspectives, and is applicable to children with varying abilities, interests, and cultural backgrounds " (Hardman, Drew & Egan, 1999, p. 17). Because a student participates in many ecological systems, an intervention must be implemented in as many of the student's ecosystems as necessary. As Edgar (1998) points out, "a marked improvement in one component or modest improvements in all components might be sufficient to allow the child to become a functioning member of the system" (p. 164).

A critical feature of the ecological perspective (Kaplan & Carter, 1995) is that it is broad in application, because it considers "a wide variety of interactive factors including the physical environment, (e.g., seating, room size, temperature, lighting, furniture) and the curriculum (e.g., what is being taught and when and how it is taught)" (p.17). An ecological intervention begins with a detailed assessment of the entire learning environment of the student, which is sometimes referred to as an ecobehavioral analysis (Rogers-Warren, 1984).

How Does the Ecological Perspective View Student Behavior?

The causes of problem behaviors do not reside in the student, but rather problem behavior is considered a result of the student not meshing well with his/her environment. For example, a student may constantly complain to the teacher about homework assignments and other classroom responsibilities because the student needs the teacher's attention. The reality may be the teacher does not adequately attend to the student at appropriate times. The result of the poor fit between the teacher's skill and the student's need for attention is that the student engages in disruptive behavior to compensate for the inadequate learning environment.

How Do I Use the Ecological Perspective in My Classroom?

Jason, a student in Mr. Mason's seventh-grade science class, is doing poorly academically and has become disruptive in the classroom in the last 2 months of school. Mr. Mason has discussed this with Jason's parents and learned Jason has also become uncooperative at home, often refusing to complete homework and return home at prescribed times. In response to Mr. Mason's concerns about Jason, the school psychologist initiates an ecobehavioral assessment to identify factors that may be causing Jason's behavior problems. Using both direct observation and interviews, the assessment will examine (a) Jason's classroom learning performance, (b) his interactions with Mr. Mason and other teachers, and (c) his behavior at home.

As a result of the analysis, the psychologist develops a multifaceted intervention designed to adjust several of Jason's ecosystems. The psychologist recommends Mr.

Mason monitor Jason's academic performance more frequently to afford him more positive attention during class. He recommends Mr. Mason ask Jason questions during class to provide him more opportunities to participate and learn. The psychologist advises Jason's parents to use a behavioral contract to increase Jason's motivation to complete homework.

Advantages and Limitations of the Ecological Perspective

Advantages.   Research demonstrates the effectiveness of the ecological approach with students with behavior problems because of the strong focus on initial assessment and translation of that information into intervention. The ecological perspective may be particularly adaptable to problems of students in middle school and high school. Because the causes of behavior problems with these students are often complex, a comprehensive restructuring of a student's relationship with family, friends, and teachers is often necessary.

Limitations.   Because the ecological perspective is a systems approach and focuses on many different areas, it is difficult for a teacher to make significant modifications in each identified ecosystem. For example, ecological interventions may require modification in a student's family relationships, involvement with community, or school activities. Although instructional factors are important considerations, the ecological perspective does not inform teachers about important instructional design features.

Interventions with an ecological focus are typically not proactive, because the teacher institutes programs such as Cooperative Discipline in *response* to behavior problems. Because an ecobehavioral assessment takes considerable time to complete, most teachers don't use this approach unless faced with very difficult behavior problems in the classroom.

SOCIAL LEARNING PERSPECTIVE

What Is It? Definition, History, and Critical Features

Proponents of the social learning perspective believe a student's behavior is influenced by more than just the learning environment or inner forces (Bandura, 1995). Instead, behavior is influenced by the interactions between the student's feelings, school and home environments, and behavior. Assertive Discipline is an example of a classroom management program based on the social learning perspective. Canter and Canter (1976) define an assertive teacher as "One who clearly and firmly communicates her wants and needs to her students and is prepared to reinforce her words with appropriate actions. She responds in a manner which maximizes her potential to get her needs met, but in no way violates the best interests of the students" (p. 9). Assertive Discipline provides a framework for the teacher to communicate to students the limits of their behavior in the classroom and clear consequences for disruptive behavior. Canter and Canter developed Assertive Discipline because they felt teachers were not adequately trained to respond effectively to disruptive behavior. Assertive Discipline requires teachers to take control of the classroom by (a) utilizing an assertive teaching style, (b) specifying behaviors expected of students and those not tolerated, and (c) developing a plan for increasing appropriate and decreasing inappropriate behavior.

According to Canter and Canter (1976), teachers develop conceptualizations of the causes of misbehavior that in reality serve only to limit their effectiveness in properly managing behavior. Moreover, teachers often attribute classroom behavior problems to factors beyond their control (e.g., emotional disturbance, brain damage, inadequate intelligence, inadequate parenting, low socioeconomic status). Teachers do not empower themselves, according to Canter and Canter, to influence student behavior in positive ways by setting firm limits.

Canter (1989) believes many professionals have misinterpreted Assertive Discipline by assuming the key element is providing negative consequences for misbehavior. The key to effective Assertive Discipline, Canter states, is "catching students being good" and applying positive consequences for appropriate behavior (p.58). Assertive Discipline is based on a balance between the rights of teachers and the rights of students. The teacher has the right to determine and request appropriate behavior from students, and students have the right to choose how to behave and to know of the consequences that will follow their behavior (Canter, 1989).

With Assertive Discipline, teachers are taught to (a) communicate their expectations clearly, (b) attend to both positive and negative student behavior actively, and (c) use consequences for both appropriate and inappropriate student behavior persistently. The Assertive Discipline approach has three major program characteristics: (a) a discipline plan, (b) consequences of misbehavior, and (c) positive discipline. Each component is discussed below.

The discipline plan.   The teacher presents class rules to students at the beginning of the school year and describes consequences for rule violations. This is an important feature of Assertive Discipline, because without it, teachers rely on spur-of-the-moment consequences for treating student misbehavior, often forcing them to negotiate and explain every consequence to misbehaving students. As Canter (1989) points out, "That is not an effective way to teach" (p. 59). By adhering to the discipline plan, Canter argues that teachers can be more consistent in their delivery of consequences. The discipline plan is sent home at the beginning of the school year to inform parents of the teacher's behavioral expectations. This explicit communication to students and parents delineates the roles and responsibilities of each participant in the learning process. It also allows teachers to enlist parental support in managing student behavior.

Consequences of misbehavior.   The feature of Assertive Discipline that is most well known and also most misunderstood is the method used to deliver consequences for student misbehavior. A misperception of Assertive Discipline is that the teacher stands in front of the class, discussing rules and consequences, and writing students' names on the board when they misbehave. In response to this misperception, Canter (1989) states, "Assertive Discipline is not a negative program, but it can be misused by negative teachers" (p. 59). In Assertive Discipline, positive reinforcement for appropriate behavior should be used in conjunction with negative consequences. Canter suggests teachers limit the number of consequences for misbehavior and use only those the teacher finds appropriate and can use comfortably. Consequences are delivered in a systematic manner.

When Assertive Discipline was first introduced, the technique most frequently used was writing the offending student's name on the board, followed by check marks. This method, it was thought, afforded explicit communication to the disruptive student about his/her behavior and provided the teacher a record of the misbehavior. However, according to Canter (1989), many teachers started to use the public display of names as a singular means of controlling students, and some students found it reinforcing to have their names displayed publicly. Canter suggests record keeping be less public and teachers use a notebook to record student names.

Positive discipline.   Teachers must reinforce appropriate student behavior when using Assertive Discipline. Without the vigilant use of reinforcement, Assertive Discipline is not effective, and the teacher can expect the management program to become negative for both students and teacher. Although positive discipline may be used for students from elementary to senior high, teachers make adjustments for age and ability differences in the delivery of positive reinforcement. Canter suggests that teachers use a three-step approach to positive discipline: instruction, practice, and correction.

How Does the Social Learning Perspective View Student Behavior?

Proponents of the social learning perspective, like proponents of the behavioral perspective, assume a student's behavior is learned as a result of interactions with others in the environment. However, behavior is also a result of interactions between personal variables of the student, external learning environment, and student behavior. A student learns behavior as a result of both direct interaction and indirect circumstance. For example, a key to Assertive Discipline is that a teacher's discipline of a student will influence the behavior of all students in the class. It is through positive influences, not negative consequences, that teachers can best affect the behavior of students in the classroom. It is also assumed that the teacher's attitude is vitally important to the success of Assertive Discipline. Through Assertive Discipline, teachers can gain the skill and confidence to identify (a) the type of classroom desired, (b) the obstacles in the classroom that prevent successful management, and (c) the plan needed to overcome the obstacles.

The assertive teacher systematically teaches students expected classroom behavior by clearly establishing appropriate behavior. Once this teaching is complete, the teacher is expected to follow through consistently with specific consequences. Positive assertions form the core of effective classroom management in Assertive Discipline, and teachers freely respond to appropriate behavior while reasserting classroom expectations.

Canter and Canter (1976) developed Assertive Discipline with the understanding that this approach "will not provide a teacher with a blueprint for every difficult classroom problem" (p.13) but is one of many options teachers have when choosing a classroom management approach.

How Do I Use the Social Learning Perspective in My Classroom?

The teacher who chooses Assertive Discipline institutes the program on the first day of the school year, after developing a discipline plan. As an initial step, the teacher reflects on his/her expectations of how students will behave in the classroom. Next, the teacher identifies unacceptable behaviors in the classroom and develops specific consequences for rule infractions.

The teacher's next step is to develop positive discipline practices. The teacher specifies what is expected from students in each learning situation and instructs students on how to follow critical directions. Because of the ability ranges of students in most classrooms, the teacher often incorrectly assumes all students know what is meant by a direction (e.g., "Everybody stay in your seats"). During the first critical phase of positive discipline, teachers state the classroom rules and clearly model what is meant by each rule. Students are then asked to restate the rules and demonstrate their understanding of the teacher's expectations. Once the teacher discusses and models the classroom rules, students practice following the rules under the teacher's guidance. During this practice, the teacher focuses attention and praise on students who are following directions. This positive approach increases the likelihood that students will continue to follow directions and provides a positive model to students who have not yet learned to comply with classroom rules.

Once the teacher is assured students have a clear understanding of the rules, negative consequences like the ones that follow are applied to misbehavior. If a student breaks a classroom rule while a teacher is presenting a lesson, the teacher gives the student a verbal warning and writes the student's name in a record book. For the next rule infraction, the student is verbally reprimanded and receives the next level of consequence (e.g., 5 minutes after school). A check mark is then placed beside the student's name in the record book. A third infraction brings with it another reprimand and yet another level of consequence (e.g., 10 minutes after school). If there is a fourth rule violation, the teacher informs the student of his misconduct and follows with a phone call to the parents. If the misbehavior continues, an administrative action is taken, and the student is sent to the principal's office. The discipline plan and negative consequences have all been determined in advance, and the student is informed of consequences for any misbehavior. Therefore, teachers are not required to explain their consequences or engage in negotiating with the student, which is considered wasting valuable teaching time.

Advantages and Limitations of the Social Learning Perspective

Advantages.   There is considerable evidence to support using the social learning perspective to manage classroom behavior problems (Bandura, 1995). However, while many teachers report the effectiveness of Assertive Discipline, there are few controlled research studies that have demonstrated its effectiveness (Chard, Smith, & Sugai, 1992). Consequently, teachers should look carefully at anecdotal reports about Assertive Discipline. Because Assertive Discipline is predicated on a set of teacher rights, teachers gain a feeling of control in their classrooms, and because communication plays a prominent role in this approach, students gain an understanding of classroom expectations. Knowledge of expectations results in fewer misunderstandings between student and teacher, which contributes to the reported effectiveness of this management approach.

Assertive Discipline can be used for a traditional 180-day school year, and the teacher can administer a classroom management program before behavior problems surface. These procedures can be used by either general or special education teachers and are likely to be effective for all students, irrespective of their diverse learning and curricular needs. Because clearly articulated guidelines are to be followed, teachers of all training backgrounds can use Assertive Discipline in their classrooms.

Limitations.   Assertive Discipline has no assessment component to help teachers evaluate their classroom for potential behavior problems. Consequently, management in this approach is largely reactive. A significant limitation of Assertive Discipline is that it does not consider one major source of misbehavior, poorly designed instructional programs, as a contributor to classroom disruption. For example, if a student's unmanageable behavior is caused by misplacement in a reading program, Assertive Discipline is not effective for rectifying the problem. It does not provide a mechanism for the teacher to evaluate critically the role of curriculum in classroom management. One could argue that Assertive Discipline is not intended or designed to address instruction.

A comprehensive monitoring system is not provided for evaluation of learning and behavioral outcomes with Assertive Discipline. The lack of careful monitoring, especially with disabled students, can pose both practical and administrative problems for the teacher. Assertive Discipline is sometimes misused by teachers who focus only on negative consequences, making the classroom an aversive learning environment for students and teachers alike. A further limitation of Assertive Discipline is that it does not accommodate students of different ages. For example, the severity of consequences is the same for younger and older students.

Assertive Discipline does not provide teachers specific guidelines on proactive management techniques. While students are presented classroom rules at the beginning of the year and consequences for not adhering to those rules, Assertive Discipline does not provide guidelines for teaching students the skills that apply to the rules.

INSTRUCTIONAL PERSPECTIVE
What Is It? Definition, History, and Critical Features

The instructional perspective is focused on managing student behavior from an instructional point of view. It is based on a rather simple proposition: The strategies for teaching and managing social behavior are no different from the strategies for teaching reading, earth science, or mathematics. Proponents of the instructional perspective believe that by their very nature, classroom and behavior management procedures are instructional, not merely behavioral or social, because they take place in the context of instruction and are designed to impart information to students. To impart information about how to behave, a teacher teaches, explains, directs, models, or otherwise communicates to a student how to behave and not behave. This process is no different than the process of teaching a concept, fact, or principle in mathematics or science.

The instructional perspective to classroom management has its origins in the development of the direct instruction model for teaching academic skills in the 1960s. Siegfried Engelmann and his colleagues developed Direct Instruction as a comprehensive system and organizational structure for looking at all aspects of instruction, including classroom organization and management, design of instructional programs, and quality of teacher and student interactions (Gersten, Woodward, & Darch, 1986). The principles of Direct Instruction have been integrated into specific, programmatic approaches for use with students of all ages and ability levels (Kame'enui & Simmons, 1997). Several examples of these programmatic approaches based on an instructional perspective include *CHAMPS, A Proactive Approach to Classroom Management,* (Sprick, Garrison, & Howard, 1998) and *Generalized Compliance Training* (Engelmann & Colvin, 1983). In addition, Kame'enui and Darch (1995) introduced *Instructional Classroom Management,* a programmatic approach applying instructional design principles to teaching students age-appropriate behaviors in the classroom and to eliminating disruptive classroom behavior.

The primary difference between an instructional approach to classroom management and all other approaches (*all* other approaches not some or a few), including the approaches listed earlier, is that an instructional approach is proactive. This means that before an action or problem occurs, *the teacher teaches carefully, strategically, and to a high criterion level of performance all information required for students to behave appropriately.* More importantly, the teacher systematically sets up numerous opportunities to reinforce what's been taught and directly communicate to students how well they are doing as reflective and problem-solving citizens.

"Teaching carefully, strategically, and to a high criterion level of performance," all that is required for students to behave appropriately, doesn't sound very different from what most teachers do now. However, the shift in a teacher's focus and thinking on a day-to-day basis is significant and necessary if instructional management is to be successful.

How Does the Instructional Perspective View Student Behavior?

The basic assumption is that teachers must first teach students how to behave in every circumstance for which appropriate behavior is expected by the teacher. This holds true whether the behavior to be taught is an academic behavior, such as naming the capitals of all 50 states, or a social behavior, such as speaking politely to adults and other students. This assumption is fundamental to the instructional perspective and carries major implications for the role of the teacher in developing teaching and behavior management programs. The instructional perspective requires the teacher to have a clear idea of how students are to perform in any activity, whether that activity is academic or social. A teacher's understanding of an academic or behavioral standard is the basis for effective instruction. This understanding is particularly important when teachers are working with students with learning and behavior problems. For example, if a student with attention deficits has difficulty learning her multiplication facts and fails to meet a designated performance standard, the teacher can evaluate a number of instructional factors such as the sequence of math facts taught, the pace of presenting new math facts, or the schedule of review of previously learned facts to determine ways to modify the teaching plan to make it more appropriate for the student. A teacher who has an instructional perspective assumes that the student, regardless of the learning problem, is capable of learning math facts and that one reason for her failure may be the organization and delivery of her instructional program. In this case, it may mean the content must be organized and delivered in a way that accommodates the attention deficit of the student. Because the student can master the content, the teacher's next steps are to modify the instructional program, re-teach the math facts, and provide enough structured practice so that the student not only learns math facts, but also can apply these facts to solve more complex arithmetic problems.

A teacher having an instructional perspective uses the same analysis when managing inappropriate social behavior. If a sixth-grade student continually talks during science class, the teacher with an instructional perspective determines whether the student has the social and study skills necessary to listen to the teacher's presentation and take detailed notes. If the student does not have these study skills, the teacher would devise a plan for teaching the student active listening skills and note taking as part of a larger intervention strategy. In this example, because the teacher adopted an instructional perspective when "thinking about" intervention options, her primary analysis of the causes of the talk-outs focused on instructional variables.

While the instructional perspective may at first appear time-consuming, in reality it is the most efficient approach for managing disruptive behavior, particularly for students with a history of learning and behavior problems. A teacher having an instructional perspective understands that unless the underlying academic and social skills are explicitly taught to students exhibiting problems, many behavioral interventions are unlikely to be successful in the long run since they don't focus on teaching students necessary prerequisite skills. The time required for teaching students *how* to perform critical prerequisite academic and social skill behaviors is time better spent than simply punishing students for being disruptive in the classroom, since punishing students does not teach students alternative behaviors.

How Do I Use the Instructional Perspective in My Classroom?

Teachers often find, for example, that transitions are difficult for students. One teacher completes an instructional analysis of the problem and determines the transition problem is the result of her failure to: (a) structure the last 5 minutes of class and teach transition behavior in the hallways, (b) clearly articulate to students expected behavior in the hallways, and (c) manage student behavior proactively.

The teacher plays an important role in managing students' transition to different learning activities.

Based on her analysis, the teacher develops an intervention strategy of four steps. First, she structures the last 5 minutes of class. Because the teacher determines her students are disruptive before they leave class, she decides to prevent hallway problems by using the last 5 minutes of class for an activity that can be better managed. The goal of this activity is to make sure all students are following classroom rules at the bell. The teacher identifies rules for behavior in the hallways and requires students to practice transition behavior until all students complete the activity appropriately. The teacher uses part of the last 5 minutes of class to review what is expected of students when they are out in the hall. Finally, the teacher monitors students as they pass between classes and delivers reinforcement as they improve their performance. The following Learning Activity will provide more insight about teacher perceptions of problem behavior and intervention strategies.

Advantages and Limitations of the Instructional Perspective

Advantages.   A growing body of research has looked at the instructional design of teaching acceptable behavior to students with learning and behavior problems. For example, research has shown effectiveness of teaching students in such diverse areas as independence, adaptive behavior, compliance, and social behavior on playgrounds. As these and other reports demonstrate (e.g., Walker, Colvin, & Ramsey, 1995), we now have evidence of effectiveness of specific strategies for teaching students behaviors that allow them to perform successfully in the classroom. Emerging evidence also demonstrates how the instructional perspective can be implemented effectively in an entire school. While preliminary evidence suggests schools can effectively adapt this perspective to school organization and classroom management, the long-term effectiveness is yet to be determined.

The instructional perspective is useful for teachers because combining teaching and management activities into one highly integrated system is economical use of a

Learning Activity

Interview With Two Teachers About Classroom Management

Purpose of Activity

To gain insight into teacher's perceptions of problem behavior

Step 1: Identify two teachers: one from a mainstream classroom, and one from a special education classroom. Conduct interviews with each teacher about his or her perceptions on the causes of classroom behavior problems and their intervention strategies. Sample questions are provided to help you start the interviews.

1. When do behavior problems typically occur?
2. What types of classroom management problems are most prevalent?
3. What is your typical strategy to control disruptive student behavior?
4. What causes students to be disruptive in the classroom?

Step 2: Once you have completed interviews with both teachers, consider the following questions and discuss them with a classmate.

1. Does the assessment of behavior problems differ between general education and special education teachers?
2. Do teachers identify possible causes of learning and behavior problems?
3. Do intervention strategies teachers describe deal with causes of behavior problems as identified by the teachers?

teacher's time. In addition, because the instructional perspective focuses on academic performance, teachers will be helping lower-achieving students compete in subject areas. Teaching and reviewing appropriate social behaviors helps students maintain these skills throughout the school year.

The instructional approach to management is adaptable and effective for students of different age and ability levels. In addition, because the instructional perspective takes into consideration a student's academic performance level, the organization of academic lessons, and the structure of the classroom, teachers in all content areas will find this approach adaptable to their particular teaching circumstances.

One of the strongest features of the instructional perspective is that it is an integral part of a teacher's regular instructional program. Teachers who adopt this perspective manage classrooms under the assumption that if students are not behaving appropriately, it is imperative for the teacher to teach necessary social and learning skills. Most importantly, this intervention perspective provides the instructional details of how to effectively teach these skills.

Limitations.　Designing effective instructional programs and teaching students appropriate behavior is the first step in proactive and comprehensive interventions.

However, the translation of this theory into practice can be difficult, as procedures dictated by the instructional perspective are often complex, time consuming, and demanding. While considerable research exists on the effectiveness of strategies used in the instructional perspective, empirical evidence of successful implementation school wide is only now emerging (Kame'enui & Simmons, 1997). Implementing a school-wide management plan demands strong leadership by a school's administration and vigilant implementation by all teachers in the school.

SUMMARY

Six current theoretical perspectives on student behavior were presented. For each of these perspectives we discussed (a) its definition, (b) how the perspective views student behavior, (c) the ways a teacher can use the perspective in the classroom, and (d) the advantages and disadvantages of the perspective. Our discussion provided specific examples of how each perspective is used when teachers are developing a teaching plan for all students, regardless of their ability levels. An analysis of the research support for each of the perspectives was a major element of this chapter. The authors argue that a teacher who is knowledgeable about different theoretical perspectives will consider a greater range of interventions when managing learning and behavior problems. While each of the six perspectives provides helpful insights for understanding student behavior, the instructional perspective, with its emphasis on evaluating variables related to teaching and learning, provides a strong, research-based link to effective interventions for students experiencing learning or behavior problems.

CHAPTER ACTIVITIES

1. List and discuss the theoretical basis, characteristics, and assumptions of each of the prominent theoretical perspectives in classroom management discussed in this chapter:
   a. behavioral
   b. biophysical
   c. psychoeducational
   d. ecological
   e. social learning
   f. instructional
2. Identify and discuss the four reasons why theory is important to understanding student behavior.
3. Identify and discuss advantages and limitations of the instructional perspective for managing students in the classroom.

REFERENCES

Adler, A. (1962). *Understanding human nature*. New York: Humanities.

Albert, L. (1990). *Cooperative discipline: Classroom management that produces self-esteem*. Circle Pines, MN: American Guidance Service.

Alberto, P., & Troutman, A. (2003). *Applied behavior analysis for teachers*. Upper Saddle River, NJ: Merrill/Prentice Hall.

Baer, D. (1988). Foreword. In F. Rusch, T. Rose, & C. Greenwood, *Introduction to behavior analysis in education*. (pp. ix–xi). Englewood Cliffs, NJ: Prentice Hall.

Bandura, A. (1995). *Self efficacy in changing societies*. Cambridge, England: Cambridge University Press.

Buskist, W., & Gerbing, D. (1990). *Psychology: Boundaries and frontiers*. Glenview, IL: Scott Foresman/Little Brown.

Canter, L. (1989). Assertive discipline: More than names on the board and marbles in a jar. *Phi Delta Kappan, 71,* 57–61.

Canter, L., & Canter, M. (1976). *Assertive discipline: A take charge approach for today's educator*. Los Angeles: Canter & Associates.

Chard, D., Smith, S., & Sugai, G. (1992). Packaged discipline programs: A consumer's guide. In G. Tindal (Ed.), The *Oregon Conference Monograph* (pp. 19–26). Eugene, OR: The University of Oregon, Behavioral Research and Teaching Group.

Cullinan, D., Epstein, M., & Lloyd, J. (1991). Evaluation of conceptual models of behavior disorders. *Behavioral Disorders, 16,* 148–157.

Dreikurs, R. (1974). *Discipline without tears*. New York: Hawthorn Books.

Dreikurs, R. (1982). *Maintaining sanity in the classroom: Classroom management techniques*. New York: Harper & Row.

Duke, D. L., & Meckel, A. M. (1984). *Teacher's guide to classroom management*. New York: Random House.

Edgar, E. (1998). Where does weather come from? A response to "Behavior disorders: A postmodern perspective." *Behavioral Disorders, 23,* 160–165.

Engelmann, S., & Colvin, G. (1983). *Generalized compliance training*. Austin, TX: PRO-ED.

Freud, S. (1938). *A general introduction to psychoanalysis*. New York: Doubleday.

Gersten, R., Woodward, J., & Darch, C. (1986). Direct instruction: A research-based approach to curriculum design and teaching. *Exceptional children, 53,* 17–31.

Hardman, M. L., Drew, C. J., & Egan, M. W. (1999). Human exceptionality: Society, school, and family (6th ed.). Boston: Allyn & Bacon.

Jones, L. (1991). *Strategies for involving parents in their children's education*. Bloomington, IN: Phi Delta Kappa Educational Foundation.

Kame'enui, E. J., & Darch, C. B. (1995). *Instructional classroom management: A proactive approach to behavior management*. White Plains, NY: Longman.

Kame'enui, E., & Simmons, D. (1997). *Designing instructional strategies: The prevention of learning problems*. Upper Saddle River, NJ: Merrill/Prentice Hall.

Kame'enui, E., & Simmons, D. (1998). Beyond effective practice to schools as host environments: Building and sustaining a school-wide intervention model in reading. *Oregon School Study Council (OSSC) Bulletin, 41*(3).

Kaplan, J., & Carter, J. (1995). *Beyond behavior modification: A cognitive-behavioral approach to behavior management in the schools*. Austin, TX: PRO-ED.

Neuwirth, S. (1994). *Attention deficit hyperactivity disorder*. National Institute of Mental Health (NIH Publication No. 94-3572) (On-line). Available: http://www.nimh.nih.gov/publicat/adhd.htm.

Rogers-Warren, A. (1984). Ecobehavioral analysis. *Education and Treatment of Children, 7,* 283–303.

Rusch, F., Rose, T., & Greenwood, C. (1988). *Introduction to behavior analysis in education*. Englewood-Cliffs, NJ: Prentice Hall.

Silver, L. (1995). *The role of medication*. Paper presented at the annual meeting of the Learning Disabilities Association, Honolulu, Hawaii.

Skinner, B. F. (1971). *Beyond freedom and dignity*. New York: Knopf.

Sprick, R., Garrison, M., & Howard, L. (1998). *CHAMPS: A proactive and positive approach to classroom management*. Longmont, CO: Sopris.

Walker, H., Colvin, G., & Ramsey, E. (1995). *Antisocial behavior in school: Strategies and best practices*. Pacific Grove, CA: Brooks Cole.

Wolery, M., Bailey, D., & Sugai, G. (1988). *Effective teaching: Principles and procedures of applied behavior analysis with exceptional students*. Boston: Allyn & Bacon.

Chapter

3

A Conceptual Framework for Instructional Classroom Management

OVERVIEW

Educators have long understood that behavior problems can keep students from functioning productively in the classroom. At the same time, there is much controversy as to the most effective instructional strategies teachers can use to effectively manage behavior of students in school. This debate has been ongoing for years. According to Berliner (1988), classroom management is the "area that the press and the public love to criticize teachers about, and it is the area that teachers have the most fear about when they begin to teach" (p. 321). However, he goes on to argue that, "We have made unbelievable strides in the last decade, having learned many of the techniques used by teachers that lead to smooth-running, on-task, cheerful classrooms" (p. 321). Indeed we have made "unbelievable strides." For example, there is little disagreement about the importance of systematically arranging and organizing the classroom (Paine, Radicchi, Rosellini, Deutchman, & Darch, 1983; Vaughn & Klinger, 1998) in ways that improve student task engagement and performance (Brophy & Good, 1986; Klinger, Vaughn, Hughes, Schumm, & Elbaum, 1998) as well as student completion of clearly articulated learning tasks (Evertson, 1989). In addition, teachers are now more knowledgeable about how to modify their instructional and classroom management strategies to accommodate diverse students. In fact Mercer, Lane, Jordan, Allsopp, and Eisele (1996) suggest, "To benefit all students, teachers must have a repertoire of instructional approaches that can help students progress from the need for explicit instruction to the ability to direct their own learning" (p. 227). Few would argue that teaching students to manage their own learning and behavior, or providing the necessary instructional support to be successful, are important features of any classroom management strategy. However, many teachers still find translating research into practice a difficult endeavor, particularly with students who exhibit behavior problems. Shores, Jack, Gunter, Ellis, and DeBriere (1993) report in a study that teachers working with students with behavior disorders provided little instructional support for responding correctly. Teachers provided support on less than 20% of the occasions in which students were requested to respond to questions. This level of instructional support is less than adequate to maintain high levels of student success during instruction.

In fact, more than a decade ago, Rohrkemper and Brophy (1980) argued the research had produced a "largely consistent knowledge base identifying effective group management techniques and linking them to teacher success in maximizing student engagement in academic activities and achievement on standardized tests" (p. 1). This knowledge base continues to be developed. Christenson, Ysseldyke, and Thurlow (1989) have discussed the degree to which classroom management strategies must be both effective and efficient: "Classrooms in which fewer behavioral problems occur tend to be ones in which established instructional routines are used, resulting in increased student cooperation and control. Students in these classrooms know when they are confused, how to obtain necessary information or assistance, where material and supplies are kept, and the procedures for bathroom breaks, sharpening pencils, and selecting the next activity upon completing an assignment. Transitions are brief in these classrooms" (p. 22). However, this knowledge is not always translated into daily instructional and management strategies by teachers. Abbott, Walton, Tapia, and Greenwood (1999) recognize a "long-standing gap between research and practice in general and special education" (p. 339), and that this research-to-practice gap has become a national concern for professionals working in the schools.

Gunter and Denny (1996) discuss the important relationship between a teacher's classroom management strategies and instructional approach. "Classroom management strategies may serve as setting events for academic and social behavior" (p. 15). However, teachers have been slow in designing instructional and behavioral interventions that are part of their instructional plan (Conroy & Fox, 1994).

A long, rich history of research has investigated the management strategies teachers use in their classrooms. Over 20 years ago, research by Rohrkemper and Brophy (1980) on teachers' strategies for dealing with problem behaviors revealed some interesting findings. The researchers found that teachers who were considered high-ability teachers for handling difficult students (a) used more rewards; (b) provided more supportive behavior, including more comforting and reassuring of students; (c) used punishment less than other teachers; and (d) were more likely to involve students in their own behavior change. These skills that characterized high-ability teachers more than two decades ago are no less important now. For example, Clarke et al. (1995) investigated the effectiveness of individualized, curricular modifications on the behavior of students with behavior problems. The study of Clarke et al. (1995) was consistent with Rohrkemper and Brophy (1980) in demonstrating that careful modification of a teacher's instructional plan resulted in more successful involvement of students and decreased disruptive behavior.

Features of an instructional classroom management approach to problem behaviors are in part derived from past research on classroom management and research on teacher effectiveness, which attempts to clarify the relations between student outcomes and what the teacher does in the classroom. As Good (1979) stated, "Teachers' managerial abilities have been found to relate positively to student achievement in every process-product study conducted to date" (p. 54). The research on instructional classroom management is even broader than teacher behavior and student outcomes because it also incorporates an analysis of task and instructional variables. However, teachers continue to report their training, both at the preservice and inservice levels, is less than adequate for managing diverse classrooms (George, George, Gersten, & Grosenick, 1995). Teachers need a clearly articulated conceptual framework to help them organize integrated and effective instructional and classroom management strategies.

A PROACTIVE APPROACH

As noted in Chapter 1, a critical feature of an instructional classroom management approach is that it is proactive. Teachers design instructional materials and teaching sequences to reduce the probability of school failure and disruptive behavior. Simply put, one acts *before* a problem occurs rather than reacting *after* the problem. As Gettinger (1988) states, "'Proactive' means to act in advance, to design a plan of action that affords an individual maximum control of a situation" (p. 228). A proactive approach to classroom management "anticipates and prepares for a situation through a plan to achieve control of the situation" (Swick, 1988, as cited in Gettinger, 1988, p. 228). Many inexperienced teachers have a limited understanding of how general teaching and classroom management requirements affect their understanding of what constitutes proactive behavior management. They don't see how instruction and classroom management can be melded to form an instructional classroom management approach.

Francis (1995) investigated how preservice teachers reflected upon different aspects of their teaching and classroom management activities. One of the subjects in her study wrote in her teaching journal about the requirements of developing a positive and proactive approach to classroom instruction and management: "I am still tending to think about . . . the preparation of a caring classroom climate. While I think this is important, there must be more to managing the learning environment than a positive atmosphere. Atmosphere alone doesn't stimulate thinking or challenge children to set higher goals" (p. 236). As teachers gain experience and begin to develop more sophisticated conceptual frameworks of instruction and classroom management, they begin to see the importance of proactive management.

Gettinger (1988) describes three "distinguishing characteristics" of a proactive classroom management approach: (a) it is preventative, (b) it integrates methods that "facilitate appropriate student behavior with procedures that promote achievement through effective instruction" (p. 229), and (c) it emphasizes group dimensions of classroom management. Proactive classroom management, Gettinger (1988) argues, "represents a broader approach to effective management than either behavioral or instructional management alone" (p. 229). However, the application of a proactive approach to instruction can be difficult for teachers to implement. Zigmond and Baker (1996) observed and interviewed teachers regarding their attempts to proactively modify instruction to increase the academic and social successes for students with learning and behavior problems in the general education classroom. They characterize one-to-one proactive instructional and management episodes—those attempts by teachers to modify the curriculum assignment or adjust instructional delivery—as "unplanned and infrequent" (p. 31).

While we agree with Gettinger's (1988) analysis of proactive classroom management, his assertion that instructional management is not a broad approach is debatable for one simple reason. No one has clearly or substantially delineated the details of an instructional approach to classroom management. This text delineates such details, at least at an introductory level.

A proactive classroom management approach doesn't require a teacher to anticipate and prevent every problem that surfaces in the classroom, for there is simply no way to anticipate some problems. In addition, as Zigmond and Baker (1996) point out, teachers who are working in inclusive classrooms often don't have the necessary time and support to implement a proactive classroom management approach in a systematic way. However, a proactive approach to instructional classroom management is not so much taking action before problems occur than it is establishing a way of thinking about behavior that solves problems before initiating an exchange or a lesson with the learner. A proactive approach to management requires a teacher to consider all aspects of the learning task: details of implementation, student learning and behavior characteristics, and assessment activities that help teachers make decisions about restructuring or reteaching the task.

In the most practical sense, we think of a proactive approach to classroom management as including the following characteristics of a teacher's behavior. The teacher:

1. Identifies, teaches, and posts rules for appropriate behavior in the classroom.
2. Periodically reminds students of the rules for behaving appropriately.
3. Creates and maintains a positive, warm, and supportive classroom environment in which students feel comfortable and academically engaged.
4. Greets students at the classroom door before class begins.
5. Arranges the physical space and materials in the classroom to prevent disruption and distractions and maximize student task engagement.
6. Systematically rewards (e.g., verbal praise) students for demonstrating appropriate behavior in the school setting.
7. Establishes a clear and consistent routine for moving about the classroom and carrying out general classroom routines and activities.
8. Works with other teachers to ensure quick and quiet transitions between classes and positive behavior management of students.
9. Facilitates the learning process by mediating and controlling learning activities and making adjustments in the instruction.
10. Accommodates student needs by adjusting schedules and lesson demands on a case-by-case basis.

The list above represents a proactive approach to classroom management primarily because it involves actions the teacher carries out either before or during a lesson to prevent a problem from surfacing. A proactive approach to classroom management, however, must extend beyond the general planning, management, and monitoring of students' social behavior. It must also consider the dimensions of the instructional process related to students' learning and academic performance and the role school-wide programs (Ashbaugh & Kasten, 1991) can serve as a positive part

Proactive classroom management includes greeting students at the door as they enter.

of effective, proactive management. Clearly, a school that is orderly and has a positive atmosphere, encouraged by strong, focused leadership, and effective instructional classroom management, contributes to the academic and teaching focus essential for successful student learning and school participation. According to Sugai (1996), a proactive approach to instruction extends to instructional and management activities at all levels of a school. Sugai (1996) organizes instructional and management proactive strategies into six basic components: (a) a clear and positive statement of purpose, (b) a set of positively stated expectations for prosocial behavior, (c) procedures for teaching school-wide expectations, (d) a continuum of procedures for encouraging displays of school-wide expectations, (e) a continuum of procedures for discouraging violations of school-wide expectations, and (f) a method for monitoring implementation and effectiveness of these procedures.

In short, a proactive approach addresses the very learning and teaching tasks and classroom activities that often set the occasion for serious behavior problems. This approach also establishes the broader context of the school and its effect on the learning and behavior of students. It incorporates the teacher preparing a lesson for an academic skill, like sound-symbol relationships, as well as a social behavior skill, like transitioning quietly from one learning activity to another. A proactive approach to instruction requires identifying those dimensions of a task or the instructional process that may be troublesome for a learner before the learner is required to engage in the target task or lesson.

To appreciate the difference between a reactive and proactive approach to classroom management, consider the following vignette. Prior to starting the lesson, the teacher carried out some of the ten activities listed earlier as representing a proactive approach to classroom management. The teacher (a) reviewed the rules with

Jon and he readily recited them (e.g., "I will keep my eyes on my work. I will give every task my best effort"); (b) created and maintained a positive, warm, and supportive classroom environment; (c) arranged the physical space and materials in ways that helped prevent Jon from being distracted; and (d) praised Jon when he demonstrated the appropriate behaviors. In spite of these attempts to be proactive, the lesson ended when Jon's verbalizations about his new puppy became excessive, and the teacher stopped the lesson and had Jon sit quietly with his head down on the desk. The teacher also ensured before the lesson that the rest of the class was working on an independent activity, which allowed the teacher to work with Jon.

Vignette of a Reactive Approach

Jon is a third grader posing a problem for his teacher, because he is very active physically and verbally. He is also falling behind in mathematics. The teacher has scheduled the task of counting by fives that requires Jon to orally state the facts (e.g., 5-10-15-20-25-30). The following interactions take place:

Teacher (T):	Hi Jon, how are you?
Jon (J):	Did you know I got a new puppy?
T:	Oh you did?
J:	Yes, I got it for my birthday and it has brown and white spots all over. It wiggles its . . .
T:	Okay, Jon. Let's get back to work. Today we're going to count by fives. What are we going to do, Jon?
J:	We're going to count by fives. My puppy is really cute, you know.
T:	Yes, we're going to count by fives. Let's start, listen, 5-10-15-20-25-30. Your turn . . . you count by five. Start with five and stop at 30.
J:	5-10-15-20-30. Do you have a puppy?
T:	Listen, Jon. I'll count by fives again. 5-10-15-20 . . .
J:	Do you have a puppy? My puppy is really cute.
T:	Listen again, 5-10-15-20-25-30.
J:	My puppy has brown and white spots all over it.
T:	Jon, I need you to count by fives. Get ready . . . count.
J:	5-10-15 . . . Do you have a puppy?

By most accounts, the teacher's efforts represent reasonable attempts to teach Jon an important skill. She didn't waste valuable instructional time and began the task immediately, even though Jon was more interested in talking about his new puppy. She focused on the task, ignored Jon's comments about his puppy, and tried to keep Jon focused as well. However, in spite of her efforts, the task deteriorated as Jon became relentless in his verbalizations. Unable to curb Jon's talk about his puppy, the teacher placed him in an "in-class time-out."

The teacher's efforts to be proactive were sabotaged by her failure to consider one important variable—the instructional task and the response requirements this task made of Jon. In this case, the teacher prepared an instructional task that was reasonable but simply the wrong one to teach at the time. The task of requiring Jon to state a verbal chain (e.g., 5-10-15-20-25-30) from rote memory (Kame'enui & Simmons, 1997) contributed to Jon's excessive verbalizations. Because of Jon's penchant for being active both physically and verbally, the verbal task of counting by fives fueled his verbalizations and provided him an opportunity to practice not only the chain of math facts, but also his strategy of using verbal tasks to become disengaged from academic work. A more appropriate task would not require any verbalizations, such as a written task in which Jon would produce a sustained written response. The teacher could have minimized Jon's excessive verbal behavior by starting with a task that required Jon to write, not talk.

The teaching focus of the instructional classroom management approach we recommend is different from many approaches to behavior management. For example, Gunter and Denny (1996) discussed the "importance of structure in effective and efficient management of the classroom environments for all students" (p. 16). They describe structure as having three focal points. The first is the physical structure of the classroom. They suggest that teachers should consider seating arrangements, the organization of the physical space of the classroom, and the proximity of the students to each other as important in a general classroom management model. The second aspect of structure Gunter and Denny discuss is the temporal structure of the classroom. They suggest the teacher must be aware of time and transitions when classroom management problems are being considered. Finally, the third component of structure in classroom management that Gunter and Denny discuss is social structure, the identification of the conventions for social behavior in the classroom. While each of these areas is important for teachers to consider when developing classroom management plans, the critical feature again missing in their analysis is instructional organization and design. Simply, how can each individual instructional task, whether the goal of that task is to teach multiplication facts or appropriate ways for students to manage stress, be organized and designed to increase successful participation and learning for students with behavior problems?

Matching the instructional task and Jon's behavior we earlier described requires intimate knowledge of at least two sets of variables: (a) Jon's past behavior in a range of instructional conditions and (b) the intricate requirements of the task, such as the response requirements placed on the learner. The instructional approach to classroom management considers the full range of task dimensions and the instructional context in development of strategies for managing children's academic and social behavior.

TASK DIMENSIONS OF INSTRUCTIONAL CLASSROOM MANAGEMENT

There are six task dimensions for teachers to consider in an instructional classroom management approach: (a) history, (b) response form, (c) modality, (d) complexity, (e) schedule, and (f) variation. Definitions and examples of task dimensions to be utilized for proactive classroom management are given in Table 3.1.

TABLE 3.1 Definitions and Examples of Task Dimensions

Task Dimensions	Features and Examples
1. **Task History:** The status of a task, the extent to which it has been taught before, and the likelihood the learner will be familiar with the task.	**New**—novel and never seen before task **Familiar**—introduced previously but not mastered **Old**—mastered and established
2. **Task Response Form:** The manner in which students are required to respond to the task or teacher.	**Yes/No**—answer *yes* or *no* **Choice**—select an answer from multiple choice **Production**—produce a response
3. **Task Modality:** The mode of response required of the student.	**Oral**—verbal talk **Motor**—physical manipulation **Written**—writing a response
4. **Task Complexity:** The extent to which a task involves multiple steps, new concepts, unfamiliar procedures, etc.	**Easy**—task not complex **Hard**—task complex
5. **Task Schedule:** The amount of time allocated to complete a task.	**Abbreviated**—task scheduled for short periods of time **Extended**—task scheduled for long periods of time
6. **Task Variation:** The sequence in which easy or hard tasks are scheduled within a lesson.	**Varied**—easy and hard tasks are varied one after another **Unvaried**—tasks are not changed in sequence

Task History

The notion that learners have a learning history regarding the acquisition of academic and social skills is well accepted (Rosenberg, Wilson, Maheady, & Sindelar, 1997). A student's learning is comprised of the full range of past events related to schooling and learning, such as acquiring information, responding to school demands, interacting with teachers, performing on tests, studying and collaborating with peers, writing reports, completing daily assignments, and so on. Task history is concerned with assessing the learner's familiarity with a particular task. In other words, the task can be new and novel to the learner, or it can be an old task for which the learner has a great deal of background knowledge and even a high level of familiarity, if not automaticity. In either case, the history a student has with a learning or behavior activity has broad implications for teaching and managing that student's behavior. A teacher can make predictions about a student's behavior in the context of an academic activity if the teacher knows the student's history of successful learning on similar tasks.

New tasks present learners and teachers a different set of problems and challenges from old tasks. New tasks require a fundamentally different kind of teaching than old or even familiar tasks. The teaching of new tasks, be they social skills, concepts, algorithms, rule relationships, or principles, assumes the learner has little or no competency for performing the tasks. The learner may have some background knowledge or pre-requisite skills related to the target tasks, but for all practical purposes, the task is new and unknown to the learner. In a sense, the learner is in a state of *unknowing* about the task, and it is the teacher's responsibility to move the learner to a state of *knowing*. In addition, the teacher has limited information about how the student will perform new learning tasks and activities, which frequently cause behavior problems simply because they are new. Because the learner has had no instruction on the new task, the teaching must be carefully planned with all dimensions of the task considered.

The more the learner knows about a task (e.g., a known, mastered task), the more demands we can place on the learner. Similarly, the less the learner knows about a task (e.g., an unknown, novel task), the fewer demands we can place on that learner. New tasks are the most difficult for learners and may set the occasion for problem behaviors. For example, if a fourth grade student with a history of learn-ing and behavior problems is presented with learning a new academic skill such as the reading rule that "if a word has an *e* at the end, you say the name of the vowel." The teacher's instruction includes asking the student to decode a new word type (e.g., *late, fate, tire, tone*). Reading this set of words creates anxiety for a student who has always experienced difficulty learning new reading skills. The reason for the stu-dent's anxiety is obvious, and after being presented with reading a difficult set of words, the student wonders how to get him- or herself out of this situation. The way many disruptive students extricate themselves from difficult new learning tasks is to act out and create enough behavior problems so the teacher's attention is focused on the student's behavior, not on whether he/she can read the words. A student's disruptive behavior often comes at the beginning of the new learning task.

Academic and social skill activities that have been previously taught and mas-tered by the learner cause less difficulty for the learner. For example, assume a stu-dent with learning and behavior problems has been effectively taught to quietly transition from one learning activity to another within the classroom. Or, a student is presented with a review lesson on how to decode irregular CVC words (e.g., *saw, tar*). These mastery-level tasks require less cognitive effort, because the learner has had extensive practice on them and is fairly automatic and fluent. In addition, old tasks require much less instructional support from the teacher. Because of the stu-dent's history of success with the particular skill, the teacher does not need to spend a great deal of time setting up the task or providing instructional prompts to promote success. The teacher's efforts when presenting previously mastered tasks are directed toward keeping the students motivated to practice the skill. In this case, the teacher's instructional planning reflects task history. Old tasks are scheduled for periodic re-view and practice, which are used to assess the learner's retention or recall of what is already known. The teacher can reasonably assume the learner understands the re-quirements of an old task, and the student can also reasonably assume he/she will successfully complete the assigned learning activity. This task history has implications for the teacher when designing an instructional and behavior management strategy.

A familiar task is one that has been introduced to the learner but has not been mastered and therefore requires further instruction, review, and practice. The de-gree to which the task is familiar to the learner depends on several factors that in-clude: (a) the adequacy with which the task was previously taught; (b) the amount of time between successive presentations of the task to the learner; (c) the learner's retention and recall of the task; (d) the sameness in content, form, context, and response demands between successive tasks; (e) the criterion level of student performance on tasks presented previously; and (f) the student's interest in the content being taught (Charlebois, Normandeau, Vitaro, & Berneche, 1999).

Gauging students' level of mastery across tasks is difficult and will require an evaluation and assessment system that is sensitive to students' daily classroom performance. The range of assessment tools and strategies is extensive and beyond the scope of this chapter. (See Chapter 5 for a complete discussion of assessment strategies.) However, determining if a task is new, old, or familiar to the learner is fairly straightforward and sets the stage for considering the full range of task dimensions that may cause potential social behavior problems. By knowing the task history for both academic and social skills activities, the teacher will be alerted to potential problems and can adjust expectations about a learner's performance on the task and, most importantly, make modifications in the instructional plan.

Task Response Form

Learners demonstrate their general knowledge of the world by providing overt, observable responses to specific tasks. Not surprisingly, these responses come in various forms, ranging from audible grunts designed to acknowledge, to thoughtful, prosaic essays intended to persuade. The student's response form is an important teaching consideration in both academic and social skills learning. For example, when young students with a history of difficulty following the teacher's directions are first taught this critical skill, the instruction can be designed so students are only required to provide oral responses to questions about the sequence of events to follow. However, when students have been taught verbal responses to following the teacher's direction, they are then required to actually demonstrate they can follow an array of teacher commands (e.g., "Students, please put your pencils down, open your reading text to page 25, and point to the first question under Part A."). Student responses are varied and come in the following forms:

1. **Yes/no choice response.** The teacher presents a question that requires a simple yes or no response from the learner. For example, the teacher asks, "Was Millard Fillmore the 20th President of the United States?" The student responds by answering, "No."
2. **Multiple choice response.** The teacher presents a question that requires selecting an answer from a set of possible responses provided to the learner. For example, "Tell me if Millard Fillmore was the 13th President, the 15th President, or the 20th President of the United States." The student selects an answer, "Millard Fillmore was the 13th President of the United States."
3. **Production response.** The teacher asks a question for which the student is required to generate a response. For example, the teacher asks, "Who was the 13th President of the United States?" The student responds by stating, "Millard Fillmore was the 13th President of the United States."

The three types of responses can be placed on an easy-to-hard continuum in which yes/no choice responses are the easiest and production responses are typically the hardest. Multiple choice response forms fall somewhere in between. This analysis applies when students are learning academic skills or social skills. The response forms vary in the amount of information provided back to the teacher and the amount of prompting and cueing carried by the response form. A yes/no choice response provides minimal information about what the learner knows, because the learner has an equal chance of getting the answer right or wrong. In contrast, a production response only offers extensive information about what the learner knows, because the learner is given little information about the correct response.

When planning any teaching task, the teacher must determine the most appropriate response form for the student. As with other task dimensions, the selection of the response form will depend on a range of considerations. For example, if the teacher plans to teach a *new task* that may be difficult for the learner, a yes/no response may be the best response form to use initially. The yes/no response is a generally weak response form, because the learner has a 50% chance of getting the answer right. For example, let's assume that a teacher has designed an instructional sequence for teaching a group of students how to apply the rule "when there is an *e* at the end of a word, you say the name of the vowel" to the following list of words:

    rode
    rod
    fat
    fate

In order to ease the level of difficulty of the reading list, the teacher begins the teaching sequence with a series of yes/no questions. Thus, the teacher points to the first word and says, "Class, is there an *e* at the end of the word?" The students respond correctly by saying, "yes." After the students have responded correctly, the teacher proceeds to teach the critical discrimination of saying the long vowel sound for the word or using the short vowel sound. The teacher's use of a relatively easy response form (yes/no) increases dramatically the students' success, and the teacher thereby increases the probability there will be fewer behavior problems during the lesson.

When an old task is reviewed, it is more reasonable for the teacher to require the learner to provide production responses, because the task is familiar, if not already mastered by the learner. Of course, in the academic domain (e.g., reading, mathematics, social studies), the desired outcomes and the learner's background knowledge are also important variables to consider in selecting the most appropriate response forms. In the social skills domain as well, the teacher must consider if the student has the necessary prerequisite behaviors for mastering the new skill being taught.

Task Modality

In addition to the response form, the response modality is important. For example, a production response can be given orally, in writing, or motorically (e.g., student uses an augmentative communication device to select words or phrases to produce a statement). Like task response forms, task modes can be placed on an easy-to-hard continuum, in which the easiest mode of response is likely to be a motor one, and the hardest mode of response is a written one. A written mode requires the learner to orchestrate a host of skills that eventually result in a permanent product, a product that displays to the audience the thoughts and competencies of the writer (Kame'enui & Simmons, 1997).

Examples of different task modalities are given below:

1. **Oral:** The student tells the teacher the name of the 13th President of the United States.
2. **Written:** The student writes the name of the 13th President of the United States.
3. **Motor:** The teacher gives the student a worksheet in which five written choices are given. The student checks the answer to indicate that Millard Fillmore was the 13th President of the United States.

The difficulty of the response modality varies from learner to learner, and the selection of the best mode depends again on the learner, the desired outcomes, the task history, and so on. However, there is one more consideration for a teacher when selecting the task modality for a learning activity. When teaching students social skills (e.g., lining up properly, using appropriate greeting with a teacher or another adult) the most difficult mode of response for most students is motor. It is easier for students to explain why it is important to line up quietly than it is to actually line up quietly.

Task Complexity

As noted in Table 3.1, task complexity is concerned with the extent to which a task requires the learner to complete a series of steps that are either new or unfamiliar. If the task is new and involves a series of steps that are complex and require the learner

When the learning task is new or difficult the teacher must provide explicit instruction.

to apply unfamiliar terms, information, or skills not mastered, then it is likely to be hard for the learner. In contrast, if the task involves one or two steps, mastered concepts, skills, or knowledge, then the task is likely to be easier for the learner. As with other task dimensions, the complexity of a task can range from easy to hard.

The complexity of a task can be made easy or hard by a number of other variables not directly related to the task itself. For example, the clarity with which the task is presented, described, and "framed" (Kame'enui & Simmons, 1997) prior to requiring students to complete it, can also influence the complexity of a task. If, for example, a teacher gives her students who have a history of learning or behavior problems an assignment to write a 5-page paper on the causes of the Civil War in the United States, without providing the instructional support for completing the assignment, then successful completion of the writing assignment is not very likely. Specifically, if the task is not properly framed, and expected outcomes and response forms are not clear, then the task will be difficult for the learner to complete successfully. If an unfamiliar task is presented immediately after the completion of another complex and difficult task, then the successive presentation of two difficult and unfamiliar tasks is likely to cause problems of fatigue and motivation. This increases the probability of learning and behavior problems.

The complexity of a task is made easy or difficult by the number and kinds of concrete examples presented to explain or demonstrate the new task. For example, if a new concept is taught using only one or two examples, then the task is likely to be difficult for the learner. If a range of greatly different examples is used to teach a new concept, the task is also likely to be difficult. For example, second grade teacher Mr. Sing is teaching solving single-digit addition problems with an unknown addend for the first time. As the figure shown here illustrates, Mr. Sing presents two problems on the board with a brief teaching demonstration.

$5 + \square = 9$ $6 + \square = 8$	
Mr. Sing says:	Student response:
"Students, you have to remember when you solve these kinds of problems to count from the little number on the left side to the big number on the right side. Whatever number you end up with is the number you put in the empty box."	
Mr. Sing shows how in the first problem to count from 5 to 9 and then fill in the missing addend. Mr. Sing asks, "Does everyone see what I just did?"	Yes
The teacher uses the same teaching routine for the second problem on the board and asks, "Does anyone have a question?"	No

As soon as Mr. Sing has completed his teaching demonstration, he hands out a 15-problem worksheet and instructs the students to work quietly and complete the worksheet. Not long after the students begin to work, students become agitated, inattentive, and begin to argue among themselves. Mr. Sing provided his students only two brief and not very helpful teaching demonstrations. The result was that his students did poorly on the worksheet and became disruptive in the process.

Tasks that are difficult, confusing, and unclear set the stage for serious behavior problems if the instruction for the task is not adequate. Task complexity is an important consideration when designing a proactive instructional classroom management system.

Task Schedule

The amount of time scheduled to teach and complete a task influences the difficulty of the task and consequent behavior. Tasks can be scheduled for extended or brief periods of time. By allocating extensive time (i.e., 45 minutes to an hour) for a particular task, the teacher is making the following set of assumptions:

1. The task is not new but is familiar to the learner.
2. The learner has all the component or prerequisite skills necessary to complete the task.
3. The task is of moderate difficulty; that is, it is not so easy as to be boring to the learner, or so difficult as to be frustrating.
4. The extended time is necessary for the learner to independently "practice" a set of skills related to an important educational outcome.
5. The response form of the task is production or a mixture of choice and production responses.
6. The mode of the task is written or a mixture of modes (e.g., oral, motor, and written).
7. The task history is that the major components of the task are familiar to the learner and established in the learner's repertoire.
8. The expected outcome of the task is substantial, clear, and aligned with educationally valid goals for the learner.
9. The task is sufficiently engaging and motivating to maintain the learner's attention and increase the probability it will be completed successfully.
10. The task involves multiple steps and components that require extended time to connect to demonstrate knowledge of a particular knowledge base or domain.

A task scheduled for an extended period of time should not be so difficult as to be punishing, or so easy as to be trivial to the learner. For example, a teacher could schedule 45 minutes to teach third grade students how to work complex division operations. Such a teaching schedule is not likely to lead to success, especially for low-performing students who have difficulty staying engaged for long periods of time. Ten minutes into the teaching routine, off-task behavior is likely to become a problem. Even if the teacher scheduled 20 minutes of teaching and 25 minutes of independent seatwork, the amount of real learning is likely to be limited. Tasks scheduled for extended periods of time must be carefully planned with specific outcomes and must consider the full range of task dimensions listed in Table 3.1.

In contrast to an extended schedule is a variable schedule in which a range of tasks, possibly even a greater number of tasks, is scheduled for brief periods of time. Instead of scheduling the teaching of a new math operation for 45 minutes, the teacher may schedule it for 15 minutes, followed by 15 minutes of work on a writing task familiar to the learner. The teacher then returns to the new math task previously introduced and reviews or practices for 15 minutes. In contrast to a traditional schedule of 45 minutes for teaching and working on mathematics only, this variable schedule is comprised of three distinct activities involving three different academic tasks.

It's important to note this is an ideal example, for in reality, teachers must account for transition time between activities. A schedule of abbreviated activities has several advantages. First, variety of academic tasks (e.g., mathematics, reading, writing) is likely to maintain the learner's attention and engagement, because there is little redundant activity, and the variation from task to task holds the learner's attention. Second, the abbreviated tasks represent succinct, obtainable goals. A task can be started and completed in a brief time to allow students a sense of accomplishment. Students are likely to feel reinforced and refreshed after completing a series of tasks, in contrast to enduring a long assignment for which the beginning and ending points are long forgotten.

Finally, a schedule of abbreviated activities allows students to review in a cumulative way information previously introduced, as the teacher teaches multiple strands of skills, rather than just one skill or content area. Specifically, a new task introduced on Monday can be reviewed in various abbreviated chunks of time (e.g., 5 minutes one day and 10 minutes the next day) every day of the week. This differs from a traditional schedule that teaches a new skill for 45 minutes on Monday and reviews it on Tuesday (if at all), before moving on to the next task and skill.

Task Variation

When multiple tasks are presented in a lesson, they create a sequence that is varied or unvaried (i.e., comprised of both easy and hard tasks, all easy tasks, or all hard tasks). Presenting difficult tasks back-to-back often sets the occasion for frustration, failure, and perhaps behavior problems. A better approach is to vary the sequence so that difficult tasks are followed by easy or moderately difficult tasks. The task variation is most important for students who experience academic learning problems and are at risk for behavior problems, while it may be unnecessary for average learners. Low-performing students must eventually be able to respond to an unvaried sequence of tasks (e.g., a series of difficult or demanding tasks).

APPLICATION OF TASK DIMENSIONS TO CLASSROOM MANAGEMENT

Kauffman and Wong (1991) have pointed out that teachers can be more effective teaching and managing students with behavior problems by employing "instructional and management strategies that are significantly different from those used by effective teachers of nonidentified students" (p. 226). The conceptual framework for modifying task dimensions discussed herein takes an initial step toward those "significantly different" strategies. Identifying, isolating, and describing task dimensions of classroom management represents only part of an instructional classroom management approach. The next step is for the teacher to translate adjustments in task dimensions into teaching plans for successful learning. In order to accomplish this goal, these task dimensions must be considered within the full context of instruction. First, all instruction, whether academic or social, takes place within a temporal framework. Specifically, Kame'enui and Simmons (1997) and others (e.g., Sprick, Garrison, & Howard, 1998) have called for designing instruction in three phases of *before instruction, during instruction,* and *after instruction.* The same analysis applied by Kame'enui and Simmons (1997) for design and development of instruction in a temporal framework can be applied to instructional classroom management. The usefulness of the instructional design analysis we recommend is that teachers can proactively tailor an instructional task for a group of students by making adjustments in the task dimensions. If a teacher is working with students who have a history of difficulty with a certain skill, he/she can modify the task dimensions to make the learning activity more manageable. On the other hand, if a teacher is working on a review task that requires less cognitive effort from the students, the teacher can modify task dimensions to increase the level of difficulty so that students remain interested and motivated. As most teachers know, providing students instruction well below their ability level as well as too far above often results in behavior problems (Jolivette, Wehby, & Hirsch, 1999).

Before Instruction

All task dimensions listed in Table 3.1 and described previously should be considered in the phase that comes before a task is presented to the learner. Adjusting task dimensions in the before-instruction phase is effective and efficient just before a lesson is taught or well before school begins. What's important is to consider the dimensions of the task before a lesson is taught and demands are placed on learners to respond. It is during the before-phase instruction that the teacher links potential learning difficulties and proactive adjustments to the teaching plan. As part of their preteaching planning, teachers should consider (a) students' ability level, (b) the structure of the task, and (c) how the task dimensions can be adjusted to increase successful learning.

Adjustments in task dimensions may require extensive adaptations to the curriculum program being used. Investigations of curriculum material shows that many commercial programs are not designed to accommodate students with learning and behavior problems (Kame'enui & Simmons, 1997). Commercial reading programs often provide too few practice trials for learning basic decoding and comprehension strategies, a sequence of skills that fosters early reading problems for some students, and insufficient review for mastery and retention. Commercial math programs for elementary students with learning and behavior problems provide similar concerns. For example, a commercial mathematics curriculum program may introduce a new operation or skill by requiring students to work with manipulatives for an extended period of time. Evans (1991) compared an algorithm-only strategy with a manipulatives strategy and found that students took an average of three times longer (i.e., average time of 75 minutes) to reach criterion level using manipulatives than an algorithm-only strategy.

For low performers, manipulating a hundred or more objects (e.g., pasta, cubes, toothpicks) is not easy and presents serious challenges that may result in students becoming frustrated with the manipulatives. Low-performing children have a difficult time focusing on a task, selecting a strategy that's effective, carrying out a strategy, sticking with a strategy, and adjusting their use of a strategy to solve a problem. These difficulties in the context of using manipulatives are compounded because students are required to keep track of many loose objects, arrange the objects into specified groups, and make the association between a symbolic system and the concrete objects. Orchestrating all these actions and objects can be very frustrating.

The following task dimensions as a group create the most difficult task scenario:

Task History:	new
Task Response Form:	production
Task Modality:	written
Task Complexity:	hard
Task Schedule:	extended
Task Variation:	unvaried

A task that is new, hard, presented for an extended period of time, has little variation in sequence, and requires a written production response is likely to set the stage for behavior problems. On the other hand, if a task is old, easy, presented for a brief period of time, has variation in sequence, and requires only a yes/no oral choice response, then it is less likely to cause behavior problems. However, if the task is too easy, students may not take it seriously because it won't be cognitively challenging. See the Learning Activity for an example of task adjustments.

In the before-instruction phase, the teacher must examine the dimensions of each task and determine the balance most appropriate for the learner and the task (i.e., it is aligned with the goals and expected outcomes of the lesson). Designing the proper mix of task dimensions depends on the outcomes specified for the learner in the skill or content area. In general, special consideration should be given to the learner's predicted performance when introducing a new task. It may be best to ease into a new and complex task by planning an easy response form (e.g., yes/no or choice), mode (i.e., oral), and an abbreviated but unvaried schedule (e.g., 3- to 10-minute presentation). As an example, Mr. Atlantis is teaching his third grade students to ask appropriate questions before their class trip to the local animal shelter because he believes the students have not gotten much out of the animal shelter trip in previous years.

Making Adjustments in Task Adjustments

For this activity, assume you are supervising first grade teacher, Ms. Tasco, instructing a group of 15 students with learning and behavior problems to decode the following regular CVC words:

sat	hit
mat	tap
hit	set
cap	tip
rap	ton
not	fun

While observing Ms. Tasco, you notice many of the students' responses are incorrect (e.g., students say *sit* for *sat,* etc.), and as the lesson continues, the students become more and more inattentive and disruptive. You also observe that Ms. Tasco's teaching approach is to point to each word and ask the students to read the entire list. This method is used for each of the 12 words on the board. After the lesson, Ms. Tasco is frustrated and asks your advice on how to better teach and manage the group of first graders. For this learning activity, list adjustments to the various task dimensions you feel would increase the success of the students during the lesson.

Task Dimension	**Adjustment**
Task response form	
Task modality	
Task complexity	
Task schedule	
Task variation	

Because Mr. Atlantis knew that asking questions about topics new to third grade students can be very difficult, particularly for students with learning and behavior problems, he eased the difficulty of the task by adjusting task complexity. First, Mr. Atlantis introduced to the class three general topics for questions: (a) how are the animals cared for in the shelter, (b) what kind of animals are cared for, and (c) what is the most fun about working in an animal shelter. Next, to further reduce the difficulty of the task, Mr. Atlantis asked each student to identify another topic that would be appropriate to talk about at the shelter. Finally, Mr. Atlantis required the students to practice asking questions on the selected topics while he provided feedback about the appropriateness of their questions. His students will learn more from the field trip because they are equipped to ask questions that are meaningful and interesting.

The sequence of a task can remain unvaried if the teaching is kept to a brief period of time. Once a new task has been introduced, the learner can be required to make a more difficult response form (e.g., production) in subsequent lessons, using a more difficult mode (e.g., written) for a longer period of time. Considerations of the dimensions of a task are likely to *prevent* behavior problems associated with difficult academic learning situations.

The before-instruction phase is the most important phase because it sets the foundation for what the teacher will do during the other two phases of instruction. What the teacher designs and plans in the before-instruction phase should unfold as planned in the during-instruction phase and then be evaluated in the after-instruction phase. After instruction, the teacher considers the extent to which his or her planning results in the desired outcomes for both learner and teacher.

Changes in the lesson and task dimensions must be considered again in the next before-instruction phase. In addition to considering the dimensions of a task, the teacher must attend to other instructional requirements before instruction, including the rules and expectations of student behavior during instruction, consequences for misbehavior, and so on. These requirements for all three phases of instruction are developed in Chapter 4.

During Instruction

The during-instruction phase is concerned primarily with delivery and ongoing management of the lesson. While all of the task dimensions should be scrutinized during this phase, the most important ones are the response form, modality, and schedule. If the task is either new or old, the teacher must monitor the degree to which students are facile in the prescribed response form and mode. Moreover, the amount of time allocated to complete the task must be monitored to determine if more time is needed or if too much time was allocated. If a problem in any of the task dimensions is diagnosed, then the teacher must determine if it is a "can't" problem or a "won't" problem. In general, it is best to adapt the task so the task dimension that is causing the problem is made easier for the learner. Disruptive behavior of students with learning and behavior problems is likely to occur during a lesson that introduces many difficult tasks at the beginning. When teachers understand the interaction between task difficulty, learning, and behavior, they can anticipate and adjust the activity during instruction. For example, Mr. Enrique presents a worksheet to his fourth grade students that requires them to write sentences that incorporate new vocabulary words. Mr. Enrique designed the writing assignment to last about 35 minutes. Immediately after the assignment is given, several students in the class begin to write, while many others sit and look confused, unsure of how to write sentences "off the top of their heads" using the new vocabulary. After a few minutes, Mr. Enrique observes that many students begin to talk among themselves and become louder.

At this point, Mr. Enrique has several options to try to get every student involved in the writing activity. While a punitive approach (e.g., "Complete the assignment in 25 minutes or receive a failing grade.") may be tempting in this situation, it rarely works. A more effective response is for Mr. Enrique to make an immediate adjustment in his teaching plan by changing the task modality. Once Mr. Enrique noticed many of the students were not starting the assignment, he could have altered his instructional approach and modified the task modality from written to oral. He might have asked the students to put down their pencils and think of examples of sentences using the new vocabulary after he provided and discussed examples of sentences using the new vocabulary. He could then invite individual students to offer their own sentences. This way Mr. Enrique provides the necessary support for students having trouble by providing the stem of a sentence for them. Once students are able to verbalize sentences using the vocabulary, Mr. Enrique provides instructional support for those students who have trouble translating their verbal sentences into written sentences. Mr. Enrique has modified the task requirements and reintroduced the learning activity by asking students to verbalize sentences using the vocabulary words. This easier response form enhances the opportunity for Mr. Enrique to give feedback and reinforcement during the activity.

The relationship between quality teaching and learning and behavior is a powerful one. Because teaching takes place in very complex contexts, with many activities occurring simultaneously, it is sometimes difficult to focus on instructional and task variables that are within teacher control (e.g., task dimensions). We have observed teachers sometimes focus on student characteristics over which they have no control (e.g., student IQ) when considering the causes of disruptive behavior. The during-instruction focus recommends teachers adjust their approach and task structure by directing attention to task dimensions while implementing a lesson.

In some cases, particularly with students who have learning and behavior problems, it may be necessary to stop the task altogether and present an entirely different task, preferably an established task or one that is "neutral" (i.e., neither too easy nor too difficult). It is unlikely for only one response form or one mode to be used during an entire lesson, but a range of response forms and modes is used. The juxtaposition of response forms and modes will require the teacher to monitor student responses and determine if the response form requires changing.

After Instruction

Including a strategy of modifying task dimensions as part of classroom management in the before and during phases represents only part of the commitment to linking instruction and classroom management. Teaching and managing the most difficult students requires a careful and thorough analysis of how to effectively adapt instruction for students who exhibit more pronounced learning and behavior problems. This analysis can best be accomplished during the after-instruction phase. The question the teacher poses for reflection is straightforward. "Based on (a) the structure of the learning activity, (b) the type of academic errors, and (c) the level of disruptive behavior, what adjustments do I need to make in the nature or structure of the task for improved learning and behavior?" Answering this question for the most difficult students can best be done after instruction, when the teacher has collected as much performance information about the students as possible. The primary purpose of an after-instruction phase is to focus teachers reflection on all aspects of teaching, from instructional design to the student's error patterns as well as evaluation of the results of a lesson or teaching sequence. We know from earlier research (e.g., Walker, Gersten, & Darch, 1988) that teachers who are most effective with stu-

Correcting and analyzing student papers is a critical feature for determining instructional plans.

dents with learning and behavior problems use an instructional approach to manage behavior. However, research shows that most teachers infrequently make adjustments in academic tasks as part of an intervention strategy for students who are disruptive (Soodak & Podell, 1994). For example, Von Brock and Elliott (1987) have shown that when behavior problems are more severe, teachers "may rely more on past experience, or personal judgement" (p. 142) than on information that could be gleaned from an after-instruction analysis.

One way teachers can increase the amount of relevant information when making decisions about new ways to teach and manage is to use the after-instruction phase as a major part of the teaching and planning process. The teacher should examine the student's performance and evaluate the six task dimensions in light of that performance. If adjustments are necessary, they should be made for the next lesson or teaching sequence, though wholesale and dramatic changes should be avoided. If dramatic changes are necessary, then the lesson and selection of task dimensions were probably poorly planned. If the teacher is unsure why students are having difficulty learning, it may be best to present the task again to the learner before making changes in the design of the lesson. Relatively minor modifications in task dimensions sometimes translate into significant learning and behavior changes. Because the learning task was the initial context for failure for the student, any task modifications that make the activity more suitable for students will help improve their overall behavior.

The appropriateness of a task dimension depends on the learner's performance on the task and not on a logical analysis of the task independent of the learner's performance. Making adjustments in task dimensions within a proactive classroom management approach is based on the teacher's knowledge of his or her craft and the learner's instructional needs. While the principles of designing instruction are derived from a substantial body of research (Engelmann & Carnine, 1982; Kame'enui & Simmons, 1997), the analysis we offer in this text is based on experience and logic. For example, logic calls for easing into a new and complex task by using an abbreviated schedule and easy response forms. However, if the learner is capable of handling a longer period of instruction and a more difficult response form and mode during initial instruction, then these task dimensions should be used. The design of a lesson plan and selection of task dimensions depend on the teacher's judgment of the learner's capability.

It would be a serious mistake to design task dimensions that are simply easy for the learner, because this may communicate to the learner that learning is not challenging. The learner will not learn if not challenged cognitively and emotionally, but learning should not be punishing and frustrating. It can be exciting for the student if the proper cognitive tension is created by designing task dimensions appropriate to the learner's ability and the educational outcomes.

SUMMARY

In this chapter, we defined, described, and provided a range of examples of the six task dimensions. The purpose of examining these dimensions is based on the premise that the nature, structure, and demands of a task can set the stage for serious behavior problems. For example, tasks that are new and complex are likely to be more difficult than tasks that are mastered and simple. Similarly, tasks that are taught for an extended period of time and require a written production response are more difficult than tasks presented briefly that require a choice response from the learner. By attending to the task dimensions and designing tasks appropriate to the learner, social behavior problems associated with difficult tasks can be avoided.

In addition, we described how the dimensions of tasks are considered within a temporal framework that consists of three phases of instruction: before instruction, during instruction, and after instruction. We argued that the before-instruction phase requires special consideration because here teachers select and design tasks appropriate to the learner's level of competence, and with appropriate instructional design a teacher can minimize classroom disruptions through increased successful engagement of students.

CHAPTER ACTIVITIES

1. Discuss the characteristics of a proactive approach to classroom management.
2. Define and give an example of the six task dimensions of instructional classroom management.
3. Discuss how the dimensions of tasks are considered within each of the three phases of instruction.

REFERENCES

Abbott, M., Walton, C., Tapia, Y., & Greenwood, C. (1999). Research to practice: A "blueprint" for closing the gap in local schools. *Exceptional Children, 65,* 339–352.

Ashbaugh, C., & Kasten, K. (1991). *Educational leadership.* New York: Longman.

Berliner, D. (1988). Effective classroom management and instruction: A knowledge base for consultation. In J. L. Graden, J. E. Zims, & M. I. Curtis (Eds.), *Educational delivery systems* (pp. 309–325). Washington DC: WASP.

Brophy, J., & Good, T. L. (1986). Teacher behavior and student achievement. In M. Wittrock (Ed.), *Third handbook of research on teaching* (pp. 328–375). Chicago: Rand McNally.

Charlebois, P., Normandeau, S., Vitaro, F., & Berneche, F. (1999). Skills training for inattentive, overactive, aggressive boys: Differential effects of content and delivery method. *Behavioral Disorders, 24,* 137–150.

Christenson, S., Ysseldyke, J., & Thurlow, M. (1989). Critical instructional factors for students with mild handicaps: An integrative review. *Remedial and Special Education, 10,* 21–31.

Clarke, S., Dunlap, G., Foster-Johnson, L., Childs, K., Wilson, D., White, R., & Vera, A. (1995). Improving the conduct of students with behavioral disorders by incorporating student interests into curricular activities. *Behavioral Disorders, 20,* 221–237.

Conroy, M. A., & Fox, J. J. (1994). Setting events and challenging behaviors in the classroom: Incorporating contextual factors into effective intervention plans. *Preventing School Failure, 38,* 29–34.

Engelmann, S., & Carnine, D. (1982). *Theory of instruction: Principles and applications.* New York: Irvington.

Evans, D. (1991). *An analysis of representations in mathematics instruction.* Unpublished doctoral dissertation, University of Oregon, Eugene.

Evertson, C. M. (1989). Improving elementary classroom management: A school-based training program for beginning the year. *Journal of Educational Research, 83*(2), 82–90.

Francis, D. (1995). The reflective journal: A window to preservice teachers' practical knowledge. *Teaching and Teacher Education, 11,* 229–241.

George, N. L., George, M. P., Gersten, R., & Grosenick, J. K. (1995). To leave or to stay? An exploratory study of teachers of students with emotional and behavioral problems. *Remedial and Special Education, 16,* 227–236.

Gettinger, M. (1988). Methods of proactive classroom management. *School Psychology Review, 17*(2), 227–242.

Good, T. (1979). Teacher effectiveness in the elementary school: What we know about it now. *Journal of Teacher Education, 30,* 52–64.

Gunter, P., & Denny, K. (1996). Research issues and needs regarding teacher use of classroom management strategies. *Behavioral Disorders, 22,* 15–20.

Jolivette, K., Wehby, J. H., & Hirsch, L. (1999). Academic strategy identification for students exhibiting inappropriate classroom behaviors. *Behavior Disorders, 24,* 210–221.

Kame'enui, E. J., & Simmons, D. C. (1997). *Designing instructional strategies: The prevention of academic learning problems.* Upper Saddle River, NJ: Merrill/Prentice Hall.

Kauffman, J. M., & Wong, K. L. (1991). Effective teachers of students with behavioral disorders: Are generic teaching skills enough? *Behavioral Disorders, 16,* 225–237.

Klinger, J. K., Vaughn, S., Hughes, M. T., Schumm, J. S., & Elbaum, B. (1998). Academic outcomes for students with and without learning disabilities in inclusive classrooms. *Learning Disabilities Research and Practice, 13,* 153–161.

Mercer, C. D., Lane, H., Jordan, L., Allsopp, & Eisele, M. (1996). Empowering teachers and students with instructional choices in inclusive settings. *Remedial and Special Education, 17,* 226–236.

Paine, S., Radicchi, J., Rosellini, L., Deutchman, L., & Darch, C. (1983). *Structuring your classroom for academic success.* Champaign, IL: Research Press.

Rohrkemper, M., & Brophy, J. (1980). *Teachers' general strategies for dealing with problem students.* Paper presented at the Annual Conference of the American Educational Research Association, Boston, MA.

Rosenberg, M., Wilson, R., Maheady, L., & Sindelar, P. (1997). *Educating students with behavior disorders* (2nd ed.). Needham Heights, MA: Allyn & Bacon.

Shores, R. E., Jack, S. L., Gunter, P. L., Ellis, D. N., & DeBriere, T. J. (1993). Classroom interactions of children with behavior disorders. *Journal of Emotional and Behavioral Disorders, 17,* 27–39.

Soodak, L., & Podell, D. M. (1994). Teachers' thinking about difficult-to-teach students. *Journal of Educational Research, 88,* 44–51.

Sprick, R., Garrison, M., & Howard, L. (1998). *CHAMPS: A proactive and positive approach to classroom management.* Longmont, CO: Sopris West.

Sugai, G. (1996). Providing effective behavior support to all students: Procedures and processes. *SAIL: Technical Assistance Journal. Oregon Special Education, 11,* 1–4.

Vaughn, S., & Klinger, J. (1998). Students' perceptions of inclusion and resource room settings. *Journal of Special Education, 32,* 79–88.

Von Brock, M., & Elliott, S. N. (1987). Influence of treatment effectiveness information on the acceptability of classroom interventions. *Journal of School Psychology, 25,* 131–144.

Walker, H., Gersten, R., & Darch, C. (1988). Relationship between teachers social behavioral expectations and their teaching effectiveness. *Exceptional Children, 54,* 36–47.

Zigmond, N., & Baker, J. (1996). Full inclusion for students with learning disabilities: Too much of a good thing. *Theory into Practice, 35,* 26–34.

Chapter
4

A Temporal Framework for Instructional Classroom Management

OVERVIEW

- Step 1: Considering the Phases of Instruction
  Aligning the Phases of Instruction
  Before Instruction: Designing Instructional Classroom Management
  During Instruction: Delivering Instructional Classroom Management
  After Instruction: Reflecting and Adjusting Instructional Classroom Management

- Step 2: Considering the Phases of the School Year
  Critical Features of a 180-Day Plan
  Phases of the 180-Day Plan

- Summary

- Chapter Activities

In the previous chapter, we described the instructional dimensions of classroom management and introduced three phases of instruction: before, during, and after instruction. In this chapter we extend the concept of proactive instructional classroom management by presenting a temporal framework for teachers to use when designing and implementing teaching and management activities. We first examine the features and intricate requirements of each phase of instruction and how they can be applied to developing classroom management programs. Management of academic and social behavior takes place within an instructional context in real time; that is, what the teacher does in the face-to-face interaction with children represents the "during instruction" phase. What the teacher does during instruction should be aligned both with what the teacher planned before instruction, as well as the expected accomplishments of the lesson anticipated after instruction.

Second, we present a 180-day model for teachers to use when planning an entire school year. The advantages of using both parts of this temporal framework is that teachers can more readily (a) predict classroom instructional and behavior problems, (b) assess for causes of learning and behavior problems, and (c) plan short- and long-term teaching strategies across the entire year. Figure 4.1 provides an overview of the temporal framework for instructional classroom management. The teacher uses this temporal framework to first consider the three phases of instruction, before, during, and after, and identify ways to proactively adjust all teaching and managing activities.

For the second step in application of the temporal framework, the teacher takes a broader perspective and considers the instructional and management implications of the phases of the school year, fall, winter, and spring. We recommend that both steps, analysis of the phases of instruction and analysis of the phases of the school year, be applied to planning for (a) assessment, (b) instruction, (c) management, and (d) school-wide programs.

FIGURE 4.1   Applying a comprehensive temporal framework.

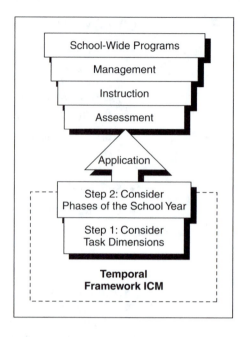

STEP 1: CONSIDERING THE PHASES OF INSTRUCTION
Aligning the Phases of Instruction

As with most events that occur outside the classroom and school, teaching follows the progression of time and unfolds in a fairly predictable manner. By thinking about teaching in a temporal framework comprised of before, during, and after phases of instruction, organization of management strategies within instruction becomes clear because a teacher focuses on specific teaching activities that are related to a phase of instruction.

Too often the primary focus of teaching is on what the teacher does during instruction. During instruction the teacher actively engages the learner and attempts to move the learner from a state of unknowing or partial knowing to a state of full or more complete knowing. This is the phase where the integrity of the teaching content and teacher-student interactions are often tested. When a teacher organizes the class for transition to the library to research a social studies topic, disruptive behavior often occurs. This time when students are instructed to put their materials away, gather materials they need for the library, and line up at the door is part of the during-instruction phase. There are important instructional implications for how teachers orchestrate these student behaviors, but the before-instruction phase may be more important in this situation. After all, during instruction the teacher merely delivers and implements what was designed and planned *before* instruction. The after-instruction phase is obviously important, because the outcomes expected of students are guided by the teacher's planning and delivery.

No single phase of instruction is more important than another. Taken together, the three phases help the teacher in comprehensive planning. Each phase helps a

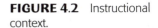

FIGURE 4.2   Instructional context.

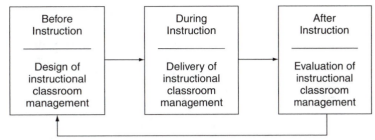

teacher identify and analyze the causes of learning and behavior problems and identify an array of positive instructional solutions. Unfortunately, teachers often have lower expectations about students with learning and behavior problems (Meltzer, Roditi, Houser, & Perlman, 1998). These negative judgments combined with time constraints teachers face managing diverse students in large classrooms, often limit teachers' thinking about solving learning and behavior problems. Teachers often feel overwhelmed by the combination of academic and behavior difficulties in a single classroom (Trent, 1998). Before, during, and after phases of instruction provide one way for teachers to engage in proactive instruction and management that helps them reach more students in their classrooms.

Because the three phases of instruction are interdependent, their application is an efficient use of a teacher's time. All three phases are both independent and connected organizational units. As Figure 4.2 indicates, linkages between the phases of instruction cannot be left to chance but must be orchestrated if the objectives for individual learners are to be accomplished. However, many teachers fail to make ongoing instructional adjustments part of their strategy to teach and manage. According to some researchers, new interventions "all but ceased in favor of continuing prior, unsuccessful efforts, and pursuing documentation activities. . . " (Wilson, Gutkin, Hagen, & Oats, 1998, p. 56). A careful analysis of the instructional task in the context of the three phases of instruction provides teachers a rich source of information for designing effective, proactive teaching and management strategies that break out of old, unsuccessful molds.

Before Instruction: Designing Instructional Classroom Management

The before-instruction phase establishes the foundation for sound instructional classroom management. The teacher must set the stage for a proactive (not reactive) instructional approach to managing student academic and social behavior for the entire school year. The teacher establishes this important foundation in the way she thinks about classroom management; talks about management to students, teachers, parents, and school administrators; and anticipates and responds to problems in the school environment and classroom. There has been increasing interest in developing teaching and management strategies that use instructional, curricular, and organizational adjustments to better manage behavior problems (Kern, Childs, & Dunlap, 1994). Researchers and teachers are beginning to understand the power in developing effective teaching and management strategies based in part on three phases of instruction. Dunlap and Kern (1996) stated, "It is important to recognize that the number of antecedent variables that relate curriculum and instruction to the occurrence of problem behaviors is potentially limitless" (p. 300).

To help teachers apply the before-instruction phase of instruction, we identify five categories of activities to consider during instruction. Within each category, we identify several essential features of proactive instructional classroom management. The list of features is not exhaustive but provides a starting point for teachers to consider assessment, instruction, classroom management, and school-wide programs.

Before-Instruction Phase

Assessment

1. Define the specific instructional objectives and learning outcomes expected at the end of the lesson.
2. Develop an assessment system for short-term and long-term planning.
3. Develop assessment strategies that help teachers link instructional solutions for learning and behavior problems.

Instructional Task Design

1. Review and determine appropriateness of the dimensions of the target task for the learners.
2. Modify selected task dimensions to accommodate learner's needs.
3. Allocate sufficient instructional time for each task and schedule time to maximize student performance.
4. Identify tasks and component skills that require preteaching.
5. Apply task dimensions to teaching interventions for learning and behavior problems.

Classroom Management Plan

1. Identify rules for student behavior in the classroom and during instruction.
2. Teach the rules.
3. Develop a plan for responding to unanticipated, but potentially serious, behavior problems during instruction (e.g., fights, tantrums).
4. Determine best use of physical space and seating of students during instruction to maximize student performance and access to instruction and teaching materials.
5. Develop a plan for monitoring student behavior during instruction.
6. Develop a system for recording student errors during instruction.

Reinforcement Plan

1. Identify appropriate dimensions of reinforcement for each specific task.
2. Develop a plan of reinforcement to maximize student performance during instruction.
3. Develop a plan for responding to academic errors that reinforces correct responses and provides corrective feedback.

4. Develop a plan of reinforcement that accommodates tasks with different levels of difficulty.

School-Wide Transition Plan

1. Identify the least-intrusive procedures to increase appropriate behavior and decrease inappropriate behavior.
2. Develop and practice management procedures to ensure effective implementation during instruction.
3. Develop an individual plan linked to a school-wide discipline plan for responding to serious behavior problems.
4. If necessary, develop prompts and cues to use punishment as a transition tool only.
5. Develop roles and responsibilities for all school personnel in a school-wide program for effective teaching and managing.

Student outcomes.   Assessment during the before-instruction phase is designed to identify the desired student outcomes before instruction begins. This sets the focus for the phases of instruction that follow and determines the instructional classroom management tools and strategies the teacher will use to move the student from a state of unknowing or partial knowing to a state of more complete or full knowing. Teachers must select instructional tools and materials designed to ensure that the target skills are in fact taught. In many cases, instructional materials must be modified to ensure that outcomes are accomplished.

Student outcomes can be stated in broad or narrow terms. Although it's not feasible or necessary for teachers to spell out detailed student outcomes for each instructional lesson, we recommend that teachers have a clear idea of the academic or social outcomes they want to accomplish by the end of each lesson. Without a clear idea of expected student outcomes, the focus and execution of the lesson is in jeopardy, especially when behavior problems disrupt the lesson. By targeting specific student outcomes ahead of time, the teacher can gauge how outcomes may set the stage for behavior problems or instructional difficulties. Once this is determined, the teacher can take the necessary steps to prevent those problems.

Task design.   As noted in Chapter 3 on task dimensions, the design of instructional tasks holds great potential for influencing student and teacher performance during instruction. An analysis of a task predicts difficulty levels of each activity in a lesson and points to which learning or behavior problems are likely to occur. In the before-instruction analysis, tasks should be reviewed against the six task dimensions (e.g., history, response form, schedule, variation, modality, and complexity). The task dimensions are scrutinized with student outcomes in mind. For example, if the outcomes and instructional objectives call for written responses from the learner, then those task dimensions must be targeted for instruction. The teacher might plan one or two relatively easy tasks so the student can practice the prerequisite skills of the harder tasks.

If a task is new and the learner's responses are weak, the teacher must be prepared to make changes in selected dimensions of the task (e.g., switch to a different response form, vary the sequence or schedule). If the task is an established one, the student's performance is not likely to be problematic (unless the task is too easy), and the teacher's readiness to change task dimensions is of less concern. This readiness to make changes in task dimensions is an example of the proactive approach required in instructional classroom management. It is also important for the teacher to note the changes in task dimensions necessary during instruction and which dimensions set the occasion for problem behaviors.

One of the most important features of the before-instruction phase is the allocation and scheduling of instructional time for each task. A traditional schedule usually consists of 30- to 45-minute blocks of time for reading, mathematics, science, and so on. A teacher teaches a lesson in reading, for example, and requires students to complete independent seatwork associated with the reading lesson. Because all of the teaching and learning activities are associated with reading, there is little variation in content and task demands. This traditional schedule often sets the stage for behavior problems because the content and student response requirements are predictable and redundant, which in turn leads to boredom and off-task behavior.

In contrast to a traditional block schedule is one in which several different topics, skills, or content areas are taught back-to-back in abbreviated time segments. The schedule below is designed for a second grade class. Instead of a 45-minute reading lesson, the time is scheduled as follows:

9:00–9:10	Review of specific errors made in previous reading lesson involving blending skills—oral small group production responses; medium to hard task. (10 minutes)
9:10–9:16	Review family of math facts—oral, production, individual responding; easy to medium task. (6 minutes)
9:16–9:32	Creative writing involving development of problem to be solved by main character—written, production response using structured story grammar writing sheets; hard task. (16 minutes)
9:32–9:36	Oral recitation of the capitals of selected states—production responses; easy task. (4 minutes)
9:36–9:45	Individual oral reading on student-selected book—oral production responses; one-to-one with teacher; medium to hard task. (9 minutes)

The schedule consists of five activities to be taught in different blocks of time. The different tasks are unpredictable in sequence, and their variation is likely to keep students engaged, motivated, and refreshed. This kind of schedule minimizes the fatigue often associated with a block schedule in which the same content is taught for an extended period of time. This schedule may not be feasible for the whole class, but it may be used on a selective basis for students with behavior problems who have a difficult time attending to a task for long periods of time.

A final strategy for preparing instructional tasks is preteaching. The teacher targets an academic or social skill that is likely to be a problem for the learner and "primes" or prepares the learner to respond to a task by providing already taught information that will allow the learner to respond successfully. The preteaching strat-

---

Task: Subtracting two-digit numbers from two-digit numbers that require renaming in the one's column (e.g., 53 − 26 = _____).

Task History: New

Task Response Form: Production

Task Modality: Written

Task Complexity: Hard

Task Variation: Unvaried

Task Schedule: 35 minutes, unvaried

(The teacher has just completed teaching students the new task and distributes a worksheet of 15 problems for students to complete independently. Some of the problems require renaming, some do not.)

Teacher: Students, the problem on the board is the same as the first problem on your worksheet. Could someone read the problem for me? (Teacher calls on Craig.)

Craig: Fifty-three minus twenty-six.

Teacher: Good job, Craig. Yes, fifty-three minus twenty-six. Remember, some problems will require you to rename. Read each problem carefully and check the numbers in the ones column to decide if you have to rename. Get started.

(The teacher monitors the independent seatwork by moving around the classroom checking on students' work.)

FIGURE 4.3 Preteaching strategy—academic activity.

egy is especially useful for tasks that are new or complex. An example of a preteaching strategy is given in Figure 4.3.

The task dimensions in Figure 4.3 justify the use of a preteaching strategy, because the task is new, complex, and requires a written response. Even though the task is taught immediately prior to the independent worksheet, the use of the preteaching strategy supports the student's transfer of the newly taught material in a context and format different from the teacher's oral and written demonstration on the blackboard. Although the preteaching strategy example in Figure 4.3 is specific to a newly taught task, it can be used for a range of new or old academic tasks.

In Figure 4.4, we apply the preteaching strategy to a motor task. In this case, the task is walking through the halls to the library. As in most preteaching situations, the teacher has already taught students the skills required to perform the task, namely walking quietly through the hallway. In Figure 4.4, the teacher preteaches going to the library because it is the beginning of the year. This is the first time the second graders will make the trip to the library, which makes the probability that disruptive behavior will occur quite high (Tulley & Chiu, 1998). For this particular task, the task dimensions are similar to the academic tasks in Figure 4.3. For example, the task is new and requires students to make an oral, motor production response. The task is easy and not varied in its schedule or sequence, which means it is taught in isolation and not in the context of other tasks or another lesson.

Task: Walking through the school hallways to the library.

Task History: New

Task Response Form: Production

Task Modality: Motor/Oral

Task Complexity: Easy

Task Variation: Unvaried

Task Schedule: 10 minutes, unvaried

(The teacher has taught the class the requirements for walking to the library. The class is about to visit the library.)

Teacher: I need everyone's attention before we leave for the library. I want to take a minute to talk to you about how I want you to behave walking down the hall to the library.

Teacher: What are some things I want you to remember when you're walking down the hall to the library?

(Child): We should walk quietly.

Teacher: Good, but what does it mean to walk quietly?

(Child): It means not talking.

Teacher: Exactly, very nice. So when you walk quietly, is it okay to talk quietly or whisper?

(Child): No.

Teacher: What's another thing to remember when you're walking down the hall to the library?

(Child): We should keep our hands and feet to ourselves.

Teacher: That's right. Watch me (teacher flails arms back and forth to each side). Am I keeping my hands to myself?

(Child): No, you're not, because you can hit someone with your arms.

Teacher: Good job. Alton, show me how to keep your hands to yourself when you walk down the hallway.

(Alton stands up and walks toward the front of the class and keeps his arms close to his sides.)

Teacher: Excellent, Alton. That's exactly the right way to walk quietly down the hall to the library.

Teacher: Before we leave for the library, let's quickly review the rules for walking quietly down the halls (teacher restates the two rules). Now, I want you to prepare to go to the library. (The teacher walks around the class while students prepare to visit the library.) I'll know by your quiet waiting and your library books on your desk, that you are ready to line up. (The teacher waits until it is quiet.) Very nice. Please line up to go to the library.

FIGURE 4.4 Preteaching strategy—nonacademic activity.

Following we list four general conditions for which a preteaching strategy may be effective.

1. Preteach rules for how to behave before making the transition to a new context that may be:
   - *unfamiliar* (visiting another teacher's classroom)

- *unknown* (field trip)
- *potentially ambiguous or troublesome* (situations that have caused problems in the past; prior to a school assembly).

  If there is any ambiguity, preteach the necessary behaviors or skills.

2. Preteach an already taught component skill prior to working a new and complex skill (e.g., teacher points to the *a* in the word *rate* and applies a rule for reading these word types, "Remember when you read this word, you say the name of this letter").
3. Preteach before returning to class after an engaging and highly reinforcing activity (e.g., awards assembly, field trip).
4. Preteach after long absences and holidays.

In order for students to be successful at complex, higher-order operations, the component steps and pieces of the complex operations must be identified and taught. Frequently, however, serious behavior problems surface during difficult lessons and activities because students are required to think about and work complex operations for which they are not adequately prepared.

Management plan. The management plan is the most traditional aspect of instructional classroom management. It is designed to control the movement of activities in the classroom in ways that allow students and teachers to move through the classroom and school with a minimum amount of disruption and unnecessary contact. A sound management plan addresses five different areas of concern: (a) rules for behaving appropriately in the classroom, (b) a systematic strategy for responding to potentially serious behavior problems, (c) efficient and effective use of physical space, (d) a system for monitoring student behavior, and (e) a system for recording student academic and social errors.

Identifying and teaching rules. Students must be informed from the very first day of school what the expectations are for behaving in classroom and school settings. The rules serve as the procedural anchor points for both teacher and learner. They specify for the learner exactly what the teacher expects under most, if not all, instructional conditions. Specifically, the rules should describe for students the behaviors (i.e., gestures, language, physical movement) to perform under certain conditions. For example, if the conditions involve walking down the hall to the library, as described in Figure 4.4, then the rules will specify the behaviors (e.g., walking quietly, keeping hands and feet to oneself).

Some teachers think it is not necessary to spend time planning which classroom rules to use. However, there are many reasons why the selection of rules and their teaching is crucial for effectively teaching and managing students who are at risk for learning and behavior problems. First, some students, particularly those with learning problems, often do not have the vocabulary knowledge to translate seemingly simple rules into behavior. For example, a first grade teacher may say to a group of students: "Everybody, listen up. Before we line up to go to lunch, I want each of you to put your pencils inside your desks and put your folders underneath your reading books. We will finish our worksheets after we return from the cafeteria. When you are done getting ready I will call your name to line up at the door!" A student would need a reasonably sophisticated vocabulary knowledge to understand how to successfully follow

Explaining and teaching classroom rules plays a significant role in effective classroom management.

this teacher's request. For example, a student would need to understand the words, *listen up, inside, underneath,* and *return.* Research has shown that for many students with learning problems, we can't assume they have this level of sophistication. The reasons listed below indicate that identifying and teaching rules is a crucial first step in successful classroom management.

- For many young students with limited formal learning experiences, the classroom is the first time they are required to work in structured group learning activities.
- For some students, the classroom is their first experience having to translate complicated instructions into behavior routines.
- For many students, following rules in the early grades marks the first time they have been held accountable for their behavior.

We have found that identifying a short list of rules to be followed is an important step for the teacher, but it is only the first step. If the conditions involve small group oral reading, then the rules should specify the required behaviors, and the teacher teaches the students how to behave in the various learning contexts. For example, "When some-one is reading, follow along with your eyes." The conditions for the rule are "when someone is reading," and the required behaviors are to "follow along with your eyes."

Rules can be very specific (e.g., "No touching others with your hands or feet at any time"), or they can be general (e.g., "Be kind to others"). The level of specificity required of rules depends on several factors, including (a) teacher (e.g., experienced versus inexperienced); (b) student cognitive level (e.g., high performers or low per-formers); (c) time of year (e.g., beginning or end of year); (d) school context (e.g., classroom, recess, bus, general school environment); (e) nature and history of school-wide discipline (e.g., poor school-wide discipline policy and history of seri-ous behavior problems); and so on. In general, rules should be designed to meet the needs of the teacher, students, and instructional requirements. However, rules aren't developed in a vacuum; they require thought and careful planning. In Table 4.1,

TABLE 4.1 Five General Questions That Guide Teachers' Thinking About Rules and Expectations

General Question	Teachers' Thinking
1. What do I want my classroom to be like?	• Do I want my classroom to be highly organized with everything in its place most of the time? • Do I want my classroom to be quiet most of the time? • Do I want children to be active and interactive with each other most of the time? • Do I need to have things quiet, or can I tolerate a great deal of activity?
2. How do I want children to treat me as a person?	• Is it acceptable for children to take issue with me and correct me when I am wrong? • Is it acceptable for children to raise their voices even when they are right and I am wrong? • Is it important for children to always, no matter what the circumstances, respond to me in a courteous manner?
3. How do I want children to treat each other?	• Is it acceptable for children to speak roughly or rudely to each other? • Is it acceptable for children to laugh at each other's mistakes? • Do I want children to be kind to each other and speak with gentle voices?
4. What kind of information or values do I want to communicate to students about being an adult, an educator, a woman, or a man in today's society?	• Do I want to demonstrate a strong work ethic in which hard work is seen as important and necessary to succeeding? • Do I want children to know that making mistakes is natural to the process of learning? • Do I want children to respect the process of asking questions, no matter how silly the questions seem to be, and do I want to encourage children to ask questions?
5. How do I want children to remember me when the last day of school arrives and I am no longer a part of their daily lives?	• What image do I want children to have when they think of me? • What feelings do I want children to have when they think of me in their later years?

Source: From *Designing Instructional Strategies: The Prevention of Academic Learning Problems* (pp. 476–477) by E.J. Kame'enui and D.C. Simmons, 1997, Upper Saddle River, NJ: Merrill/Prentice Hall.

Kame'enui and Simmons (1997) offer five general questions that guide teachers' thinking about rules and expectations.

As Kame'enui and Simmons (1997) suggest, there are no right answers to these questions. The answers are personal to each teacher and are shaped by a teacher's teaching and life experiences. The answers, nevertheless, should reflect the teacher's genuine attempt to provide students with the best educational context possible. The purpose of posing these questions before the beginning of the school year is to ensure that ample time and consideration are given to them. The following learning activity, if completed, will help the reader develop their own philosophy of instruction and classroom management.

Whatever the conditions, it is not feasible for rules to be so specific that they cover all possible behavioral conditions. More important than the rules themselves is the process teachers use to identify the rules best suited for their classrooms and the teaching of the rules, using examples and nonexamples to communicate requirements of the rules. The teaching of rules communicates to students what is important and valued.

Using a Tool to Develop a Management Philosophy

Purpose of Activity

Students Begin Developing Their Philosophy of Teaching and Classroom Management

Step 1: Read each of the five questions presented in Table 4.1.

Step 2: Consider how you would develop both your instructional and classroom management programs when answering each of the questions listed in Table 4.1. Indicate what type of classroom (e.g., general education, special education) and grade level you aspire to teach or are currently teaching. Be sure your responses reflect working in the classroom you have described.

Step 3: Develop and write specific answers to the questions posed in Table 4.1. Give very specific answers that reflect your current thinking about how you will plan your teaching and management program.

Step 4: Once you have responded to the questions, be prepared to discuss why you think your approach will be helpful in developing both your academic and classroom management programs. For example, does your philosophy lend itself to developing an instructional, proactive approach to classroom management?

Step 5: Be prepared to present your responses to the class for discussion and debate.

Reinforcement plan. In Chapter 6, we describe the features of reinforcement and their correspondence to the dimensions of tasks. We conceptualize reinforcement as activities to increase valued behaviors. Because the most frequent interactions a teacher has with students are instructional ones, instructional interactions must be viewed and treated as "reinforcement" opportunities. By increasing instructional opportunities, we increase reinforcement opportunities. Effective teaching sets the occasion for reinforcement by leaving less to chance. Part of effective teaching is designing a reinforcement plan that considers not only student behavior, but the dimensions of the task and the pattern of errors associated with specific tasks and student performance.

A carefully designed reinforcement plan aligns the dimensions of a task (e.g., history, response form, modality, complexity, schedule) with the dimensions of reinforcement (e.g., intensity, schedule, type, timing). For example, a brand new task will require a different kind of reinforcement than a familiar, well-established task. Specifically, a familiar task should require reinforcement that is delayed, less intense, and less frequent. In contrast, a new task may require a range of reinforcers (e.g., social, tangible, activity) that are delivered immediately, more frequently, and with greater intensity. The details for developing a reinforcement plan are described in Chapter 6.

Remediation plan.   The purpose of the remediation plan is to acknowledge the need for "remediating" or correcting behavior problems. Such a plan is in contrast to the proactive, preventative instructional strategies that serve as the basis of the instructional management approach described and advocated previously. However, when problems can't be prevented, it is imperative for teachers to have a clear understanding of the procedures for decreasing the problem behavior; these procedures are commonly known as punishment procedures. Wolery, Bailey, and Sugai (1988) define punishment as "a functional relationship between a stimulus or event and a decrease in the occurrence of a behavior (p. 336). In general terms, when the teacher presents or withdraws a "stimulus," and the target behavior *decreases,* punishment has occurred. In spite of the galaxy of meanings associated with the word, punishment (e.g., time-out, yelling, wall sits), the technical definition of punishment refers to the relationship between events in the environment (e.g., what the teacher says and does) and the resulting decrease in the target behavior. Therefore, if a target behavior decreases in the future, the preceding events could be characterized as "punishing stimuli" (see Chapter 8 regarding punishment). As Kame'enui and Simmons (1997) point out, punishment and reinforcement are not defined by the actions of the teachers or school administrators, but by the reactions of children.

Only by understanding the technical requirements and features of punishment is it possible to implement remediation strategies to correct behavior problems. However, an instructional management approach conceptualizes punishment or remediation as "transition" strategies or tools. If used correctly, punishment can be an effective tool for decreasing or stopping inappropriate behaviors. However, merely stopping a misbehavior is not enough, because it does not provide the learner with information about how to behave appropriately. Punishment or remediation strategies must move a child quickly from a punishment context to a positive context of reinforcement and instruction. But the movement must be swift. By thinking about punishment as a transition tool, the teacher is in a mindset to move quickly from instruction "through" remediation and back to instruction and reinforcement.

Finally, the use of punishment procedures should be linked to a school-wide discipline plan (see Chapter 10). Punishment or remediation procedures should not be used in isolation but in the broader context of school goals and expectations.

During Instruction: Delivering Instructional Classroom Management

The during-instruction phase in an instructional management plan is concerned with three categories of activities: managing instruction, delivering instruction, and modifying instruction. The features in each category are listed as follows.

During-Instruction Phase

Managing Instruction

1. Present and reinforce rules and expectations at beginning of session as to how students are to behave during instruction.

2. Preteach task requirements as necessary.
3. Monitor students throughout the instructional session by providing prompts and feedback when necessary.
4. Record persistent academic errors.

Delivering Instruction

1. Present information at a pace that maintains student attention and engagement.
2. Provide students ample opportunities to respond.

Modifying Instruction

1. Make adjustments in task dimensions (e.g., task modality, response requirements, task complexity) based on student performance.
2. Take note of academic errors and implement correction procedures consistently and appropriately.

Managing instruction. The pace of presenting information and monitoring student performance during instruction can be very demanding, especially considering the hundreds of interactions that occur daily in a classroom. In order to orchestrate an effective, efficient, and engaging delivery of instruction, a well-established and well-designed instructional management plan must be in place, and the teacher must have confidence in the instructional tools and management strategies to be used. The management of behavior during instruction is anchored to four dimensions of managing instruction: (a) presenting and reinforcing the rules to ensure clear expectations of student behavior, (b) preteaching difficult task requirements to ensure successful performance, (c) monitoring student performance and providing prompts and feedback when necessary, and (d) recording persistent errors in an effort to gauge the effectiveness of the teaching presentation.

The presentation of rules and expectations is essential to sound instructional classroom management, because the expectations, when clearly specified for learners, set the "ground rules" for their response to instruction and task requirements. Although widely acknowledged as important, teaching of rules in clear and unambiguous terms is not easily accomplished. The general practice is for teachers to merely recite the rules by "telling" them to students, based on the assumption that students already "know how to behave" and that teaching what is already known is simply not necessary (i.e., it may appear redundant and silly in some cases). Though, some students may know how to behave under certain instructional conditions, it's unlikely all students will know how to behave under "all" instructional conditions when the teacher is present. Even if students know how to behave during instruction, it is important that the teacher clarify and affirm expectations to establish a personal presence and communicate the importance of the expectations and rules. An example of a rule-teaching sequence is described in Figure 4.5. Rules change as the year progresses and students' ability levels increase. Rules are designed to set the stage for teaching and managing during the first phase of the school year and are taught and practiced until students understand them and can apply them effortlessly. However, after students have been taught classroom rules and routines and demonstrated mastery of them, teachers use rules to remind students of classroom routines

Task: Speak kindly to others.

Task History: New

Task Response Form: Production

Task Modality: Oral

Task Complexity: Easy

Task Variation: Unvaried

Task Schedule: 5–7 minutes, unvaried

(It's the first day of class and the teacher has spent the first 30 minutes greeting her third grade class and discussing her expectations, the academic content and skills to be covered during the year, and general procedures for moving about in the classroom and school.)

Teacher: I need everyone's attention. I want to talk about how I want you to behave in and out of this classroom. Here's a rule I'd like you to follow when you are talking and working with each other. The rule is "Speak kindly to others." What's the rule to follow when you're talking and working with each other?

Student: Speak kindly to others.

Teacher: Yes, the rule is to speak kindly to others.

(At this point, the teacher may want to solicit examples from students of what it means to speak kindly to others. In addition, the teacher may want students to generate negative examples of speaking kindly to others [e.g., speaking harshly and abruptly]. Following the examples volunteered by students, the teacher should continue with the following steps.)

Teacher: I'll show you exactly what I mean by the rule, "Speak kindly to others." (Teacher approaches a student and looks directly into the student's face and speaks in a kind and direct tone). "Joshua, may I borrow your pencil for a second?" (Joshua nods his head).

(The teacher approaches another student and speaks in a flat but polite tone of voice): "Alice, yesterday I gave you cuts at recess to play wall ball, but not today. Sorry."

(The teacher approaches another child and speaks in a gentle, but firm voice): "I'm sorry, Bobby, I would loan you my pencil, but the last time you didn't return it."

Teacher: Now I'll show you what it looks like when you don't speak kindly to others. (Teacher approaches Bobby again and speaks in a harsh and loud tone): "I'm sorry, Bobby, I would loan you my pencil, but the last time you didn't return it."

(The teacher approaches another child and speaks in a flat, cold, abrupt tone): "What are you looking at? Do I owe you money or something?"

(The teacher approaches another student and asks in a harsh tone): "Where's my pencil?"

(The teacher speaks to the entire group): "Okay, I want you to watch and tell me if I'm speaking kindly to others?" (Teacher approaches Joshua and speaks in a kind tone): "Where's my pencil?"

(The teacher presents several positive and negative examples and asks students): "Am I speaking kindly to others?" (Students respond by answering *yes* or *no*.)

FIGURE 4.5   Format for teaching rules.

and their responsibilities. Teachers spend less time teaching students rules but use the fact that students are following classroom rules and routines as an avenue to academic success.

Rules should be taught during the first instructional sessions (i.e., small group, large group, class lectures) of the school year. By teaching the rules at the beginning of the instructional session and school year and reinforcing them throughout the year, the teacher communicates to students the importance of rules in instruction. Successful communication of the teacher's expectations depends on the frequency and clarity with which they are taught. The teaching of rules should be designed and delivered in the same way as any other skill, concept, operation, or piece of knowledge. Simply telling students the rules is inadequate instruction. Teaching the rules of how to behave requires (a) a clear statement of the rules, (b) the selection of positive and negative examples of each rule, (c) the immediate and delayed assessment of students' knowledge of the rules, and (d) opportunities to practice the rules in natural contexts (e.g., classroom, hallway, library).

In the example on teaching rules, the task is a new one and requires students to make oral production responses to an easy task. In addition, the teaching sequence on rules requires the presentation of concrete examples, both positive and negative, designed to communicate the boundaries of the expected behavior (e.g., speaking kindly to others). Design of the teaching sequence for teaching rules is no different than one designed for teaching a concept.

As noted earlier, the preteaching of complex tasks is effective in preparing learners to respond successfully to difficult tasks. For example, new rules can be "pretaught" immediately prior to their application.

Prompts and feedback are essential means of monitoring student performance during instruction. A range of teaching prompts includes (a) verbal—written and oral, (b) facial, and (c) physical. The use of a particular prompt depends on a number of factors that vary according to the dimensions of the task (e.g., new or old, easy or difficult); the learner (e.g., age and developmental level); the learner's performance (e.g., working and completing the task); and the context of instruction (e.g., small group, large group, classroom, library). For example, during the first few weeks of school, it is appropriate for the teacher to use verbal and gestural prompts to remind students of the rules and teacher expectations (e.g., "Jennifer, I appreciate you staying on task and working on your writing assignment." The teacher gestures to get John's attention by pointing to John's paper. "John, I'd like you to begin your writing assignment.")

It is important to record persistent student errors during instruction. Error patterns should inform the teacher about the instruction in general and the specific task and management requirements. However, persistent errors can be managed during instruction only through a general correction procedure of modeling the correct response, assisting the child with the production of the response if necessary, and requiring the learner to produce the response independently. Persistent errors require a fundamental adjustment in the design of the instruction, which must be considered in the before phase of instruction. Persistent errors signal limitations on the part of the student and the teaching sequence: (a) lack of prerequisite knowledge and component skills to complete the target task, (b) inability to produce a complex response requirement, (c) inability to understand the task requirements, (d) lack of reinforcement, (e) fatigue, and so on.

If errors occur frequently during an instructional session, the teacher should stop presenting the target task and switch to a neutral (i.e., not too easy or too difficult) task with an entirely different set of task requirements (e.g., oral instead of written responses, choice instead of production responses). To continue presenting a task that is too difficult can lead to serious behavior problems. Once the teacher has determined the problems inherent in the design and delivery of the difficult task, then the requirements of the task can be taught separately, prior to reintroducing the entire task.

Delivering instruction.   Two features of instruction often associated with problem behavior during instruction are the pace of instruction, and opportunities for responding. In a study designed to evaluate the effects of pacing instruction, Darch and Gersten (1985) found that rapidly paced instruction increased both the levels of on-task behavior and correct responses during reading of five disruptive students. This demonstrates the broad effects pacing can have on both behavior and academic learning. As Darch and Gersten (1985) state, "The powerful effects of pacing and praising can be important in allowing students to succeed in the early stages of remedial education programs" (p. 302). However, if the pace of instruction is either too fast or too slow, students become distracted and frustrated, which sets the stage for behavior problems. The appropriate pace of instruction depends on the nature of the tasks and the learner, but in general, it should be brisk. The pace for complex tasks may need to be slowed, especially when they involve multiple steps and complex student responses. If the task is strictly verbal (e.g., a verbal chain such as days of week, months of year, mathematics facts), the pace should be fairly brisk.

Students should have ample opportunity to respond during instruction to give the teacher a measure of the student's engagement in the lesson. If students are not given an opportunity to respond, the stage may be set for problem behaviors.

After Instruction: Reflecting and Adjusting Instructional Classroom Management

The final phase of instructional classroom management is that of reflecting upon instruction after it is completed. The after-instruction phase is the time to adjust instruction for the next before-instruction phase. This phase helps teachers reframe learning and behavior difficulties as instructional problems (Wilson et. al., 1998). Teachers can use the after-instruction framework to develop new approaches with the features listed below.

After-Instruction Phase
Reflecting on Instruction
  1. How do you feel about the lesson?

Assessing Instruction
  1. Were students able to perform the task at an appropriate criterion level?
  2. Were there any serious or persistent behavior management problems?

Modifying Instruction

1. Is there a pattern to student academic errors?
2. Are behavior problems associated with specific task dimensions?
3. Was the instruction motivating for students?
4. Did the lesson accommodate students' individual differences?

Reflecting on instruction.   After instruction, the teacher must take time to reflect on the lesson. The reflection can be focused on a specific task dimension or on the general instructional session. The primary purpose of reflection is to provide teachers an opportunity to examine their feelings about the instructional session.

Assessing instruction.   One of the most important considerations in the after-instruction phase is assessing the instruction based on student performance in the during-instruction phase. The teacher must determine the answers to questions like, "Were students able to perform the task at an appropriate criterion level?" If students aren't able to reach the target criterion level set by the teacher for the task, then the task may be too difficult or the criterion inappropriate. Students' failure to reach criterion level performance may set the stage for problem behaviors. At first the problems may be minor, but sustained failure over time will take its toll on students (and teachers) and create management problems. If students aren't reaching criterion-level performance, it's unlikely they are accomplishing the objectives of the lesson.

Another important consideration is to identify serious or persistent behavior problems that occurred during instruction. Identifying the problems is only the first step of the process, because to remediate them, it is essential to determine how the problems are associated with specific instructional task requirements. This requires an analysis of task dimensions and student responses. Strategies to address persistent behavior problems are instructional ones (e.g., reteaching component skills, clarifying rules and expectations, preteaching), and punishment should be used only as a last resort.

Modifying instruction.   In order to modify instruction in an effective and efficient manner, it is important to determine if there is a pattern to students' academic errors and if behavior problems were associated with specific task dimensions. The modification of task dimensions is not easy and will require continued teaching and testing to discern the task requirements that are causing problems for students.

Finally, as part of the after-instruction routine, we recommend that teachers determine if students' individual differences (e.g., culture, disability) have been accommodated during instruction. Teachers must be knowledgeable about and sensitive to students' cultural, and linguistic differences. Some research has been completed that supports the notion that instructional adjustments should accommodate a student's race or ethnic background (Franklin, 1992; McIntyre, 1992). Teachers must consider the full array of instructional and management options when individualizing instructional and management programs.

A list of factors to consider and suggestions for modifying instruction for students with diverse instructional and classroom management needs follows. The suggestions in this list serve as a starting point for teachers to make instructional and management adjustments for students.

Teachers are most effective if they understand and accommodate for individual differences among students.

Managing for Individual Differences

Factors to Consider

- As demographics change in the United States, students with diverse cultural and linguistic backgrounds comprise an increasing segment of the school population.
- There is evidence of an interaction between the teacher's rate of reinforcement and the race, gender, or disability of the student.
- Evidence suggests that punishment procedures are used more frequently with students from diverse backgrounds and students with disabilities than with other students.
- Students with disabilities and students from low-income homes are at greater risk for dropping out of school.

Individualizing Strategies

- Use multiple assessment approaches (e.g., written, oral) to accommodate students with diverse cultural and linguistic backgrounds.
- Monitor rates of reinforcement to insure equitability across all students (e.g., ethnicity, gender).
- Teach students how to be sensitive to students from diverse ethnic, cultural, and linguistic backgrounds.
- Develop training/information packages for parents from diverse cultures about special programs (e.g., special education, gifted and talented education) available at school.

STEP 2: CONSIDERING THE PHASES OF THE SCHOOL YEAR

For Step 2—conceptualizing and implementing a temporal framework for instructional classroom management—teachers use a broad perspective to consider implications of the phases of the school year on teaching and planning. While Step 1 in our model asks teachers to look at the phases of instruction as a basis for a task-by-task analysis, teachers look at the full expanse of the school year in Step 2. This longer view will allow teachers to predict learning and behavior problems associated with each of the three seasonal phases of the academic year. In the remainder of this chapter we discuss the teaching and classroom management implications of the three phases of the school year.

Critical Features of the 180-Day Plan

Managing behavior always takes place within the context of time. Too often the management of social and academic behavior is considered in either immediate terms (e.g., "How do I stop this behavior right now?") or future terms (e.g., "What management strategies will stop the problem behaviors from occurring in the future?"). The typical approach is to conceptualize a management strategy for a specific problem and apply it until the problem either increases or decreases, when the teacher tries another strategy or stops trying altogether. The teacher often has no overall plan of management strategies to use over the course of the school year.

If we think about behavior management in instructional terms, we must consider terms we use to teach a cognitive skill, operation, or strategy. Like academic learning, classroom management and teaching of social behavior take place in phases. When a student learns an academic skill such as story grammar to comprehend narrative stories, the initial learning takes time and requires teacher assistance, practice, and feedback. The teacher supports the student's independent application of the story grammar strategy over time. During the initial phases of instruction, the teacher provides the environmental support in the form of direct instruction, modeling, and frequent feedback and guidance. After the initial phase of acquisition, the learner requires less teacher support and direction. During this "scaffolded" instruction, the learner attempts to apply the strategy independent of the teacher, who offers support at strategic or necessary points of the student's strategy application. Eventually, the learner reaches a state of full independence, the strategy is mastered, and instructional support is not needed.

Instructional classroom management must be conceptualized in similar "phases." Like instruction, behavior management takes place over the course of a full school year, about 180 school days. Therefore, an instructional management plan must be conceptualized as a 180-day process that begins at least a few days before the first day of school and ends after the last day of school. Later in the chapter, we offer a rationale for starting before school and stopping one day after school ends. For now, a 180-day instructional classroom management plan provides the teacher a general blueprint for managing the classroom for the entire school year.

The development of a 180-day plan encourages teachers to think about the entire school year and not just the first two weeks of school or the long winter months. More importantly, the 180-day plan allows teachers to plan strategically and confidently for a full year of school, helping them anticipate periods of potential crisis (e.g., before holidays) and be proactive about managing problem behaviors. The 180-day plan also acknowledges certain realities of teaching and managing behavior. First, behavior management is easier at the beginning of the school year than at the end, for obvious reasons: (a) teachers and students are "energized" by the new school year, (b) students are likely to be neutralized by the novelty of a new school year, (c) teaching and learning fatigue are minimal, and (d) students have yet to "test" the boundaries of acceptable and unacceptable behavior. Second, by linking phases of the year with causes of behavior problems, teachers can be proactive by anticipating when problems will occur.

One problem with developing management plans for the beginning of the school year alone is that students are typically compliant. By conceptualizing behavior management in a 180-day plan, all periods of the school year are given full consideration. A 180-day plan is a general blueprint of strategies likely to be effective at different times during the year. The plan acknowledges the covariation between the time of the year, student behavior, teacher behavior and expectations, and student academic and social performance. Teachers are likely to respond to inappropriate behavior differently in February than in September.

Phases of the 180-Day Plan

The 180-day plan consists of three phases, each comprised of three months of the school year. The conceptual basis of the 180-day plan is also valid in schools with year round instruction. In schools that have adopted year round instruction, student behavior continues to covary with the time of the year. The instructional management plan for the first phase (i.e., first three months) of the school year will be fundamentally different from the plan for the last three months of the school year. The first phase of the 180-day plan parallels the acquisition-of-skills phase of learning, because the primary objective is to "teach" students how to behave in the classroom and school contexts. The third phase of the 180-day plan parallels the maintenance-and-transfer phase of academic learning, because the primary objective is for the learner to retain rules and expectations and transfer them to new and untaught contexts.

Figure 4.6 provides an overview of the predictive power of a temporal framework that considers the phases of the school year. Each phase is often associated with specific causes of learning and behavior problems. For example, we can predict with a level of confidence that during the first part of the academic year, the fall months, many learning and behavior problems are a result of a lack of adequate instruction. Many students violate classroom rules and routines because they are not adequately taught the expectations of the classroom. For example, a student may frequently disrupt other students when she completes an assignment rather than shift her attention to another assignment because she may not have been taught to monitor other tasks that need to be completed. As Figure 4.6 shows, the teaching consists of providing many teacher-modeled demonstrations of how a student selects and finishes uncompleted work. The instructional solution also involves the teacher using precise reinforcement whenever the student transitions from one completed task to another.

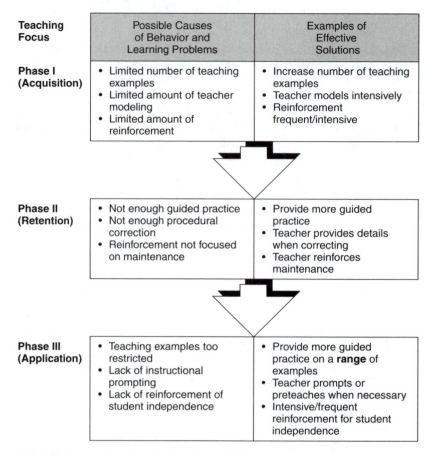

Teaching Focus	Possible Causes of Behavior and Learning Problems	Examples of Effective Solutions
Phase I (Acquisition)	• Limited number of teaching examples • Limited amount of teacher modeling • Limited amount of reinforcement	• Increase number of teaching examples • Teacher models intensively • Reinforcement frequent/intensive
Phase II (Retention)	• Not enough guided practice • Not enough procedural correction • Reinforcement not focused on maintenance	• Provide more guided practice • Teacher provides details when correcting • Teacher reinforces maintenance
Phase III (Application)	• Teaching examples too restricted • Lack of instructional prompting • Lack of reinforcement of student independence	• Provide more guided practice on a **range** of examples • Teacher prompts or preteaches when necessary • Intensive/frequent reinforcement for student independence

FIGURE 4.6   Using the 180-day plan to link instructional solutions to learning and behavior problems.

At the beginning of the school year many students with a history of learning and behavior problems question teachers about whether they "really have to" complete a learning assignment or not. It may take several weeks of teaching for some students to learn that negotiating assignments with the teacher is not a successful strategy to avoid assignments.

Prediction and understanding of causes of problems during the school year are without value if we don't also discuss teaching and classroom management strategies to develop proactive instructional interventions. As seen in Figure 4.6, during Phase I, when students are first learning a skill or concept, we recommend that teachers use many teaching examples, with intensive modeling followed by frequent reinforcement. In Figure 4.6, the same analysis of predicting causes of problems and linking effective solutions can be completed for each of the three phases of the school year. Applying a 180-day plan, as we discuss in the following sections of this chapter, allows teachers to consider implications of the phases of the academic calendar throughout the school year.

Phase I of the 180-day plan: The fall months. The primary focus of the first phase of the 180-day plan is to teach students appropriate classroom behavior. The first phase of the 180-day management plan is designed to organize instruction so students are taught the rules and routines. Figure 4.7 presents a blueprint that specifies the management strategies the teacher will use for each week of the first three months of the school year. In the beginning of the school year, the classroom management plan is almost exclusively instructional, as students are first being introduced to expectations of the teacher and school. The primary role of the teacher is to assess for instruction and teach students what behaviors are acceptable and what behaviors are unacceptable. While the role of assessment and teaching is obvious for some teachers, too often students who require the most intensive instruction for successful learning receive less instruction. For example, McWilliam and Bailey (1995) have shown that preschool children with disabilities were engaged for less time and at less sophisticated levels than children without disabilities.

First month (September). The first month of the management plan focuses on instruction. The teacher carefully instructs students in appropriate classroom behaviors, and nothing is left to chance. In Figure 4.7, we recommend teachers organize the classroom to decrease opportunities for disruptive behavior. Assessment plays a prominent role in this phase of the 180-day management plan, as this is how the teacher identifies the academic and social skills needs of students. By assessing students on their ability to correctly follow rules and routines of the classroom, the teacher doesn't waste time teaching skills the students perform consistently. The major management activity for the first month is to teach only those skills students need, such as how to quietly transition from one class activity to another or how to properly turn in completed homework. These behaviors are established through instruction and strengthened through reinforcement.

Careful teaching ensures that students are not merely exposed to a teacher's classroom rules and routines, but that the teacher models exactly how a rule is followed or how a routine is completed. Careful teaching offers many opportunities for the teacher to reinforce students, which results in a more positive classroom atmosphere and more successful students. This basis for proactive teaching and management serves as the foundation for instructional classroom management and allows children to succeed throughout the year.

Second month (October). The focus of the second month of the management plan shifts slightly from teaching new skills to reinforcing and strengthening previously taught skills. Teachers continue to teach students appropriate behavior when necessary, but a significant amount of the teacher's time is spent helping students establish appropriate behavior patterns. As shown in Figure 4.7, we recommend teachers review classroom rules and preteach behaviors students continue to find difficult. For example, if students fail to make quick and quiet transitions from one instructional group to another, preteaching should continue. Students with learning and behavior problems will require extensive preteaching and review of all classroom rules and routines.

In the second month, there is a slight shift in the teacher's reinforcement strategy. Rather than only reinforcing students when they comply with specific classroom rules, teachers reinforce other appropriate behaviors as well. For example, when students are working independently, the teacher reinforces the accurate completion

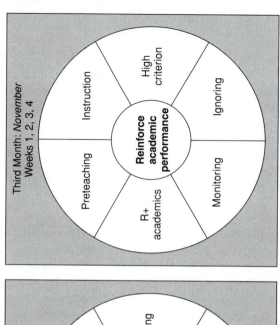

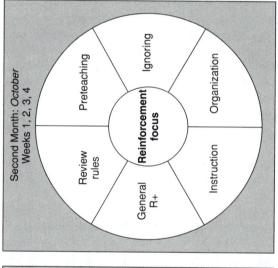

R+: Positive reinforcement

FIGURE 4.7 Phase I of the 180-day plan: The fall months.

of the assignment rather than working "quietly." This shift in reinforcement is subtle but important. The teacher is carefully and systematically teaching students that if they follow rules (e.g., working quietly) their performance will improve. The intent is to help students understand the relation between effort and performance.

If it is necessary to establish instructional control by using punishment strategies, we recommend teachers select strategies that are the easiest to implement. For example, it would be inappropriate for the teacher to use exclusionary time-out at this time in the school year, but the teacher might instead use ignoring all types of reinforcers to teach appropriate behavior. This way, the teacher continues to emphasize instruction as the primary management tool, helping the classroom continue to be a positive learning environment.

Third month (November).   The teacher continues to reteach appropriate behavior by demonstrating, reinforcing, and practicing what is expected. If some students are not consistently following classroom rules, the teacher should upgrade instructional procedures and increase the amount of time that students have to practice these skills. Instruction is still the key management strategy in this part of the plan. However, the majority of the teacher's effort should be geared toward reinforcing *academic performance* of the students. Figure 4.7 demonstrates fundamental teaching techniques for upgrading instruction. The teacher increases the number of examples for teaching the skill and provides explicit models of how to complete the skill, extensive guided practice, and intensive reinforcement.

Linking the instructional program to the management program is a primary goal of this component of the management program. Our instructional emphasis is designed to teach students the relationship between improved social behavior and increased academic performance. To help accomplish this goal, we recommend the teacher use reinforcement strategies to acknowledge the improved academic performance of the students. For example, a teacher merely says, "Good job" to a student who has just completed one assignment and has moved on to another for the first time without teacher prompting. The teacher is not taking advantage of an instructional and reinforcement opportunity but should, instead, structure verbal praise so the student will see the positive consequences of working efficiently. In this example, the teacher might say, "Maria, smart idea going to your math assignment. Using your time efficiently will make a difference in your grade! Keep it up!"

During this part of the management plan, students must begin to understand that every effort is being made to help them succeed in school. Students learn expectations of them in both academics and behavior. Even for very young students, the teacher must emphasize improved academic performance through reinforcement. If the teacher uses an instructional program that is properly designed, all students should achieve success that is reinforced.

During November, we recommend the teacher begin to increase the criteria of acceptable performance. Students should no longer be reinforced each time they comply with a classroom rule or complete an assignment but should earn reinforcement for complying with rules for longer periods of time or in difficult learning contexts. This does not suggest that students exhibiting behavior problems be excluded from opportunities for reinforcement. As we have stated throughout the text, the teacher must continually modify the instructional program so that each student is successful.

Monitoring student performance plays a significant role in this part of the management program. Monitoring is particularly important because of the increased emphasis on reinforcement of academic performance. The teacher must carefully monitor the behavior of the students to determine what academic and behavioral skills need to be taught. For low-performing students, monitoring provides the teacher information to upgrade the instructional and management programs. Without careful monitoring, teachers may not be able to design an instructional and management program to meet the needs of all students.

Phase II of the 180-day plan: The winter months. The focus of Phase II of the 180-day management plan is to develop mastery of behavioral skills and academic competencies so that students can become independent learners. Figure 4.8 features teaching techniques that foster retention of a skill, which is the next step toward independence for students. In the three months of this phase, December, January, and February, students must develop fluency with the behaviors they were taught during the beginning of the academic year. Students must develop fluency or automaticity responding to both academic assignments and rule/routine-following behaviors. Primary tools teachers use during this time are instruction, scheduling of instruction, and higher expectations for appropriate behavior and reinforcement. During these months, the instructional emphasis begins to switch to teaching students to be independent, self-directed workers. Students are no longer reinforced each time they follow a classroom rule or complete an assignment. Instead, the students learn that the teacher's expectations are growing over time. During this phase, the students play a significant role in monitoring their own behavior so that they can make subtle management adjustments. As Kame'enui and Simmons (1997) state, "The assumption at this point is that children are fully aware of the teacher's expectations and need few reminders. Children, in effect, have mastered the skills of how to behave in the school environment, and the teacher shifts the responsibility of management to the students" (p. 479). As Figure 4.8 denotes, during this phase the teacher wants to rely on guided practice, systematic corrections that provide the students the steps to follow to comply with rules and routines, or structured reinforcement.

Fourth month (December). December, the first month of Phase II, is characterized by instructional procedures that initially foster mastery and maintenance of appropriate classroom and school behavior. To accomplish this, the teacher begins to restructure the instructional program so that students are required to work independently, but still under close monitoring by the teacher. In this phase of the management plan, the teacher plays a less prominent role in directing learning and social activities. The teacher's primary focus is to teach and reinforce instances of independent and self-reliant behavior (see Figure 4.8). This is an important shift in instructional emphasis, because as students grow older, they are expected to develop independent work skills. Most programs do not directly teach students these skills, and students are expected to develop independence naturally. In fact, as Wilson, et al. (1998) point out, teachers often do not make instructional modifications that will foster independent learning for students with behavior problems. The structure of the 180-day plan in instructional classroom management emphasizes teaching students to be independent learners.

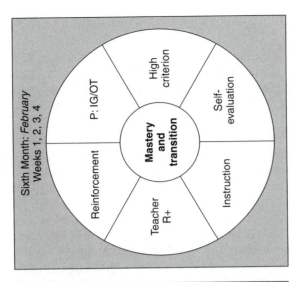

Sixth Month: *February*
Weeks 1, 2, 3, 4

High criterion · Self-evaluation · Instruction · Teacher R+ · Reinforcement · P: IG/OT

Mastery and transition

Fifth Month: *January*
Weeks 1, 2, 3, 4

Self-evaluation · Teacher R+ · Instruction · High criterion · P: IG/OT · Review · Reinforcement

Reteach and reinforce

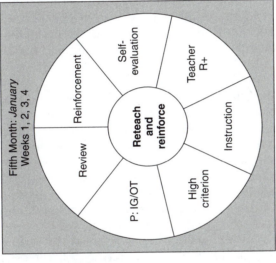

Fourth Month: *December*
Weeks 1, 2, 3, 4

Change R+ · Self-evaluation · P: IG/OT · High criterion · Instruction · Maintenance

Instruction focus

R+: Positive reinforcement
P: Punishment (IG = Ignoring; OT = Owing-time)

FIGURE 4.8 Phase II of the 180-day plan: The winter months.

The structure of the reinforcement program also changes in December. Skills that have been previously taught (e.g., old, familiar tasks) are reinforced less frequently, if at all. Instead, new behavioral and academic skills performed at a high criterion level are the focus of the reinforcement program. Students are heavily reinforced for attempting to perform in ways that enable them to become more independent. For example, a student who is extraordinarily shy is reinforced for any spontaneous attempt he/she makes to meet other students. Or a student who rarely asks content-related questions during class is reinforced for asking questions that allow the completion of an activity independently. The teacher vigilantly uses powerful reinforcers to maintain these new behaviors that signal the student is becoming a more independent learner in the classroom. The requirements for earning reinforcers have slowly changed, and the teacher looks for students who behave like mature, independent learners and quickly reinforces that behavior.

The role of punishment changes during this phase of the management program. In Figure 4.8, we recommend using quiet-time and owing-time strategies when necessary. Behavior problems during this phase require more powerful interventions. By this time in the academic year, the assumption is that students understand what the teacher's expectations are in the classroom. Behavior problems that continue in December need to be stopped with powerful strategies like quiet-time and owing-time.

Fifth month (January).   In most settings, students return to school in January from a holiday vacation, energized and ready to tackle the remainder of the school year. For some students, however, returning after a long vacation is difficult. Students who have learning and behavior problems often forget classroom expectations and school rules. Just as some students will not retain certain academic content (e.g., multiplication facts) after vacation, others may forget classroom rules and the teacher's expectations. Much of the plan for January is to reintroduce classroom rules and routines while helping students regain mastery of academic content.

We recommend teachers reteach students how to comply with the teacher's expectations as soon as the students return to school. The teacher should not wait to see if students remember rules and routines but should model rule-following behavior and provide students time to practice the rules. Rule teaching continues until all students are consistently following rules, usually within a few days. Instructional time used is well spent, for this is a more efficient use of time than trying to reestablish the skills later with punitive procedures. The teacher should periodically prompt students to follow rules and provide practice throughout the month. Reteaching classroom rules enables the teacher to teach students more advanced social and academic skills in the months that follow.

Once students have regained mastery of classroom rules and routines, the focus of the instructional program shifts to maintenance of the social and academic skills taught during the first three months of the school year. The teacher reinforces instances when students demonstrate independent behavior and when behavior problems occur, the teacher implements a consistent plan to decrease the frequency of the behaviors. In Figure 4.8, we recommend the teacher use quiet-time and owing-time strategies in response to disruptive behaviors. These strategies are powerful, if applied consistently, and will be effective in controlling most behavior problems during this phase of the school year.

The demanding job of teaching becomes increasingly demanding during the winter months. There are reasons why this phase of the school year is particularly demanding for teachers and students. First, as we have discussed throughout this section of the text, teaching students to become independent learners is a difficult task. Successful teaching requires students to be closely monitored by the teacher when they begin to work independently. Also, the demands of the curriculum change during this phase, and students are expected to complete more difficult tasks. As February approaches, many teachers begin to feel the stress of the academic year. As Sprick, Garrison, & Howard (1998) point out, no matter how much time a teacher spends preparing for the school day, there are always papers to grade, meetings to prepare for, and instructional materials to develop. The management of behavior problems adds to the stress of many teachers, and fatigue associated with active teaching and management become apparent during this time. We recommend that teachers build in reinforcers for themselves as part of the teaching schedule.

Sixth month (February).   The management plan for February has two purposes. First, management activities are designed to maintain previously learned behavioral skills and foster the student independence. Second, management activities in February are designed to prepare students for the final phase of the school year, the spring months. The teacher's first task is to ensure that students have developed mastery of behavioral skills so they can demonstrate them in new learning contexts (Gutkin, 1993). The teacher's second task for February is to make sure students have prerequisite skills for the learning demands of the third phase of the academic year.

Figure 4.8 presents the specific teaching strategies emphasized in February. Reinforcement and instruction continue to play a prominent role in the management plan. As always, we recommend teachers focus on teaching students new social skills while helping them develop mastery on previously taught competencies. Even though students have had several months to learn and practice classroom rules and routines, some students will periodically engage in disruptive behavior.

Teachers can decrease the frequency of behavior problems during this phase by reviewing classroom expectations with students at least once a week. After this review, the teacher consistently reinforces appropriate behavior. This may seem indulgent, and some may ask, "Why should a teacher have to remind students of school and classroom expectations this far into the school year?" Commercial academic programs present the most difficult learning tasks at this time in the school year. Academic skills are complex, and it is assumed the student is performing at mastery level on all prerequisite skills. As a consequence, students are at greater risk for learning difficulties, which puts them at risk for behavior problems. When students must struggle with difficult material that is new to them, they often become disruptive. Periodic review of classroom expectations helps maintain appropriate student behavior, even in the context of difficult learning tasks.

We also recommend teachers continue to teach students to be independent in the classroom. A common feature of commercial academic programs is that by February, students are required to work independently on difficult learning activities. Many commercial programs reduce the teacher's role to that of monitoring student performance. Direct teaching of skills is not emphasized in this phase of the academic year. Even young students are expected to be much more self-directed by this time. Therefore, it is important that teachers help students make the transition to independence by carefully structuring tasks and using reinforcement to increase the frequency of successful independent behavior.

Phase III of the 180-day plan: The spring months.   March ushers in the final three months of the management plan (see Figure 4.9). The variety of school activities scheduled for students during these months is considerable. Schools schedule field trips, plan special events within the classroom, and organize school-wide assemblies during this time of year. Many students, particularly low-performing students, have difficulty participating in these events without becoming disruptive, causing them to have less successful learning opportunities and fall further behind their peers. It is not unusual for teachers to exclude some students from participation in these activities because of potential behavior problems. Teachers can decrease the probability that students will become disruptive in these settings by preteaching expected behaviors before students participate in specific events.

Seventh month (March).   The focus of the management plan during March should be on teaching students appropriate behavior for special events and activities. The instructional program is expanded to teach students appropriate behavior for different settings. During this month, the teacher should list scheduled field trips, special classroom learning activities, and school-wide programs, as well as schedule time to instruct students on the expected behaviors in these different settings. For example, if the teacher has arranged a field trip to the post office, he/she should first introduce the activities that will occur on the field trip (e.g., bus ride, tour of the post office, lunch). For each separate activity, teachers identify the expected behaviors for the students. If students are going to ride the bus to the post office, the teacher should explain and demonstrate appropriate bus behavior, as well as appropriate behavior at the post office.

During the teaching and practice sessions, the teacher should use powerful reinforcers to expedite learning, and during the trip the teacher should use high-frequency verbal praise for students who are following rules. After the field trip, the teacher should review the trip with the students and discuss what they have learned.

Eighth month (April).   The focus of the management plan for April is similar to March. We recommend teachers continue to teach students appropriate behavior for new contexts. In addition, students should be reinforced when they demonstrate independent learning skills and social behavior. It is important for teachers to provide students opportunities to be independent, with minimal teacher guidance.

Ninth month (May).   Students are not taught many new skills in May because of the approaching end of the academic year. We recommend teachers evaluate students' performance throughout the year and provide students more practice on academic and social skills that have yet to be mastered. We suggest 10 to 15 minutes per day be dedicated to review activities. Teachers can begin to consider ways to improve their management plan for the year to come by recording ideas while the past year is still fresh in mind.

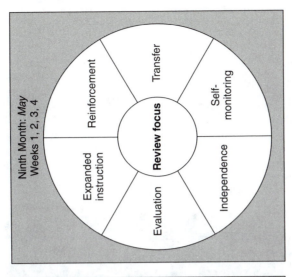

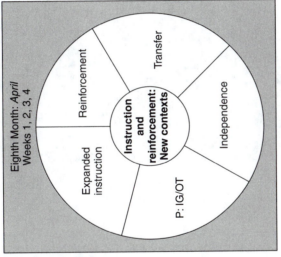

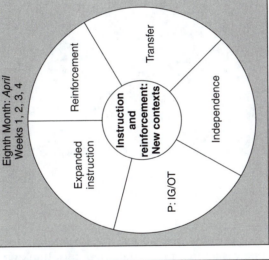

R+: Positive reinforcement
P: Punishment (IG = Ignoring; OT = Owing-time)

FIGURE 4.9 Phase III of the 180-day plan: The spring months.

Teachers must instruct students how to behave for special events and activities.

SUMMARY

In this chapter, we propose a temporal framework for instructional classroom behavior. The first part is a three-phase framework for thinking about and planning instructional classroom management. The framework consists of before, during, and after phases of instruction and allows the teacher to gauge the students' instruction and management needs in each phase. By relying on this temporal framework, the teacher will be able to respond to students' instructional classroom management needs in ways that link teaching and managing behavior before instruction begins, during instruction, and after instruction.

Moreover, by attending to the requirements of each phase of instruction, the teacher sets the stage for a proactive approach to instruction.

The second part of this framework is a three-phase 180-day classroom management plan. In Phase I, the fall months, we offer strategies for initially teaching students appropriate behavior. The focus of Phase II, the winter months, is on strategies teachers use to help students maintain previously taught behaviors. Phase III introduces procedures for teaching students to independently transfer behavioral skills to new contexts. We argue that the advantage of using the temporal framework is that teachers can more readily (a) predict classroom instructional and behavior problems; (b) assess for causes of learning and behavior problems; and (c) plan for effective, proactive instructional solutions.

CHAPTER ACTIVITIES

1. For each of the five questions that guide the teacher's thinking about rules and expectations in the classroom (Table 4.1), discuss your expectations for your classroom.
2. Choose a content area (e.g., social studies, science) and develop a 45-minute lesson that would help eliminate behavior problems. For this lesson, provide the time allotments for each lesson segment along with a discussion of the specific teaching and learning activities.
3. List and discuss the major components of each of the three phases of instruction.
4. List and discuss the major classroom management activities for each month of all three phases of the 180-day plan.

REFERENCES

Darch, C., & Gersten, R. (1985). The effects of teacher presentation rate and praise on LD students' oral reading performance. *British Journal of Educational Psychology, 55,* 295–305.

Dunlap, G., & Kern, L. (1996). Modifying instructional activities to promote desirable behavior: A conceptual and practical framework. *School Psychology Quarterly, 11,* 297–312.

Franklin, M. E. (1992). Culturally sensitive instructional practices for African American learners with disabilities. *Exceptional Children, 59*(2), 115–122.

Gutkin, T. B. (1993). Moving from behavioral to ecobehavioral consultation: What's in a name. *Journal of Educational and Psychological Consultation, 4,* 95–99.

Kame'enui, E., & Simmons, D. (1997). *Designing instructional strategies: The prevention of academic learning problems.* Upper Saddle River, NJ: Merrill/Prentice Hall.

Kern, L., Childs, K., & Dunlap, G. (1994). Using assessment-based curricular intervention to improve the classroom behavior of a student with emotional and behavioral challenges. *Journal of Applied Behavior Analysis, 27,* 7–19.

McIntyre, T. (1992). A primer on cultural diversity for educators. *Multicultural Forum, 1*(1), 6, 13.

McWilliam, R. A., & Bailey, D. B. (1995). Effects of classroom social structure and disability on engagement. *Topics in Early Childhood Special Education, 15,* 123–147.

Meltzer, L., Roditi, B., Houser, Jr., R., & Perlman, M. (1998). Perceptions of academic strategies and competence in students with learning disabilities. *Journal of Learning Disabilities, 31,* 437–451.

Sprick, R., Garrison, M., & Howard, L. (1998). *CHAMPS: A proactive and positive approach to classroom management.* Longmont, CO: Sopris West.

Trent, S. (1998). False starts and other dilemmas of a secondary general education collaborative teacher: A case study. *Journal of Learning Disabilities, 31,* 503–513.

Tulley, M., & Chiu, L. H. (1998). Children's perceptions of effectiveness of classroom discipline techniques. *Journal of Instructional Psychology, 25,* 189–197.

Wilson, C. P., Gutkin, T. B., Hagen, K. M., & Oats, R. G. (1998). General education teachers' knowledge and self-reported use of classroom interventions for working with difficult to teach students: Implications for consultation, prereferral intervention and inclusive services. *School Psychology Quarterly, 13,* 45–62.

Wolery, M., Bailey, D., & Sugai, G. (1988). *Effective teaching: Principles and procedures of applied behavior analysis with exceptional students.* Boston: Allyn & Bacon.

Chapter

5

Instructional Classroom Management Assessment

OVERVIEW

Assessment activities in classroom management include the information-gathering techniques a teacher uses to document behavior problems and determine their causes. According to Foster-Johnson and Dunlap (1993), an effective assessment approach will help teachers translate this information "into logical, positive and effective intervention strategies" (p. 45). An assessment plan is developed to organize assessment activities, systematize information gathering, and develop a mechanism for program refinement. Assessment in classroom management has at least three primary purposes: (a) to determine the causes of ongoing behavior problems so the teacher can develop interventions immediately, (b) to help the teacher refine the entire instructional program so that the probability of misbehavior is decreased, and (c) to increase effectiveness of behavioral intervention strategies by improving instruction.

For this chapter, we have designed an assessment model that includes procedures that teachers implement as part of their instructional program. Instructional classroom management assessment is not intended to provide comprehensive assessment information; rather, it enables the teacher to place assessment activities in the context of instruction so that instructional solutions to behavior and learning problems can be developed. Unlike other approaches, the assessment activities and questions we propose link assessment to instruction. Many teachers think of assessment in behavior management as an entirely separate activity from instruction, which we believe is ineffective in developing successful behavior management programs.

WHY DEVELOP AN ASSESSMENT PLAN?

Several compelling reasons lead us to develop a behavioral assessment plan integral to the teaching program. First, a careful assessment of classroom organization, behavior management, and instructional design before instruction allows the teacher to develop a teaching program that actually decreases the potential of behavior problems. Farmer, Van Acker, Pearl, and Rodkin (1999) suggest that programs designed to enhance the social skills of students need not focus on the behavior problem, but should focus on assessing for information on how to best change the entire context of learning. If assessment is completed carefully and systematically, it can be an effective tool in preventing classroom behavior and learning problems.

Second, if an assessment plan is in place, the teacher can respond to a behavior problem humanely and effectively and develop an instructional program that teaches students how to behave appropriately. Therefore, assessment helps the teacher increase the achievement of students and improve social behavior. A detailed assessment plan causes the teacher to make proper refinements in the teaching program. In addition, increased learning and prosocial behavior is maintained and supported in classrooms that practice ongoing assessment and effective instruction (Gresham & MacMillan, 1997).

In many assessment approaches, the teacher is taught to evaluate the behavior of the student only when he or she is disruptive. Special and general education teachers who work with students with behavior problems do not make the connection between effective instruction and student behavior. According to Gunter and Denny (1998), "research indicates that effective instructional strategies may not be employed commonly in classrooms for students with behavior problems, whether those classrooms are for special or regular education" (p. 46). The common focus on behavior management is on only one dimension of the teaching equation—the learner. The teacher often documents and identifies student misconduct (e.g., rates of on-task behavior, frequency of talk-outs, and percentage of correct responses). In another approach, the teacher uses a standardized instrument, perhaps a checklist, to determine the seriousness of a problem. These instruments do not provide the teacher with information to help determine causes of behavior problems and separate assessment from instruction, which limits the usefulness of the information to the teacher.

This chapter introduces an assessment model tailored for instructional classroom management. We describe the features of the Instructional Classroom Management Assessment Model and the assessment activities for each of the different phases of instruction. The proposed model expands the focus of assessment to include instructional and noninstructional variables that may contribute to disruptive classroom behavior. The purpose of this model is to provide a link between assessment and instructional activities. To achieve this goal, we describe procedures that can be used to assess the instructional task, the learner, the setting, and the curricular materials.

TRADITIONAL ASSESSMENT IN BEHAVIOR MANAGEMENT

Most assessment models are used in one of two ways. First, many assessment activities are designed for a specific classroom management approach and lack an instructional focus, causing the activities to have limited application to instructional classroom management assessment. For example, a series of teacher worksheets serves as the assessment tool for Canter's assertive discipline program. Teachers respond to a series of discipline-related questions such as, "For which students have you failed to set sufficiently firm consequences?"; "In general, how do you verbally respond to the student's behavior that you want?" (Canter & Canter, 1992).

Dreikurs, Grunwald, and Pepper's (1982) system of logical consequences also has an informal system of assessment built directly into the program. The teacher is directed to answer several key questions related to the refinement of the consequences for misbehavior (Lopez-Reyna & Bay, 1997). For example, "What is the goal of the student's disruptive behavior?" and "What are the logical consequences of the student's behavior?" These questions are obviously narrow in focus and do not guide the teacher to systematically evaluate the entire teaching program. In each of these assessment models, the evaluation questions do not provide teachers the necessary information to develop instructional solutions to behavior problems.

Another large group of assessment activities is derived from generic models not associated with specific classroom management programs. Within this group, the behavioral approach and the standardized testing approach are cited most frequently and have important applications to the model of assessment we present in this chapter. Functional assessment (Sugai & Horner, 1994), as we discuss in Chapter 7, is a method for identifying behavior problems, causes, and intervention strategies likely effective in eliminating problems. Functional assessment, with its emphasis on uncovering environmental factors that motivate students to misbehave, is a tool to use in instructional classroom management.

Behavioral assessment focuses on the student's behavior, with less emphasis on the instructional and curriculum variables that have an impact on the student's behavior. A behavioral analysis of a behavior problem will often yield information on the frequency of the behavior, the context in which the problem behavior surfaces, and the duration of the behavior. This information is important to consider when developing strategies to react to classroom management problems. However, behavioral measures are less helpful in providing the teacher with information on the instructional aspects of a behavior problem unless a functional assessment answers questions about the impact of teaching examples, the pacing of instruction, and the relationship between a teacher's instructional program and the behavior of students.

Kame'enui and Simmons (1997) suggest that the purpose of norm-referenced assessment is to determine a learner's degree of deviation from the norm group. Norm-referenced measures in behavior management present information on how a student is behaving relative to his or her peers under standardized testing conditions. In general, these tests do not provide the teacher instructionally relevant information on how to manage students in the classroom.

LIMITATIONS OF ASSESSMENT MODELS IN BEHAVIOR MANAGEMENT

There are four significant limitations to current assessment in behavior management: the failure to (a) link assessment to instruction, (b) provide information to help the teacher develop proactive classroom management procedures, (c) assess all phases of instruction, and (d) incorporate assessment activities within the normal teaching routine. Each of these limitations is discussed as follows.

Linking Assessment to Instruction

First, most assessment models fail to link assessment activities to procedures for improving instruction. For example, when discussing how teachers should first implement assertive discipline, Canter recommends discipline planning at the end of the day or week; wherein teachers focus attention on existing or potential behavior problems (Canter & Canter, 1992). This recommendation focuses the assessment strictly on the student's behavior without a call for a detailed instructional assessment of the behavior problem. Canter's approach limits effectiveness; for if a teacher's first assessment activity in response to disruptive behavior is to count the off-task behaviors, then the teacher fails to link this information to instructional solutions to the behavior problem. If classroom disruption is in part caused by inadequate instructional materials or teaching methods, then an assessment model must assess these areas. Traditional assessment in behavior management fails to guide the teacher to develop instructional solutions to classroom behavior problems.

Developing Proactive Procedures

A second limitation to most assessment models is they fail to provide teachers information for proactive classroom management. Instead, teachers implement assessment activities in response to classroom disruption. In assertive discipline for example, the teacher is not directed to assess the instructional environment and teaching materials. Teachers instead are asked to evaluate how they respond to disruptive behavior, with no suggestion that behavior problems might be related to the instructional program. If the assessment focus is on the behavior of the student, the teacher is not looking to solve classroom management problems proactively and usually reacts instead. Without an examination of the contribution instruction makes to disruptive behavior, the teacher does not modify teaching procedures to maximize student learning.

Considering the Phases of Instruction

Many assessment models are not *dynamic;* that is, they do not provide a flexible framework for assessment of behavior problems for each specific phase of instruction. Because the focus is narrow (e.g., keying in on the consequences of misbehavior, as in the Dreikurs, Grunwald, and Pepper [1982] model), teachers are locked into a rigid model that may not have relevance to their particular classroom problems. Furthermore, assessment procedures are not differentiated for the before, during, or after phases of instruction (Kame'enui & Simmons, 1997). In addition, most assessment models do not provide assessment activities tailored to the various phases of the 180-day school year, offering the same management activities at the beginning of the year and the end of the year.

Incorporating Assessment into Teaching

Finally, most assessment models are designed so that evaluation activities are supplemental, not primary, to the teacher's instructional responsibilities. Because instruction is not usually linked to behavior assessment, many teachers assume assessment is completed only in response to behavior problems. Because teachers are not trained to consider that behavior problems can be caused by weak instruction or poorly designed curriculum, many teachers have not learned to assess behavior within their normal instructional activities.

Instructional classroom management, however, considers the curriculum, the task, and the context in which misbehavior occurs. The purpose of assessment in instructional classroom management is to gather information necessary for improving both academic and social behavior of students.

FEATURES OF THE INSTRUCTIONAL CLASSROOM MANAGEMENT ASSESSMENT MODEL: LINKING ASSESSMENT, MANAGEMENT, AND INSTRUCTION

The Instructional Classroom Management Assessment Model provides for proactive assessment that is comprehensive and linked to the teaching plan. If the features of the assessment model are not consistent with the features of the instructional and behavioral model, then linking the teaching, management, and assessment models is premature.

Proactive Assessment

The old assumption that an ounce of prevention is worth a pound of cure is certainly true in classroom management. One important feature of the Instructional Classroom Management Assessment Model is that it identifies instructional features a teacher should consider to determine the causes of misbehavior.

Comprehensive Assessment

To be effective, an assessment model must be comprehensive. The teacher must include assessment questions that sample activities that occur before, during, and after instruction. The assessment model must also reflect the structure of the instructional

Graphing daily performance scores enables a teacher to make appropriate instructional and management decisions.

plan. The teacher is engaged in assessment activities throughout the school day as part of the regular teaching routine, not as separate, isolated activities. The teacher routinely evaluates the classroom organization, the behavior management strategies, and the adequacy of the instructional program as part of her or his teaching.

Assessment Linked to Instruction

The obvious critical feature of the Instructional Classroom Management Assessment Model is that assessment activities are linked to instruction. The evaluation questions a teacher asks in each of the three phases of the model are tied directly to achievement and compliance. Once teachers have collected assessment data, the information can be used to make changes in the instructional program.

Assessment Integrated School Wide

Instructional classroom management assessment is integrated into a school-wide assessment approach. Chapter 10, "School-Wide Discipline and Instructional Classroom

Management: A Systems Approach," presents an assessment model for monitoring and evaluating the (a) administrative policies, (b) procedures, and (c) practices of a school-wide management model. A major feature of school-wide management is that teachers use a proactive instructional program designed for the entire school year.

THE INSTRUCTIONAL CLASSROOM MANAGEMENT ASSESSMENT MODEL

The language of most assessment models reflects separation between instruction and assessment. Most assessment models in behavior management focus on control, with little information on how to teach students alternatives to misbehavior. The Instructional Classroom Management Assessment Model focuses on developing instructional procedures to teach students appropriate classroom behavior. The foundation for developing teaching programs in behavior management is the assessment plan the teacher uses to make program adjustments.

The three-phase Instructional Classroom Management Assessment Model is presented in Figure 5.1, before instruction, during instruction, and after instruction. Each phase employs a three-level assessment approach that examines class organization, behavior management, and instructional design. The triangles denote that initial assessment activities are completed with broad strokes, across all three phases, asking questions that assess organization first. Next, behavior management questions are posed. To complete the assessment plan, the teacher focuses on specific instructional design features related to classroom management. Finally, the information collected

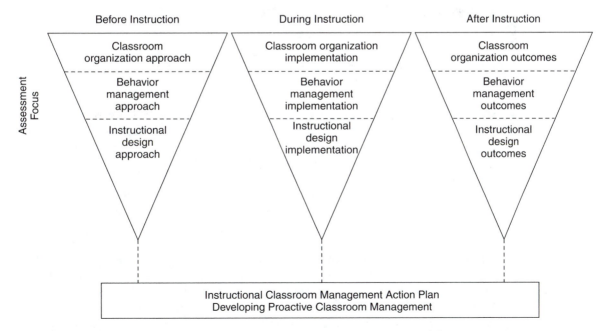

FIGURE 5.1   Three-phase instructional classroom management assessment model.

> **Goal:** To evaluate, revise, and reconsider the general problems in the organization and administration of instruction
> **Phase:** Before Instruction
> **Focus:** Approach to classroom organization
>
> ### Evaluate/Revise/Reconsider (ERR)
>
> 1. Does the classroom organization and structure allow for smooth transition between groups, classes, or activities?
> 2. Are students completing their assignments at a high criterion level of performance?
> 3. Are students happy, cooperative, and considerate of each other and the teacher?
> 4. Is adequate time allocated for instruction in critical academic areas?
> 5. Is the plan for organizing and managing the classroom proactive?
> 6. Is the physical arrangement of the class designed to facilitate optimal learning?
> 7. Do students receive clear and systematic feedback on their work and classroom/school behavior?
> 8. Have classroom routines been established to facilitate order?

FIGURE 5.2   Before-instruction level 1: Classroom organization assessment.

during assessment is converted into a plan for developing proactive modifications in the areas of classroom organization, behavior management, and instructional design.

Assessment Before Instruction

The before-instruction phase focuses primarily on preparing instructional activities that must be in place before instruction is delivered. Assessment in this phase begins long before students enter the classroom by collecting information on classroom organization, behavior management, and instructional design.

Classroom organization.   In Figure 5.2, specific questions are posed for each level of assessment within each phase. In the before-instruction phase, the questions prompt the teacher to examine his or her approach to classroom organization before students arrive in the classroom at the beginning of the school year.

If adjustments are warranted, then the target feature needs to be revised. For example, the teacher may need to revise the amount of independent seatwork assigned or the criterion level of performance expected of students during independent seatwork or homework.

An important part of the Instructional Classroom Management Assessment Model for each phase of assessment is the *evaluate/revise/reconsider (ERR)* process which asks teachers to evaluate, revise, and reconsider their responses to each question. This three-step process allows for a systematic and organized approach to assessment. During evaluation, the teacher asks the eight assessment questions related to classroom organization, increasing the probability of positive academic and behavioral outcomes in the classroom. The assessment questions cover activities in transition, instruction, and

Instructional assessment of academic performance is the basis for linking assessment and instruction.

organization. To evaluate each question, the teacher need not engage in a formal and lengthy evaluation process but should target a particular behavior (e.g., transition between classroom activities, assignment completion) and decide if adjustments are required. For example, the teacher asks question number 2 (see Figure 5.2): "Are students completing their assignments at a high criterion level of performance?" If this needs attention, the teacher revises the teaching plan to reflect the necessary change. The teacher may conclude that the number of independent worksheet assignments is too great and make the appropriate adjustment during the revise step. Once a revision is completed, the teacher enters the reconsider step and evaluates the revision in the context of other changes made in the teaching and management plan. This is an important step, because changes in one area of a teaching plan may require adjustments in another.

The teacher uses the three-step procedure (ERR) for each of the remaining assessment questions. For example, the teacher poses question 1: "Does the classroom organization and structure allow for smooth transition between groups, classes, or activities?" The teacher must consider the location of instructional groups and instructional materials to determine the likelihood of quick student transitions from one activity to another. If classroom organization does not facilitate easy student movement and quick teacher preparation for each instructional group, then it must be modified.

Behavior management approach.   The second level in the before-instruction phase (see Figure 5.3) focuses on the behavior management approach. As illustrated in Figure 5.1, the assessment focus becomes narrower, with the teacher asking questions directly related to issues in behavior management. Why does the teacher wait until after classroom organization has been evaluated before addressing behavior management? Classroom organization concerns the entire classroom and school environment and allows the teacher to cast a broad assessment net to address potential management and instructional problems. In contrast, the behavior management and instructional design strands are narrower in scope.

Goal: To evaluate, revise, and reconsider specific problems in the management
plan of the classroom
Phase: Before Instruction
Focus: Approach to behavior management

Evaluate/Revise/Reconsider (ERR)

1. Are the classroom rules clear, established, and posted in the classroom?
2. Is a delivery system in place for praising, acknowledging, and rewarding students'
   academic accomplishments and social responsibilities?
3. Is a mechanism in place for responding to serious behavior problems?
4. Is a systematic process in place for recording and documenting behavior problems?
5. Is the punishment system designed primarily as a transition tool?
6. Are classroom routines clearly defined, established, and posted in the classroom?

FIGURE 5.3   Before-instruction level II: Behavior management assessment.

The six assessment questions key the teacher to the following critical areas: (a) the presence of classroom rules, (b) the use of reinforcement, (c) the process for responding to severe or chronic behavior problems, (d) data collection procedures, (e) the role of punishment in the classroom, and (f) establishing classroom routines.

There are three reasons for focusing on these areas before instruction. First, employing a mechanism to determine the appropriate use of reinforcement and punishment is critical if we conceptualize classroom management as basically a teaching endeavor. A management system will not work effectively over an entire academic year if classroom rules and reinforcement and punishment approaches are not appropriate. Second, we recommend the teacher place emphasis on the mechanism for responding to serious and chronic behavior problems. Without an effective process for managing this type of behavior, the teacher will find it hard to maintain a positive learning environment for all students in the class.

We also recommend the teacher follow the three-step assessment process: evaluate/revise/reconsider (ERR). The teacher first asks an assessment question (e.g., "Is a delivery system in place for responding to serious behavior problems?"), and if a revision in the teaching plan is recommended, the teacher makes the required adjustment. Finally, the teacher considers the change in the context of other changes made for this assessment phase. For example, if the teacher determines an adequate system is not in place for recording and documenting serious behavior problems, an adjustment must be made in the organization of the behavior management approach. By making this change before serious behavior problems occur, the teacher proactively manages the classroom.

Instructional design approach.   The final level of assessment in the before-instruction phase (see Figure 5.4) requires the teacher to evaluate his or her approach to instructional design as part of the preinstructional activity. This assessment evaluates the instructional program to be used, required student responses, and the teacher's role during the presentation of new content. A teacher can exert instructional

---

Goal: To evaluate, revise, and reconsider the specific features of instruction
Phase: Before Instruction
Focus: Approach to instructional design

Evaluate/Revise/Reconsider (ERR)

---

1. Is it necessary to add more examples of the target skill to the lesson?
2. Is it necessary to change the sequence of examples in the target lesson?
3. Will students require more practice examples of the new target skill?
4. Will students require a new schedule of instruction that involves sequencing the easy, familiar task with the new, difficult, and unfamiliar task?
5. Will students require highly prompted, teacher-directed guidance, which includes frequent reinforcement and mastery performance on progressively more difficult segments of the new skill?
6. Are instructional materials adequately designed to meet the needs of the lowest-performing student?
7. What preskills are required of students in order for them to learn from the target lesson?
8. What is the required criterion level of mastery for the lesson? (e.g., Are students required to master x number of problems at 100 percent accuracy? 85 percent accuracy?)
9. Will students require guided instruction from the teacher during the first part or segment of the lesson?
10. Will students require more time or less time to work on a new or difficult part of the lesson?
11. Is it necessary to make the student response format easier? (oral-choice response before written-choice or production responses).
12. Will students be directed by the teacher during the target lesson in a large group, small group, or independently?
13. Does the target lesson involve *new* skills, operations, or strategies for the learner?
14. Are clearly defined procedures developed for teaching rules and routines?

FIGURE 5.4   Before-instruction level III: Instructional design assessment

control over students only if the curriculum approach facilitates clear and sound instruction.

The 14 assessment questions for this level are presented in Figure 5.4. We recommend the teacher answer each question to determine if the instructional program will foster learning. It is especially important to examine these assessment questions when students are presented with new or more varied instructional content. To assess effectively, the teacher looks at the specific structure of classroom academic programs. For example, question 6, "Are instructional materials adequately designed to meet the needs of the lowest-performing student?", requires the teacher evaluate curriculum programs at a technical level (e.g., the number of practice examples, the sequence of instructional examples, and time scheduled for teaching the skill). Behavior problems are more likely to develop if the program is technically inadequate.

> **Goal:** To evaluate, revise, and reconsider specific problems in the behavior management plan for the classroom
> **Phase:** During Instruction
> **Focus:** Implementation of behavior management
>
> ――
> **Evaluate/Revise/Reconsider (ERR)**
> ――
>
> 1. Are classroom rules posted so all students can easily see them?
> 2. Are all learning materials organized so students can easily use them?
> 3. Are all data collection materials clearly developed and placed for easy access?
> 4. Is adequate time allocated for teaching new and difficult concepts?
> 5. Are learning activities set up for efficient transition during lesson?
> 6. Are students interacting positively and enthusiastically to the lesson?

FIGURE 5.5   During-instruction level I: Classroom organizational assessment.

Assessment During Instruction

The assessment plan for the during-instruction phase focuses on the teacher delivering instruction. As in the before-instruction phase, questions are related to the classroom organization, behavior management, and instructional design, but the focus of assessment is on implementing the instructional program. If assessment information is used correctly, the teacher can improve classroom behavior while also increasing students' academic performance. In the Instructional Classroom Management Assessment Model, classroom organization questions are asked first, followed by questions on behavior management and instructional design.

Implementation of classroom organization.   In Figure 5.5, six assessment questions about implementation of classroom organization are presented. The teacher continues to follow the ERR system to ensure that assessment activities will be administered systematically. Assessment information derived from these questions will help the teacher make adjustments in the teaching program if behavior problems surface in the classroom. The focus is on how the teacher can facilitate effective organization while teaching.

We recommend the teacher pose these questions early and often in the school year to adjust the teaching program accordingly. Even if behavior management problems are not evident, the teacher is wise to collect assessment data periodically, which may indicate changes needed in the program as the school year progresses. For example, the answer to question 6, "Are students interacting positively and enthusiastically to the lesson?" can change to reflect students' placement in instructional programs. A student may be enthusiastic during one instructional unit but relatively unenthusiastic during another. The teacher can use this assessment information to adjust classroom organization.

Implementation of behavior management.   The next area of assessment in the during-instruction phase is in behavior management (see Figure 5.6) and uses

Goal: To evaluate, revise, and reconsider specific problems in the behavior management plan for the classroom

Phase: During Instruction

Focus: Implementation of behavior management

Evaluate/Revise/Reconsider (ERR)

1. Do you review and reinforce the rules?
2. Are students attending to, following along with, and responding to the lesson?
3. Is the rate of reinforcement high, and is it delivered contingently?
4. Is punishment used too frequently to control inappropriate behavior?
5. Is the process for recording data simple and unobtrusive?
6. Are students interacting positively and enthusiastically to the lesson?

FIGURE 5.6   During-instruction level II: Behavior management assessment.

six questions to cover a wide range of activities. If the answer to, "Do you review and reinforce the rules?" is "No," the teacher must begin to review and systematically reinforce the stated rules. Many behavior problems occur because the teacher does not review and reinforce students who follow classroom rules. A negative answer to any of the remaining questions also points to the need for significant changes in behavior management. The basis for behavior problems may be in low levels of student attention (question 2), low rates of teacher reinforcement (question 3), inappropriate use or high rates of punishment (question 4), and inappropriate data collection procedures (question 5). Insufficient student enthusiasm and involvement in the lesson can lead to classroom disruption as well (question 6).

Understanding the multiple factors that contribute to a student's reluctance to work is a key feature of instructional classroom management.

Goal: To evaluate, revise, and reconsider the specific features of instruction
Phase: During Instruction
Focus: Implementation of instructional design

Evaluate/Revise/Reconsider (ERR)

---

1. Does the pacing of instruction maintain student attention?
2. Are students given adequate think time?
3. Are students meeting the specified criterion level of performance?
4. Are the procedures for correcting academic errors effective and timely?
5. Is the amount of teacher direction and prompting adequate? Is it too much or too little?
6. Are the instructional examples clear and unambiguous?
7. Is the student response form acceptable or is it too difficult?
8. Is the lack of prerequisite knowledge and skills interfering with acquisition of new knowledge?
9. Are academic errors occurring at too high a rate?
10. Are students following the directions during independent learning activities?
11. Are rules and routines taught using effective instructional procedures?

FIGURE 5.7 During-instruction level III: Instructional design assessment.

Instructional design implementation. The final focus of assessment for the during-instruction phase (see Figure 5.7) is in the area of instructional design. How instructional materials are designed, the manner in which a teacher presents the content, and the sequence of teaching examples are variables that have great influence on student behavior.

The focus of the questions in the instructional design area is narrow and centers primarily on instructional variables. The 11 assessment questions incorporate three areas of concern: (a) teacher presentation techniques, (b) student responding, and (c) instructional content. Three questions relate to the teacher's presentation of material (i.e., pace of instruction, think time for students, amount of teacher involvement). If a teacher adequately presents material to students, they are more likely to follow classroom rules and perform closely to the levels expected by the teacher. Research suggests that proper teacher presentation techniques positively influence the behavior of students and their academic performance (Kame'enui & Simmons, 1997).

The teacher is able to assess the quality of student responses by answering question 3 ("Are students meeting specified criteria?"), question 7 ("Is the student response form acceptable?"), and question 10 ("Are students following directions?"). Disruptive behavior can be prompted by the type of responses students are asked to make. For example, if students with insufficient writing skills are asked to write lengthy responses to questions, they may respond with inappropriate behavior.

Five questions (4, 6, 8, 9, and 11) directly assess the instructional content of the lesson to determine if behavior problems are a result of the lesson structure. The

---

Goal: To evaluate, revise, and reconsider the general problems in the organization and administration of instruction

Phase: After Instruction

Focus: Outcomes of classroom organization

Evaluate/Revise/Reconsider (ERR)

---

1. Did you accomplish the goals you set at the beginning of the lesson?
2. Is more instructional time required to meet learning objectives?
3. Does the plan for managing instructional transitions need to be revised?
4. Does the criterion level of performance need to be revised to match the learning objectives?
5. Do the instructional materials need to be adapted, modified, or replaced completely?
6. Do other classroom rules need to be identified and taught?

FIGURE 5.8   After-instruction level I: Classroom organization assessment.

teacher must determine if the content of the lesson should be modified to prevent or eliminate disruptive behavior. For example, if the teacher fails to provide students detailed corrections to errors during instruction (question 4), social and academic problems may arise.

Assessment After Instruction

In the Instructional Classroom Management Assessment Model, the final phase of assessment occurs after instruction is completed. It focuses on the outcomes of the instructional and management program. By following the three-phase cycle of assessment, the teacher ensures the assessment plan will be continuous throughout the unit of instruction, allowing for ongoing modification of the instructional program.

Classroom organization assessment.   As with the before and during phases of assessment, after-instruction assessment begins with the teacher evaluating classroom organization, with the focus on *outcomes*. The six questions for this assessment component are presented in Figure 5.8.

These questions are expansive and help the teacher examine results and determine if an adjustment in organization of the program is necessary. For example, has the teacher accomplished the goals set at the beginning of the lesson? If not, the teacher must reassess instructional goals and perhaps the classroom design and structure.

Important to this assessment phase is the teacher's evaluation of student performance records. The teacher looks at criterion-referenced tests administered during the instructional program to determine instructional expectations and goals that have not been met.

Goal:	To evaluate, revise, and reconsider specific problems in the behavior management plan of the classroom
Phase:	After Instruction
Focus:	Outcomes of behavior management

Evaluate/Revise/Reconsider (ERR)

1. Are the rules appropriate for the current learning objectives?
2. Is the reinforcement system effective?
3. Is the mechanism for managing serious behavior problems effective?
4. Is the student monitoring system effective?
5. Are the punishment procedures acceptable?

FIGURE 5.9   After-instruction level II: Behavior management assessment.

During this assessment phase the teacher determines if instructional time was adequate to meet instructional goals. Increasing instructional time in difficult content areas may be a way to increase student performance. Transitions and adequacy of instructional materials are also assessed at this time. Outcomes in classroom organization should be assessed at the completion of each instructional unit. This assessment demands little time, and program adjustments made will be important in preventing and decreasing behavior problems and for improving student performance.

Behavior management assessment.   Assessment in behavior management outcomes is the next evaluation the teacher completes. Five questions for assessment of this area are presented in Figure 5.9.

The teacher assesses the effects of reinforcement techniques, the classroom monitoring system, classroom rules, and punishment procedures. These assessment questions should be asked at the completion of each instructional unit. It should be emphasized here that even if the teacher has not encountered behavior problems, it is important to complete all assessment activities and answer all questions to make transitions from one instructional unit to the next more effective.

Instructional design assessment.   The 11 questions for this final assessment are presented in Figure 5.10. This assessment will take more time than the first two levels of this phase. The 11 questions for this final assessment require the teacher to reflect on instructional design outcomes. The teacher takes both a short-term and long-term view of management and determines if adjustments are necessary to maintain the cooperation of students for the course of the school year. The first five questions have a short-term focus and center on daily outcomes. For example, in question 1, the teacher determines the role instructional pacing plays in behavioral and academic outcomes. The teacher's attention is on outcomes from the daily lesson or the unit of instruction. Similarly, question 4 asks if the sequence or number of instructional examples needs adjustment to improve student performance.

The last six questions focus on instructional design and require the teacher to look beyond the daily lesson or unit of instruction. Question 6, for instance, requires

---

Goal: To evaluate, revise, and reconsider the specific features of instruction
Phase: After Instruction
Focus: Outcomes of instructional design

Evaluate/Revise/Reconsider (ERR)

1. Does the pacing of instruction need to be adjusted?
2. Do students require more think time?
3. Are the procedures for correcting academic errors effective and appropriate?
4. Does the instructional lesson require more examples or a different sequence of examples?
5. Do prerequisite knowledge and skills need to be taught?
6. Does the criterion level of performance need to be increased in relation to the learning objectives?
7. Is more (or less) teacher direction and prompting required?
8. Are the student response forms appropriate?
9. Is the plan for teaching students to work independently effective?
10. Are students transferring learned skills (behavioral and academic) to new learning contexts?
11. Do procedures for teaching classroom rules and routines need to be modified?

FIGURE 5.10   After-instruction level III: Instructional design assessment.

the teacher to assess criterion levels of performance in relation to the target learning and behavioral objectives. In this case, the teacher must look beyond short-term objectives and focus on whether criterion levels of performance need adjustment to increase performance. Question 10 ("Are the students transferring learned skills to new learning contexts?") and question 11 ("Do procedures for teaching classroom rules and routines need to be modified?") are examples of long-term assessment questions. In this case, the teacher looks for evidence of transfer of learning. All assessment questions for outcomes of instructional design must be asked frequently throughout the school year. For help in developing alternative assessment questions for diverse students, see the Learning Activity on page 123.

INSTRUCTIONAL CLASSROOM MANAGEMENT ASSESSMENT CHECKLIST

Figure 5.11 presents a checklist of the instructional classroom management assessment previously described. To utilize the checklist, teachers employ a three-point rating scale to prioritize necessary teaching modifications quickly. For example, after a teacher completes the before-instruction phase of assessment and answers each of the questions for classroom organization, behavior management, and instructional design, she completes the appropriate sections of the checklist. If the teacher finds the skill being evaluated is not in need of change, then a 1 (Acceptable) is checked,

ASSESSMENT FOCUS				INSTRUCTIONAL PHASE					

Classroom Organization BEFORE DURING AFTER

Teaching Modifications	1 2 3		1 2 3		1 2 3
Transitions to Group .... ☐☐☐		Facilitating Transitions ...... ☐☐☐		Are Goals Accomplished ... ☐☐☐
Completion of Assignments . ☐☐☐		Student Responses .... ☐☐☐		More Teaching Needed .... ☐☐☐
Students' Attitudes .... ☐☐☐		Error Data Collected .... ☐☐☐		Transition Plan .... ☐☐☐
Allocated Instructional Time . ☐☐☐		Monitoring Individual Work .. ☐☐☐		Criterion Level .... ☐☐☐
Proactive Management Style ☐☐☐		Student Arrangement ...... ☐☐☐		Instructional Materials ..... ☐☐☐
Classroom Arrangement ... ☐☐☐				
Feedback System .... ☐☐☐				

Behavior Management BEFORE DURING AFTER

Teaching Modifications	1 2 3		1 2 3		1 2 3
Classroom Rules .... ☐☐☐		Review Rules .... ☐☐☐		Revise Rules .... ☐☐☐
Reinforcement .... ☐☐☐		Are Students Attending..... ☐☐☐		Reinforcement System ..... ☐☐☐
Severe Behavior Problems . ☐☐☐		Rate of Reinforcement ..... ☐☐☐		Serious Behavior Problems . ☐☐☐
Data Collection .... ☐☐☐		Rate of Punishment .... ☐☐☐		Punishment System .... ☐☐☐
Punishment .... ☐☐☐		Data Collection Procedures . ☐☐☐		Monitoring System .... ☐☐☐
		Student Interactions .... ☐☐☐		

Instructional Design BEFORE DURING AFTER

Teaching Modifications	1 2 3		1 2 3		1 2 3
Examples .... ☐☐☐		Appropriate Pace .... ☐☐☐		Paving Adjustments .... ☐☐☐
Sequence .... ☐☐☐		Think Time .... ☐☐☐		Think Time .... ☐☐☐
Practice .... ☐☐☐		Criterion Performance ..... ☐☐☐		Criterion Level .... ☐☐☐
Instructional Schedule ..... ☐☐☐		Error Corrections .... ☐☐☐		Error Correction .... ☐☐☐
Use of Prompts .... ☐☐☐		Teacher Direction .... ☐☐☐		Teacher Direction .... ☐☐☐
Instructional Materials ..... ☐☐☐		Instructional Examples ..... ☐☐☐		Student Response Form ... ☐☐☐
Criterion Levels .... ☐☐☐		Student Response Form ... ☐☐☐		Prerequisites .... ☐☐☐
Guided Instruction .... ☐☐☐		Prerequisite Skill .... ☐☐☐		Students' Independent Work ☐☐☐
Time Adjustments .... ☐☐☐		Rate of Errors .... ☐☐☐		
Student Response Format .. ☐☐☐		Do Students Follow		
Teacher Role .... ☐☐☐		Directions .... ☐☐☐		
Type of Target Skill .... ☐☐☐				
Type of Student Response .. ☐☐☐				

Rating System
1 = Acceptable
2 = Monitor
3 = Change

FIGURE 5.11 Classroom management action plan: translating assessment data into management changes.

Learning Activity

Develop Alternative Assessment Questions for Diverse Students

Purpose of Activity

To understand how teachers must accommodate students with diverse backgrounds

Step 1: List all factors related to diversity that teachers should consider during instructional classroom management assessment. Gender and disability are two factors frequently thought of as contributing to diversity. Name as many others as you can think of.

Step 2: For each of the factors you have identified, list why this factor requires accommodation during instructional classroom assessment.

Step 3: Develop a series of three to five assessment questions in each of the three phases and levels described in this chapter. Make sure that your questions are closely tied to the teaching and management program. Discuss how your questions will help teachers plan for diverse students with learning and behavioral problems.

indicating no teaching modifications are needed. If the teacher finds teaching modifications necessary, either 2 (Monitor) or 3 (Change) is marked. For example, if a teacher evaluates classroom rules and find they need nonimmediate adjusting, he/she will check "Monitor." The teacher will modify classroom rules only after priority changes (i.e., those indicated by checking 3 for "Change") are made.

We recommend a classroom teacher begin the school year with an assessment of the before-instruction phase to determine if her approach to classroom organization, behavior management, and instructional design is conducive to effective instructional classroom management. Because a teacher's assessment plan should be tied to instruction, we also recommend the formal evaluation of the before-instruction phase be done periodically, whether there are behavior problems or not. Changes based on information collected for this phase will help the teacher keep the teaching program updated during the school year.

Assessment of the during-instruction phase focuses on classroom organization, behavior management, and instructional design. Among the program components evaluated during this phase of instruction are students' attitudes, reinforcement systems, use of instructional prompts, type of student response, and mastery levels. We recommend the teacher evaluate implementation once the instructional program is in place and use the checklist throughout the year and not just in response to a behavior problem. Continuous use of assessment will allow for a proactive approach to classroom management.

Outcome measures are the focus of assessment activities during the after-instruction phase. During this assessment routine, the teacher evaluates outcomes in both behavioral and academic areas. As part of the assessment for this phase, the teacher evaluates academic measures (e.g., tests, quizzes, worksheets) completed by students.

ADAPTING INSTRUCTIONAL CLASSROOM MANAGEMENT ASSESSMENT

An important feature of instructional classroom management assessment is that it can be easily adapted to specific needs of teachers. We encourage teachers to modify assessment procedures described in this chapter when necessary, because this assessment model is not a comprehensive diagnostic tool.

Add Assessment Questions When Necessary

The assessment questions we pose should not be considered exhaustive or comprehensive. They simply serve as a guide to the teacher when assessing the classroom for developing effective interventions and refining instructional programs. We encourage teachers to add their own questions to any of the assessment phases to increase the suitability of the model.

Use With Individuals and Student Groups

Instructional classroom management assessment can be used with individual students or with groups. When groups of students are assessed, we recommend the teacher pay close attention to the lower-performing students in the group to determine the adequacy of classroom management and instructional procedures.

Combine With Other Assessment Procedures

We also recommend teachers combine instructional classroom management assessment with other assessment activities if they are interested in collecting alternative assessment information. For example, instructional classroom management assessment can be used effectively in conjunction with functional assessment procedures (Blair, Umbreit, & Bos, 1999), critical incidence log recordings or functional assessment (Sugai & Horner, 1994), or with any type of curriculum-based assessment activities (King-Sears, Burgess, & Lawson, 1999).

SUMMARY

In this chapter, we presented an Instructional Classroom Management Assessment Model. We first identified the features of the assessment model and then presented assessment activities and questions for the before, during, and after phases of instruction. A three-level assessment approach for each phase examined class organization, behavior management, and instructional design.

The chapter concluded with a discussion of how teachers can translate assessment information into an action plan for making management changes. A checklist provides teachers a way to summarize and organize assessment information.

CHAPTER ACTIVITIES

1. Discuss limitations of traditional assessment models in classroom management.
2. Develop a set of five supplemental assessment questions for each of the three phases of instruction.
3. Visit either a regular or special education classroom and assess the behavior of two students using the Instructional Classroom Management Assessment Checklist (Figure 5.11). Next, develop teaching and management modifications from the assessment data for each of the three phases of instruction (i.e., before, during, after). Be specific when you discuss your teaching and management modifications.

REFERENCES

Blair, K. C., Umbreit, J., & Bos, C. (1999). Using functional assessment and children's preferences to improve the behavior of young children with behavior disorders. *Behavior Problems, 24,* 151–166.

Canter, L., & Canter, M. (1992). *Assertive discipline: Positive behavior management for today's classroom.* Los Angeles: Canter & Associates.

Dreikurs, R., Grunwald, B., & Pepper, F. (1982). *Maintaining sanity in the classroom: Classroom management techniques* (2nd. ed.). New York: Harper & Row, Publishers.

Farmer, T. W., Van Acker, R. M., Pearl, R., & Rodkin, P. C. (1999). Social networks and peer-assisted problem behavior in elementary classrooms: Students with and without disabilities. *Remedial and Special Education, 20,* 244–256.

Foster-Johnson, L., & Dunlap, G. (1993). Using functional assessment to develop effective, individualized interventions for challenging behaviors. *Teaching Exceptional Children, 25,* 44–50.

Gresham, F., & MacMillan, G. (1997). Social competence and affective characteristics of students with mild disabilities. *Review of Educational Research, 67,* 377–415.

Gunter, P. L., & Denny, R. K. (1998). Trends and issues in research regarding academic instruction of students with emotional and behavioral disorders. *Behavioral Disorders, 24,* 44–50.

Kame'enui, E., & Simmons, D. (1997). *Designing instructional strategies: The prevention of academic learning problems.* Upper Saddle River, NJ: Merrill/Prentice Hall.

King-Sears, M. E., Burgess, M., & Lawson, T. (1999). Applying curriculum-based assessment in inclusive settings. *Teaching Exceptional Children, 31,* 30–38.

Lopez-Reyna, N., & Bay, M. (1997). Enriching assessment: Using varied assessments for diverse learners. *Teaching Exceptional Learners, 29,* 33–37.

Sugai, G., & Horner, R. (1994). Including students with behavior problems in general education settings: Assumptions, challenges and solutions. In J. Marr, G. Sugai, & G. Tindal (Eds), *The Oregon Conference Monograph, 6,* 102–120. Eugene, OR: University of Oregon.

Chapter

6

Using Reinforcement to Increase Student Motivation

OVERVIEW

Reinforcement of student performance is a major management activity. How reinforcement techniques are used will determine—in large measure—the success of the instructional management program. When teachers are primarily positive in their interactions with students, the stage is set for increased academic achievement and improved student conduct. The use of positive reinforcement takes a prominent role in instructional classroom management. It serves as a component for teaching academic and social skills and is a major factor in developing our school-wide management approach. Teachers who fail to use reinforcement as part of their instructional routine or those who rely substantially on punishment to control the behavior of students will, in the end, create disruptive, underachieving, and resentful students. In spite of the pivotal role of reinforcement in instruction and behavior management, teachers sometimes don't use positively focused strategies in response to students' misbehavior (Martin, Linfoot, & Stephenson, 1999).

In this chapter we examine reinforcement within an instructional context by describing a comprehensive reinforcement plan for teachers and for integration into daily teaching routines. First, we present the details of how to organize reinforcement activities into a plan of action that is proactive and part of the regular instructional program. Next, we discuss the features of reinforcement and how teachers can link specific reinforcement activities to task dimensions. Reinforcement is appropriate to teaching both academic information and social behavior skills in the context of general education classrooms of students with different learning abilities and behavioral skills.

WHY DOES REINFORCEMENT SOMETIMES FAIL?

If reinforcement is such a powerful teaching and management device, why isn't it always effective in controlling the behavior of students? The answer to this question is rarely easy because of the complexity of classroom instruction and schooling. However, an example of what often occurs in classrooms helps illustrate the limitations of a conventional approach to behavior management.

> Sam, a learning disabled student, is frequently disruptive in his reading class. He refuses to complete assignments and follow directions and is frequently in arguments with other students. Sam's outbursts often occur without provocation or are initiated when the teacher, Mr. Barnbrook, hands out an assignment for Sam to complete. Because Mr. Barnbrook has been trained to use a variety of reinforcement techniques, he assiduously applies several of these techniques once a behavior problem occurs. For example, Mr. Barnbrook praises other students for sitting quietly and acknowledges Sam's effort when he starts to work. He even developed a point system to reinforce all students for completing written assignments. However, Mr. Barnbrook still can't reliably control Sam's disruptive behavior.

Why was Mr. Barnbrook's approach to reinforcement ineffective? One problem is that he failed to establish a comprehensive instructional reinforcement plan that was linked to instruction and implementation at the very beginning of the school year. In such a plan, the teacher considers the instructional task when developing reinforcement procedures. More specifically, the teacher considers how to adjust reinforcement so students will have success with the most difficult learning activities. This is done proactively, before the students are actually engaged in learning activities.

Without an organized approach to reinforcement, the use of isolated reinforcement techniques is likely to be ineffective in the long term.

An instructional reinforcement plan provides information for:

- using reinforcement procedures proactively
- aligning reinforcement with task dimensions
- coordinating the use of various reinforcement procedures
- integrating instruction and reinforcement activities into a comprehensive plan

For example, Mr. Barnbrook used reinforcement in a *reactive* manner. That is, he used reinforcement techniques only in response to Sam's bad behavior. In fact, when Sam's behavior deteriorated further, Mr. Barnbrook quickly developed a point system, but it was not coordinated with any other management or instructional strategies.

Another problem was that Mr. Barnbrook did not consider the features of the instructional task when he developed his teaching and reinforcement strategies. For example, Mr. Barnbrook did not determine if the written assignment given Sam was an activity that was easy or hard, new or old. Using this task information, Mr. Barnbrook might have pretaught certain parts of the assignment and provided intensive reinforcement for Sam's completion of the most difficult parts of the writing activity, thereby decreasing learning and behavior problems.

Because Mr. Barnbrook did not have an overall plan, he was not able to link reinforcement to instruction. More importantly, he had not conceptualized reinforcement as part of instruction but instead treated reinforcement as a set of activities and actions separate from instruction. Furthermore, Mr. Barnbrook never considered how difficult assignments might have been instrumental in creating Sam's disruptive behavior. His failure to link his behavioral management program to instruction limited the power and reach of the reinforcement activities and this limited Mr. Barnbrook's ability to influence Sam's academic and social behavior. Corno (1992) provides insight into how a focused, programmatic approach to reinforcement is necessary for teachers to be successful with students who have a history of learning and behavior problems. "Persistence in the face of difficulty and willingness to attempt again after trouble are aspects of motivation for learning that have been addressed in the literature for years . . . unless teachers are willing to build into their curricula opportunities for revising early trials, and, indeed, to reinforce them systematically (through appropriate incentives and nonevaluative feedback), the increasing comfort with revision as an enduring attitude toward school work is unlikely to occur" (p. 77).

CONCEPTUALIZING REINFORCEMENT AS INSTRUCTION

It is important to define again what is meant by reinforcement. There are many different descriptions of reinforcement. Alberto and Troutman (1999) describe reinforcement as "a relationship between two environmental events, behavior (response) and an event or consequence that follows the response" (p. 220). Kerr and Nelson (1998) explain that positive reinforcement "occurs when the presentation of a consequence maintains or strengthens behavior over time" (p. 109). According to Rusch, Rose, and Greenwood (1988), positive reinforcement "refers to the process of presenting a stimulus as a consequence of a response that results in an increase in the probability that the behavior will increase in the future" (p. 217). While these definitions and descriptions differ slightly in emphasis, each consists of two critical elements important to conceptualizing reinforcement as part of instruction.

First, the primary concern with reinforcement is increasing a learner's behavior, not for now, but for the future. As Kame'enui and Simmons (1997) note, the teacher in effect is "behaving now for later." For all practical purposes, what the teacher does *now* can be viewed as a risky roll of the die, because there is no guarantee that the teacher's immediate actions in response to a particular behavior will lead to increasing the learner's positive behavior in the future. In short, it is a game of chance and probabilities. Specifically, will the behavior occur in the absence of instruction and will the stimulus chosen to reinforce the behavior actually work? This game of chance need not be based on pure luck. If every teacher-student interaction represents a chance to increase the probability of the student winning in the game of learning, then what's required is to take advantage of every *opportunity* for reinforcement. Therefore, the most frequent opportunities available to the teacher for reinforcement are those involving instruction. Simply put, as teachers, we want to maximize the opportunities or chances to influence the learner's behavior in a positive and powerful way in the future. In order to influence the future we must act now and take advantage of every instructional opportunity to shape the learner's behavior.

The second important element of reinforcement is that it involves presenting a "stimulus as a consequence of a response" (Rusch et al., 1988, p. 217). The technical jargon conceals an important feature of reinforcement; that is, a stimulus that serves as a reinforcer can be anything. The reinforcer can be a beautiful flower or an ugly one presented as a good-natured joke. It can be simply a small piece of paper or a fancy, perfumed sticker that beeps. Obviously, what's important is not the stimulus itself, but the response that it follows and the effect the stimulus has on the next response! Teachers can be very creative in how they select reinforcers and how they structure the reinforcement process.

From reinforcement definitions presented earlier, teachers may get the impression that they must wait around for the learner to make "responses" in order for reinforcement to take place. They believe the process of reinforcement is nothing more than "reacting" to the learner. In the traditional reinforcement model, the teacher waits for the learner to respond, and the teacher simply reacts with a stimulus as a consequence of the response. As with most traditional reinforcement approaches, Mr. Barnbrook set up his reinforcement plan as a reaction to Sam's misbehavior. This approach was ineffective because it simply reacted to Sam's behavior and failed to create opportunities to teach Sam behaviors that could be reinforced. This is not to suggest that teachers should not react to behavior problems. We suggest, however, that responding to problems is only part of a comprehensive approach to teaching and managing behavior problems.

What the traditional reinforcement approach fails to consider is the opportunities available to the teacher to create, stimulate, initiate, and teach students to respond. Effective teaching naturally sets the occasion for reinforcement by leaving less to chance. If the teacher wants to reinforce students' appropriate behavior, such as talking politely to other students, then the teacher must ensure that this behavior occurs. This is accomplished by teaching the skill to students and then providing opportunities to practice it. If this is done, teachers will have *increased* opportunities for reinforcement. The increase in reinforcement helps motivate students, decreasing disruptive behavior. As Corno (1992) points out, the result of increased opportunities for learning and reinforcement helps students become more "learning oriented," because they engage in more attentive behavior, offer more "quantity and quality of effort," and "feel better about themselves as learners." In the instructional reinforcement plan that we discuss in this chapter, the teacher initiates the process of reinforcement by creating opportunities for instruction and learning, which is in contrast to waiting around for the learner to respond at will, either positively or negatively. This model is one that is particularly important for teachers who work with students with learning and behavior problems. Sprick, Garrison, and Howard (1998) also discuss the importance of proactive classroom management in preventing behavior problems. "When you focus a majority of your time and energy on promoting responsible behavior by using effective instruction, providing appropriate positive feedback, and ensuring that there are not negative results for students when they behave responsibly, you will prevent most misbehavior from ever occurring" (p. 30).

THE INSTRUCTIONAL REINFORCEMENT PLAN: ITS PURPOSE AND ROLE IN INSTRUCTIONAL CLASSROOM MANAGEMENT

Unlike many classroom management approaches that focus on a series of reinforcement techniques, our approach focuses on the development of an instructional reinforcement plan that helps teachers integrate their teaching and reinforcement activities. In the section that follows, we present the features of an instructional reinforcement plan incorporated into daily teaching activities.

An Integrative Purpose

A major role of the instructional reinforcement plan is to integrate all reinforcement techniques and activities. The plan should help the teacher decide which reinforcement techniques to choose and how to integrate reinforcement with instruction. Reinforcement activities are often used without regard for developing a coherent strategy, causing teachers to have little patience with a technique that does not work immediately. They then substitute a new reinforcement activity prematurely. Teachers often use a point system to increase the completion of assigned independent work, as Mr. Barnbrook did. If the implementation of the point system fails to improve the student's performance quickly, the teacher often responds in one of two ways: (a) the reinforcer (e.g., the number of points for the completion of the assignment) is increased to improve the motivation of the students or (b) the point system is replaced with a more elaborate system. Sometimes this approach teaches students that misbehavior is associated with increased rewards, obviously not the lesson we want to teach students. The reinforcement plan should help teachers develop a management plan that maximizes the effective use of reinforcement as an instructional tool. Teachers should prioritize the use of reinforcement procedures, specify guidelines for modifying a reinforcement strategy, and choose a reinforcement strategy that "fits" the academic task.

Increasing Academic Performance

The purpose of the instructional reinforcement plan is to increase the academic performance of all students, thereby increasing the teacher's opportunity to reinforce. One could ask, "Why isn't the main purpose of the reinforcement plan to eliminate classroom behavior problems?" In instructional classroom management, if the teacher provides instruction that meets the needs of every student, behavior problems are dramatically decreased. Coleman and Vaughn (2000) investigated effective instructional and behavior management programs with students with behavior problems and concluded that if interventions are to be successful they "must be implemented in ways that not only reduce anticipation of failure on the part of the students, but also maintain high levels of interest and engagement" (p. 101). Most students performing at their potential tend not to have behavior problems.

If behavior problems do exist, the teacher will probably need to modify the teaching plan as part of an overall strategy for managing disruptive behavior. We recommend that the teacher use "aggressive" reinforcement procedures during regular teaching routines. The teacher should consider the learning task, the teaching context, and the history of the learner when developing a reinforcement strategy. Reinforcement is a teacher's primary method of diverting students with early signs of learning and behavior problems from more severe problems that lead to school failure, antisocial behavior, and rejection by teachers and peers (Golly, Sprague, Walker, Beard, & Gorham, 2000). For example, if a student with an attention deficit is being taught sound-symbol relationships during decoding instruction, the teacher must use reinforcement procedures that increase the student's attention and participation, as well as correct responses. Reinforcement is used not only to support a student's correct responses, but also as part of a broad objective for helping the student develop learning strategies for academic success. As Brigman, Lane, Switzer, Lane, and Lawrence (1999) say, ". . . researchers have consistently reported that applied learning skills such as listening, attending, following directions, and cognitive strategies, as well as social skills, are essential for school success" (p. 323).

Using Reinforcement for the School Year

Conventional reinforcement systems tend to employ the same activities at the beginning and end of the school year. This ignores the different instructional demands that teachers face at different times of the school year. Martin and Pear (1996) point out that reinforcement can have immediate and/or long-term effects on the performance of students. This has broad implications for designing an effective reinforcement plan for the entire school year. For example, many of the tasks students are required to complete during the last 3 months of the school year are either familiar (e.g., introduced previously) or old (e.g., mastered). The reinforcers the teacher chooses during this time should be appropriately linked to the task being completed. Familiar and old tasks, as we discuss later in this chapter, are best taught using less intensive forms of reinforcement. In these tasks, it is not necessary or helpful for a teacher to use intensive reinforcement approaches if the tasks are already learned.

Reinforcement as Instruction

For teachers to be effective classroom managers, they must use reinforcement techniques to *teach* students the social and academic behaviors that translate into improved performance levels. As Sprick et al. (1998) argue, students misbehave for a reason. Teachers know that students are disruptive for many reasons, but one is that students with learning and behavior problems misbehave because they lack the academic and social skills to function adequately in schools (Brigman et al., 1999).

Creating opportunities to reinforce students' appropriate behavior is part of a proactive classroom management approach.

Quite simply, some students may not understand the classroom rules, know how to follow directions to complete assignments, or know how to cooperate with class-mates and teachers. In order to provide students with these critical skills, the teacher must instruct students in behaviors to increase academic performance and coopera-tion. Some teachers feel they should not have to teach students basic entry skills by second or third grade, because they should already know school rules. While this sentiment is understandable, an effective strategy for teachers must include teaching students the academic and social skills they don't know. For example, to prepare stu-dents to complete independent work activities, students should be taught how to (a) use resource materials in the classroom, (b) determine whether the work they have completed is accurate, (c) ask for assistance during independent activities, (d) check their own work, and (e) know what to do if they complete the inde-pendent work early. Using reinforcement as instruction has other benefits as well. Cameron and Pierce (1994) report that students have increased interest in subject matter and increased enjoyment in a learning activity when reinforcers are contin-gent on improved performance on relevant tasks.

DIMENSIONS AND PROCEDURES OF REINFORCEMENT

Before describing the melding of task dimensions with reinforcement, a knowledge of reinforcement is essential. In this section, the dimensions of reinforcement are de-scribed. They include categories of reinforcers, frequency of reinforcement, sched-ule of reinforcement, intensity of reinforcement, and structure of reinforcement.

Categories of Reinforcement

Like most who write about reinforcement, we have organized our discussion of re-inforcers into three categories: tangible, social, and activity. Table 6.1 presents an

TABLE 6.1 Categories of Reinforcers

Reinforcer	Advantages	Disadvantages
Tangible	Easy to deliver	Ethical issues
	Effective with low students	Cost
	Effective with young students	Disruptive
Social	Easy to deliver	Obtrusive
	Useful in most settings	Disruptive
	Useful with most students	
Activity	Powerful with many students	Time consuming
	Supplements instruction	Disruptive
	Acceptable to most teachers	Requires scheduling

overview of each, including the advantages and disadvantages of each category. Following the table, we discuss how teachers can best use each category of reinforcers.

Tangible reinforcers. Tangible reinforcers are physical objects given to students as a reward for good behavior (Sprick et al., 1998), including food (edible) and other items (nonedible). Edible reinforcers often used are popcorn, raisins, crackers, cookies, and candy. Nonedible reinforcers include stickers, small toys, books, award certificates, and so on. Tangible reinforcers are used with students of all ages and ability levels.

This category of reinforcement combines two qualitatively different types of reinforcers, primary and secondary. Primary reinforcers, such as foods and liquids, are biologically important to human beings and are described as natural, unlearned, and unconditioned. In contrast, secondary reinforcers do not have biological importance to individuals and are used to eventually replace primary reinforcers. These reinforcers include social praise and tangible reinforcers (Alberto & Troutman, 1999).

There are some advantages to using tangible reinforcers. Food reinforcers, in particular, can be effective when a teacher is working with low-performing primary or elementary students. Edible reinforcers are particularly effective with young students who have severe learning and behavior problems. However, Alberto and Troutman (1999) say that for primary reinforcers to be useful, the student "whose behavior is to be reinforced must be in a state of deprivation in relation to that reinforcer" (p. 228). For example, if a teacher is teaching a young student with behavior disorders to line up quietly and is using candy as the incentive, this reinforcer is less effective if the student has just had lunch. Teachers should choose carefully when to use edible reinforcers.

Tangible reinforcers are most effective when teachers are trying to teach young, inattentive students entry-level skills. The use of tangible reinforcers should not be extensive or prolonged, as they are best used to transition to less obtrusive reinforcers. Once the student has established a positive learning and behavior pattern,

Allowing students to engage in certain types of learning activities contingent upon completing assignments can be reinforcing.

we recommend the teacher switch to social or activity reinforcers. We also recommend teachers pair verbal reinforcement with tangible reinforcers, which facilitates a smooth transition to social reinforcers. These are less intrusive and more appropriate in school settings for students with mild learning and behavior problems.

Tangible reinforcers have several disadvantages when used in a school setting. Most teachers do not like to use tangible reinforcers in a systematic fashion because they consider them bribery. Another disadvantage of tangible reinforcers is that even if they are effective, results are often short lived and may have little motivating power as students get older. For example, Maehr (1991) found that school-wide recognition has more influence on student motivation than classroom/task-based reinforcers for upper elementary and junior high school students. Finally, teachers are usually required to purchase tangible reinforcers.

Although tangible reinforcers have a limited role to play in classroom management, they can be an important tool, especially with low-performing students working on difficult tasks. We recommend teachers use tangible reinforcers primarily as an incentive to get unmotivated students started on difficult tasks.

Social reinforcers. Social reinforcers involve interactions between two or more people (Sprick et al., 1998). If the student finds the attention from interactions rewarding, teacher-student interactions are likely to increase. The most common form of social reinforcer in the classroom is teacher praise. Other examples are pats on the back, positive facial expressions, and positive telephone calls home to the student or parent. Principals, teacher aides, parents, and classmates can also serve as effective social reinforcers. We recommend teachers be specific and detailed when giving verbal praise to students. Be sure to specifically tell the student what he/she did to earn the reinforcer and why the positive behavior was important. Table 6.2 shows three examples of what to say and what not to say when using verbal praise. Effective forms of verbal praise are precise statements to students

TABLE 6.2   Examples of Appropriate and Inappropriate Verbal Praise

What to say	What not to say
"John, excellent job lining up quietly. Now we can get to the library quickly."	"Excellent job, John."
"Alfreda, you scored 100% on your spelling test. Great improvement!"	"Alfreda, keep working hard."
"Miranda, excellent job finishing the assignment by yourself. Working independently will help you in your other classes."	"Miranda, thanks for working quietly. I'm impressed!"

about their appropriate behavior and how continued good work will pay off for them in the classroom.

The most effective forms of praise tell the student specifically what the appropriate behavior was. This is important in working with students with learning and behavior problems, as these students often do not understand what is appropriate behavior. Exacting verbal praise provides students the precise feedback they need to learn appropriate behavior for the future.

Social reinforcers have many advantages in the classroom. First, they are easy to use and do not consume instructional time when delivered appropriately. Most elementary students and many older students find attention from the classroom teacher rewarding and are likely to work hard to receive this attention. In fact, it is doubtful that many students do not find social reinforcers rewarding. An important advantage to using them is that they can be easily tied to academic performance and effectively delivered in instructional situations. Social reinforcers are a versatile tool to use with either individuals or groups of students, regardless of age.

Even though social reinforcers can be an effective tool, there are disadvantages associated with their use. For a handful of students, social reinforcers are simply not rewarding or effective. In some cases, excessive use of social reinforcers can interfere with the delivery of instruction, particularly with secondary students or those who are very active and easily distracted. This can result in decreased student performance.

Social reinforcers are effective in most beginning instruction activities and play a major role in helping students generalize skills to new learning contexts. Social reinforcers should be utilized throughout the academic year. We recommend teachers use many forms of social reinforcement, particularly with lower-performing students. It is effective to combine handshakes, pats on the back, or hugs with verbal praise.

Activity reinforcers.   An activity reinforcer is any academic or nonacademic activity children are allowed to do as a reward for appropriate behavior. Examples of nonacademic reinforcers include using a tape recorder, listening to a record, playing a board game, and so on. Academic activities that serve as reinforcers are those that involve learning, such as tutoring another student, practicing previously learned math skills, reviewing stories, or reading to a teacher. It is important to remember these activities are *potential* reinforcers. The teacher must determine if the activity or privilege increases the targeted behavior. Academic activity reinforcers are recommended whenever possible, as this is one way to increase academic engaged time.

There are several advantages to using activity reinforcers, such as helping students develop mastery of difficult skills. If, for example, a student is allowed to practice previously learned math skills as a reward for completing other assigned tasks, the extra practice is helpful in developing mastery of math skills. Activity reinforcers increase opportunities for the teacher to reinforce students during learning activities, and they are helpful in altering the routine and reduce the monotony of the instructional session. For example, students with learning disabilities who have decoding problems require intensive instruction to learn sound/symbol relationships and sound blending. Careful placement of activity reinforcers is one method teachers can use to help students maintain enthusiasm during these reading tasks. Activity reinforcers can also provide an opportunity for the teacher to instruct students in how to cooperatively work with classmates. In addition, activity reinforcers can be used with students of all ages and ability levels. The teacher must simply select activities that carefully match the student's ability and age level.

One disadvantage of activity reinforcers is that they can prove disruptive and detract substantially from the teacher's instructional program if not used properly. It also may be difficult to ease students back into the regular instructional schedule after nonacademic activity reinforcers.

For low-performing students who also exhibit behavior problems, we recommend the teacher initially use nonacademic reinforcing activities, such as having students perform a skit, or be class monitor for the day. These students respond positively to nonacademic rewards, whereas academic reinforcers can be used with more advanced students. Examples of reinforcement activities can be found in the Learning Activity on page 139.

Schedule of Reinforcement

The schedule of reinforcement refers to the frequency with which reinforcers are delivered in a particular environment (Martin & Pear, 1996). Reinforcement can be high, moderate, or low in frequency. When a response is continuously followed by a reinforcement, it is called *continuous reinforcement*. For this schedule, the teacher reinforces each correct academic response or target behavior. In a beginning reading task, the teacher reinforces the student each and every time he/she identifies a correct letter-sound correspondence. If the target behavior was to increase the frequency of polite statements made by a student, the teacher would reinforce each instance of this behavior with a clear, focused verbal-praise statement. For example, in response to a student letting another student leave the room first, the teacher says, "Shanika, thank you for letting Max leave the room first. That was very polite of you." In less frequent schedules, the teacher reinforces the target behavior only occasionally. This is referred to as intermittent reinforcement (Alberto & Troutman, 1999).

The schedule of reinforcement can affect the behavioral and academic performance of students. Regardless of the type of reinforcer that is used by the teacher, the frequency of reinforcement influences a student's behavior in profound ways. We recommend teachers follow two rules when determining frequency of reinforcement.

The first rule is to use reinforcement as frequently as necessary to achieve the objectives of the lesson.

However, teachers should take care to remember that frequent reinforcement is not always the most effective. For example, if the teacher is maintaining high academic performance and student cooperation with relatively low rates of verbal praise, it is not appropriate for the teacher to increase praise.

The second rule is for teachers to consider the skill level of the student when determining the frequency of reinforcement.

If the student is poorly motivated and having difficulty learning basic skills, then the teacher is advised to use a high frequency of reinforcers, at least during the initial teaching routine. However, regardless of the level of the student, we recommend the teacher slowly and systematically decrease the frequency of reinforcement once the student begins to perform adequately. This is particularly important for teachers who work with students with disabilities. Teaching students to work for less reinforcement from the teacher is an important part of an effective transition program.

Intensity of Reinforcement

The intensity of reinforcement refers to the strength of the reinforcement, which can be measured in quantity or incentive value. Reinforcement can be high in intensity (i.e., high in number or value) or low in intensity. We recommend that high-intensity reinforcement be used in difficult learning situations such as complex writing assignments, difficult math computations, or complex social skills like talking politely to adults. When students are presented with previously mastered material, the teacher can use less intense forms of reinforcement (i.e., less in number or value). Periodically changing the intensity of reinforcement is an instructional technique that improves the motivation of some low-performing students. Changes in reinforcement intensity helps increase the attention of distractible students (Darch, Miller, & Shippen, 1998).

We observed a teacher working with a young student in special education who was highly distractible and unmotivated during math class. This student was learning numeral identification (5 through 10) and counting from a number other than 1 (e.g., counting from 4 to 7), both important prerequisite skills. To accommodate this distractible student, the teacher increased the level of intensity of the reinforcement by being more enthusiastic in the delivery of verbal praise and by adding a pat on the back and a handshake for appropriate behavior. The positive changes in the student's performance were immediate and dramatic under this intensive reinforcement condition.

Timing of Reinforcement

There are three basic times when students can receive reinforcement on academic activities. First, students can be reinforced when they begin a learning activity. A teacher can also reinforce students when they are working on a series of activities, or when

Counting Positive and Negative Statements Made by a Teacher During Class

Purpose of Activity

To understand the relationship between teacher verbal behavior and student behavior and to determine how a teacher is attending to students

Step 1: Select a teacher who will allow you to observe in his/her classroom. Set your observation time for 30 minutes for each session.

Step 2: When recording the teacher's positive and negative statements, use the following recording code to document the attending behavior of the teacher.

C = Whole class   M = Male   F = Female

Remember to circle the code designation if the student is in special education. Use the recording form presented here. Each time the teacher makes a positive or negative comment, determine if the comment was made to a male or female student or to the whole class. If the comment was positive to a female student and focused on an academic activity, mark an **F** under the positive category under the academic heading. Remember, if the student who receives the comment is in special education, circle the **F.** Continue this recording procedure for the entire observation.

Recording Teacher's Management Statements

Time: Recording begins: _____   Recording ends: _____

Grade level: _____   Number of special ed. students: _____

Teacher: M F

	Positive Statements	Negative Statements
Academic Behaviors		
Social Behaviors		

Codes
C = Whole class   M = Male   F = Female
# Circle code designation if statement is directed to students with disabilities

---

Step 3: Using the information from the completed data form, determine the ratio of positive and negative statements by answering the following questions:

What is the ratio of positive to negative comments across all categories?
How many positive and negative comments were made about academic performance?
Has the teacher distributed comments across male and female students?
Have students with special education needs received positive comments about their social behavior or their academic performance?

they complete an entire unit of instruction. Each method has a place in effective classroom management. Reinforcement at the beginning of a learning task is best suited for students who are highly distractible and have a history of learning and behavior problems. Reinforcement during a series of academic tasks is best suited for students who are (a) low performing and need frequent support during learning activities and (b) inattentive during the teaching of new concepts, skills, or operations. In each situation, the teacher should use frequent reinforcement to maintain the student's motivation and attention to the task. Students who are at greatest risk for disruptive behavior require instructional and management support (i.e., reinforcement) as early as possible. Golly et al. (2000) provide an analysis of why early instructional and management support is essential for students at risk for learning and behavior problems: "To divert such children from a destructive path leading to school failure and rejection by teachers and peers, it is essential to intervene as early as possible in the trajectory that so often results in acquisition of an antisocial behavior pattern" (p. 180). Reinforcement applied at the end of an instructional unit is best suited for students who are approaching or have achieved mastery level on a task. Reinforcement at the end of the unit is also appropriate for students who are learning to generalize new skills.

Integrating Reinforcement and Instruction

The classroom will be more efficiently organized if reinforcement and instruction are integrated. To establish a relationship between reinforcement and instruction, we recommend teachers use the three steps that follow.

Step 1: Before initiating instructional activities, develop a comprehensive list of potential academic and nonacademic reinforcers.
Teachers should have a comprehensive list of social, activity, and tangible reinforcers. Because reinforcers are defined only by their effect upon behavior, it is possible for even learning activities to motivate students. Not all students will need to be managed with nonacademic tangible, social, or activity reinforcers. Teachers sometimes assume that only certain activities function as reinforcers. Because of the diverse backgrounds of students, their disparate learning abilities and reinforcement and learning histories, teachers must have at their disposal a diverse set of reinforcers to meet the individual needs of students. When generating a list of reinforcers, we recommend teachers consider reinforcers linked to both classroom and school rules. Verbal praise is a reinforcer only if it increases the behavior it follows. To accommodate differences among students, it is important to develop an extensive set of reinforcers as part of instructional classroom management planning. We suggest learning activities as reinforcers whenever students find them motivating, as this increases the amount of time students are engaged in academic activities.

Step 2: Consider the type of activity when selecting a reinforcer.
During the school day, students are generally engaged in one of three activities: teacher-directed instruction, independent academic activities, and social activities (e.g., collaborative or cooperative groups). We recommend using the most powerful incentives during instructional activities. Because the potential for disruption is the greatest when students learn or practice new or difficult material,

or when they learn complex social skills, students will need frequent encouragement. When students are engaged in social activities (e.g., recess, class parties), less powerful reinforcers like praise can maintain appropriate behavior.

Step 3: Restructure reinforcement as students become motivated and skillful.

Varying the reinforcers is a management strategy to effectively manage students with learning and behavior problems. If the same reinforcer is used continuously during an instructional unit, its effectiveness will decrease and have little impact on student performance. When this happens, students are likely to act out when learning content or skills that are difficult for them. If teachers vary reinforcers, they can more effectively maintain student attention during the teaching of complex material. Varied reinforcement has been shown to be an effective tool for teaching complex comprehension skills to students with learning and behavior problems (e.g., Rabren, Darch, & Eaves, 1999).

When choosing reinforcers to use during instruction, the time of the school year should be considered. For example, tangible reinforcers (e.g., tokens, candy), are best utilized at the beginning of the school year, preferably during the first 2 to 3 weeks, while less obtrusive social reinforcers (e.g., eye contact from the teacher) are most effective from the middle to the end of the school year. Also, the schedule, intensity, and timing of reinforcement can be altered as skill levels of students increase. Altering the reinforcers during the course of the school year is an important step to planning instruction for the entire school year.

ALIGNING REINFORCEMENT AND TASK DIMENSIONS

The melding of reinforcement with instruction requires a close analysis of instruction as a first step. This analysis is complex because of the numerous dimensions of instruction, including time (e.g., before, during, and after phases of instruction); task features (e.g., complexity of tasks, sequence of examples); knowledge form (e.g., concepts, rule relations, principles, cognitive strategies); student response forms (e.g., demands placed upon students to respond); time allocation (e.g., 15-minute periods versus successive 40-minute periods of instruction); grouping structure (e.g., one-to-one, small group, large group, cooperative structure); and so on (Kame'enui & Simmons, 1997).

We have already introduced the phases of instruction (i.e., before, during, after) in Chapter 4 as the temporal framework for thinking planning instruction. The phases imply that what the teacher does to preempt or respond to behavior problems is determined in part by the phase of instruction. The temporal framework serves as a prompt for the teacher to think proactively about classroom management.

In addition to the phases of instruction, another major consideration is task dimensions. By considering the various dimensions of a task within the context of instruction, the teacher is in a better position to align reinforcement activities with instruction. More importantly, the teacher can *create instructional opportunities for reinforcement* and use reinforcement in a powerful way to increase learning in the future. In the sections that follow, we discuss how teachers can align the task dimensions discussed in Chapter 3 (e.g., task history, response form, task modality, task complexity, task schedule, and task variation) with the dimensions of reinforcement.

Task History and Reinforcement

An important task feature for teachers to consider when selecting a reinforcement strategy is task history. The teacher must determine if the activity assigned to the student is a new, familiar, or old task. Table 6.3 presents the alignment of task history with the specific dimensions of reinforcement (e.g., category, frequency, time, and intensity).

The extent to which a task has been taught in the past (i.e., task history) is important in determining how to select and structure reinforcement during instruction. As noted in Table 6.3, new tasks, those that have not been previously introduced, require powerful, varied reinforcement. This is particularly true for low-performing students who need a considerable amount of support and encouragement when learning new, difficult material. During this kind of instruction, students are most distractible and become easily disruptive. For example, if a teacher is presenting a lesson on how to decode VCe words (e.g., *time, game, hope*) for the first time to low-performing students, we recommend selecting reinforcers from each of the three categories (i.e., social, tangible, or activity) and using different ones to reinforce difficult responses, such as decoding small differences in words (e.g., *hope* vs. *hop*). In this case, the purpose of reinforcement is to help the student respond correctly and immediately. The emphasis is to increase learning and motivation by designing instruction that ensures the success of all students. Given the difficult nature of this reading skill, the teacher must select reinforcers that will maximize the student's at-

TABLE 6.3 Alignment of Task History and Reinforcement

Task Dimension	Reinforcement Dimension
Task History	*Category/Frequency/Time/Intensity*
a. New	Social, tangible, or activity High frequency Immediate High intensity
b. Familiar	Social Less frequent Immediate or delayed Low intensity
c. Old	Social Less frequent Delayed Low intensity

Difficult learning activities require effective instruction and use of reinforcement to maintain students' attention.

tention and motivation. In addition, the reinforcement should help students focus on the relevant features of the academic and social skills being taught. This is especially important when students with learning and behavior problems are learning complex academic skills such as reading comprehension or sophisticated behavior such as establishing friendships in the classroom.

Varied reinforcement can be an effective strategy. The teacher may initially decide to use stickers (tangible reinforcers) as reinforcement for a high rate of correct responding and follow the lesson with a reading game (activity reinforcer) so that students can practice reading VCe words in another context. With a game activity as a supplement to the regular reading lesson, students have increased opportunities for learning, and the teacher has additional opportunities to reinforce students when they are reading VCe words. The teacher might also include high-frequency verbal praise (social reinforcer) immediately following correct responses during the reading lesson and reading game. This intensive reinforcement approach helps maintain student motivation during a predictably difficult learning task. Because many less-able students approach new tasks reluctantly, proper use of reinforcement will help the teacher maintain instructional control during potentially disruptive learning activities.

Task Response Form and Reinforcement

Another important task feature for the teacher to consider when developing the reinforcement plan is the student response form. By considering the response form, the teacher proactively selects instructional and reinforcement procedures appropriate for the task. As discussed in Chapter 3, certain response forms are more demanding and more likely to cause learning problems and disruptive behavior. Table 6.4 presents the alignment of the three response forms with the dimensions of reinforcement.

TABLE 6.4 Alignment of Response Form and Reinforcement

Task Dimension	Reinforcement Dimension
Task Response Form	*Category/Frequency/Time/Intensity*
a. Yes/No	Social Less frequent Delayed Low intensity
b. Choice	Social, activity Moderate frequency Immediate or delayed Moderate intensity
c. Production	Social, activity, tangible High frequency Immediate High intensity

Different types of response forms require differential reinforcement techniques. Tasks that require the student to generate Yes/No responses (e.g., *Teacher:* Is the ball red? *Student:* Yes.) are easier than production responses (e.g., *Teacher:* Tell me about the ball. *Student:* The ball is red.). Teachers can predict the reinforcement necessary according to the task's response form. Students with a history of learning and behavior problems are at risk for these problems when the response form is demanding. For example, in many high school science classes, much of the work assigned to students is independent reading of textbooks. Once the reading has been completed, teachers often require students to write lengthy essays (e.g., production responses) based on the reading selection (Kame'enui & Simmons, 1997). During this independent writing, students with poor writing and organizational skills may become disruptive (Darch et al., 1998).

An example of a high school science lesson illustrates the relationship between response forms and reinforcement. After completing a reading assignment on ocean currents and how they affect weather patterns, the teacher requires students to write an essay on the influence of currents on weather in states along the Pacific Ocean. During other similar assignments, several students became disruptive at the beginning of the writing period, causing problems for the entire class. Many of the students were hesitant to begin writing and seemed confused about how to organize the material and their thoughts. In this situation, the purpose of the reinforcement plan is to: (a) get students started quickly in writing the essay, (b) help students use the assigned reading passage as a basis for developing the essay, and (c) decrease the probability of disruptive behavior. Aligning the correct forms of reinforcement with the essay task may help accomplish these goals.

In this case, the teacher might first provide students an outline designed to help them organize their essays. Once students start using the outline to organize their

TABLE 6.5 Alignment of Task Modality and Reinforcement

Task Dimension	Reinforcement Dimension
Task Modality	*Category/Frequency/Time/Intensity*
a. Oral	Social Less frequent Delayed Low intensity
b. Motor	Social, activity Moderate frequency Immediate or delayed Moderate intensity
c. Written	Social, activity, tangible High frequency Immediate High intensity

thoughts, the teacher can reinforce this prewriting activity with intensive verbal praise for writing a topic sentence and organizing secondary information. It is important to note that the teacher uses the most powerful reinforcers to help students "get started" on the essay and greatly decrease the probability that students will become disruptive at the beginning of the lesson. Next, the teacher maintains high-frequency verbal praise as the students continue working on the written assignment. Whenever possible, the teacher provides corrective feedback to the lower-performing students. Follow-up reinforcers can also be utilized, such as displaying the completed essays in the classroom for students and visitors to read.

Task Modality and Reinforcement

The mode of response required of the student is an important dimension for teachers of all grade levels and content areas to consider.

Teachers must consider the task modality when structuring their reinforcement program. As noted in Table 6.5, reinforcement is structured quite differently for written tasks than for oral ones. It is much easier for most students to verbally answer the teacher's questions than it is to complete written assignments. Therefore, when students are completing written assignments, reinforcement should be of high frequency, immediate, and of high intensity. Less extensive reinforcement is necessary during oral and motor tasks, because these tasks are easier for most students to complete.

Many elementary teachers use flash cards to provide drill and practice for students who have experienced problems with math facts (e.g., addition, multiplication). Teachers follow this drill with a timed test, where students write answers to the multiplication problems as quickly as possible for a timed period. Teachers report that some students become distracted and frustrated with their inability to write numbers quickly and legibly and sometimes disrupt class.

When low-performing students are required to complete a written, timed-test, the potential for off-task behavior is increased considerably. Written tasks are hard, and timed tasks are even more difficult and stressful for students. When teachers time a task that require students to use a difficult response mode, it is necessary to plan reinforcement carefully. The purpose of reinforcement for the math activity above is to (a) reinforce the completion of small segments of work, (b) increase accuracy of math facts, and (c) increase the rate of problems completed. We recommend teachers break down the task into smaller segments and reinforce students when targeted problems are completed. We also recommend the teacher stand in close proximity to the students and provide encouragement and physical prompts (e.g., pats on the back) as students work math problems. The delivery of these reinforcers should be done frequently and enthusiastically throughout the lesson. If the reinforcement plan is implemented correctly, the teacher can expect improved performance on the math facts and fewer disruptive behaviors. Designing instruction with reinforcement in mind increases opportunities for learning.

Because of increased use of computers and other forms of technology in the classroom (Brown, 2000), teachers must now consider the novelty of the student's response form when learning information delivered by computers. When students are first engaged with computer learning activities, reinforcement should be frequent and focused on helping students learn the proper procedural steps. Students with learning and behavior problems are less likely to be familiar with the mix of technology and progressive teaching methods (Kozma & Croninger, 1992).

Task Complexity and Reinforcement

Task complexity is defined as the extent to which a learning activity has multiple steps, presents new concepts, or involves unfamiliar procedures. The more complex the task, the greater the chances are the student will have learning and behavior problems. Teachers can help students avoid some of these difficulties by carefully aligning reinforcement with task dimensions. In Table 6.6 we provide a reinforcement plan for managing easy and hard tasks.

TABLE 6.6 Alignment of Task Complexity and Reinforcement

Task Dimension	Reinforcement Dimension
Task Complexity	*Category/Frequency/Time/Intensity*
a. Easy	Social Less frequent Delayed Low intensity
b. Hard	Social, activity, tangible High frequency Immediate Moderate intensity

Teachers must consider a reinforcement strategy for easy tasks as well as hard tasks. When easy tasks are taught, behavior problems may occur during review and expanded teaching activities, as well as when students are first taught to generalize these skills to new learning contexts. Therefore, when students are working on easy tasks, one purpose of reinforcement is to foster the transfer of skills. When teachers are developing instructional sequences for transfer, the schedule of reinforcement must be carefully crafted.

An example of spelling instruction is used to highlight the importance of aligning reinforcement with task complexity. Words that are phonetically regular, (e.g., *sat, bland*) are easier for students to learn than irregular words (e.g., *could, one*). However, when students are learning to spell phonetically regular words, a difficult and important part of the instructional strategy is to teach students to spell these words in new situations (e.g., on themes and tests) (Darch & Simpson, 1990). Therefore, when teaching an easier task, the focus of the reinforcement program must include developing generalized spelling skills. In order to develop transfer, the teacher should provide periodic verbal praise whenever a student spells target words correctly in all written assignments. By doing so, the teacher systematically increases the likelihood the student will spell correctly across a variety of learning situations. In this case, reinforcement helps the student use spelling skills across a variety of tasks. Correct spelling of phonetically regular words (i.e., an easy task) in difficult learning contexts should be reinforced whenever possible. The teacher can give written feedback to students on the accuracy of their spelling in all written assignments. This delayed, low-intensity feedback is instrumental in developing transfer and improving students' motivation and learning.

Task Schedule and Reinforcement

Task schedule is another variable for teachers to consider when developing a reinforcement plan. The amount of time it takes for a student to complete a task predicts those activities that may result in learning or behavior problems. Table 6.7 provides a reinforcement plan for abbreviated (i.e., tasks scheduled for short periods of time)

TABLE 6.7 Alignment of Task Schedule and Reinforcement

Task Dimension	Reinforcement Dimension
Task Schedule	*Category/Frequency/Time/Intensity*
a. Abbreviated	Social Less frequent or moderate frequency Delayed Low or moderate intensity
b. Extended	Social, activity, tangible High frequency Immediate High intensity

and extended (i.e., tasks scheduled for long periods of time) tasks. In general, abbreviated tasks will be easier for students to complete and are less likely to foster disruptive behavior. Extended tasks, however, can be fraught with complications for both students and teachers. For students, the length of these tasks often produces fatigue and frustration because of their difficulty in managing time efficiently to complete the activities. Proper alignment of reinforcement during an extended task is a crucial element of an effective instructional reinforcement plan.

Activities assigned by teachers for independent work are usually long enough to be considered extended tasks, especially in high school classrooms. Studies that have investigated the organizational structure of classrooms (Kame'enui & Simmons, 1997) have documented the use of extended tasks during independent learning activities. Some of the most significant classroom management problems occur during these independent learning times (Darch et al., 1998). As noted in Table 6.7, we recommend teachers use carefully planned reinforcement procedures when students are required to work on extended tasks.

During social studies classes, teachers often structure the day's lesson so that students independently read a selection from the textbook and complete extensive worksheets. Consequently, students will often work on extended assignments independently for the entire class. The teacher's structure of reinforcement will determine if students work effectively. First, the teacher should use a variety of reinforcers. For example, the teacher could use verbal praise to initially engage the students in the reading activity. While students are reading, the teacher moves among the students to ask specific comprehension questions. This allows the teacher to (a) make sure students are comprehending the material and (b) increase the opportunities for reinforcement during the learning activity. To preempt behavior problems at the beginning of the lesson, the teacher should concentrate on checking the progress of low-performing students.

The teacher should also reinforce students when they transition from one activity to the next. For example, when students move independently from an oral reading assignment to written work, the teacher should immediately praise them. Many students have difficulty starting a new task after completing another extended learning activity. Using reinforcement proactively may prevent students from becoming disruptive at the beginning of these tasks.

Task Variation and Reinforcement

The alignment of reinforcement with varied and unvaried tasks is an important part of the reinforcement plan. Unvaried tasks are a series of tasks that are not changed during an instructional sequence. Many instructional programs are designed so students are required to work a lengthy sequence of similar tasks. For example, in elementary math programs, students are typically given a large number of problems of the same type to complete during a specified period of time. For many students, the successful completion of unvaried tasks is difficult. In contrast, a varied task sequence is one that alternates easy and hard tasks in an instructional sequence. Table 6.8 describes the features associated with aligning reinforcement and task variation.

An example taken from a clinical setting helps illustrate the importance task variation has in instructional classroom management. A teacher implemented a lesson designed to teach sound-symbol relationships to a group of remedial readers. The

TABLE 6.8   Alignment of Task Variation and Reinforcement

Task Dimension	Reinforcement Dimension
Task Variation	*Category/Frequency/Time/Intensity*
a. Varied	Social
	Less frequent or moderate frequency
	Delayed
	Low or moderate intensity
b. Unvaried	Social, activity, tangible
	High frequency
	Immediate
	High intensity

teacher designed a 20-minute lesson in which the only learning activity was oral reading of individual sounds. The teacher pointed to a letter, then asked the students as a group to say the sound. This activity continued for the entire 20-minute lesson. During the lesson, the students' behavior became increasingly disruptive. Students were not attending to the lesson, several engaged in verbal arguments, and others refused to participate in the activity. In addition, many students were not able to identify the letter sounds accurately.

In discussing the lesson and modifications in his teaching, the teacher indicated it might help to increase the frequency of reinforcement and the amount of time devoted to the activity by presenting more sounds to the students to increase their practice time. In essence, he wanted to take a lengthy lesson that presented a sequence of difficult, unvaried tasks and make it longer. Would the students perform better during the revised lesson? Probably not. An alternative strategy is to present a series of varied tasks (e.g., easy, hard). For example, reinforcement during the hard tasks would be of high frequency, delivered immediately, and incorporate several different types of reinforcers to maintain student motivation. During the easy tasks, reinforcement would be less intrusive and designed to build student confidence. By integrating the instruction and reinforcement this way, the teacher can expect improved performance from students.

SUMMARY

This chapter began with a discussion of why reinforcement sometimes fails as an effective management tool and how teachers can conceptualize reinforcement as instruction. The instructional reinforcement plan was presented next to help teachers integrate all reinforcement techniques and activities. The dimensions of reinforcement presented included the categories, frequency, schedule, intensity, and structure of reinforcement. The chapter concludes with a detailed discussion of how teachers can align reinforcement and task dimensions. Classroom examples are presented to highlight this discussion.

CHAPTER ACTIVITIES

1. For each of the three categories of reinforcement:
   a. Provide a description of reinforcers of that type
   b. List the advantages and disadvantages
   c. Provide three examples of reinforcers
2. Discuss how a special education teacher can individualize his or her reinforcement program for students who are culturally or linguistically different.
3. Interview a teacher to determine how he or she attempts to align reinforcement and task dimensions. Compare the teacher's methods to align reinforcement and task dimensions with those that are discussed in the text.

REFERENCES

Alberto, P., & Troutman, A. (1999). *Applied behavior analysis for teachers* (5th ed.). Upper Saddle River, NJ: Merrill/Prentice Hall.

Brigman, G., Lane, D., Switzer, D., Lane, D., & Lawrence, R. (1999). Teaching children school success skills. *Journal of Educational Research, 92,* 323–329.

Brown, M. (2000). Access, instruction, and barriers: Technology issues facing students at risk. *Remedial and Special Education, 21,* 182–192.

Cameron, J., & Pierce, D. (1994). Reinforcement, reward, and intrinsic motivation: A meta-analysis. *Review of Educational Research, 64,* 363–423.

Coleman, M., & Vaughn, S. (2000). Reading interventions for students with emotional/behavioral disorders. *Behavioral Disorders, 25,* 93–104.

Corno, L. (1992). Encouraging students to take responsibility for learning and performance. *The Elementary School Journal, 93,* 69–83.

Darch, C., Miller, A., Shippen, P. (1998). Instructional classroom management: A model for managing student behavior. *Beyond Behavior, 9,* 18–27.

Darch, C., & Simpson, R. (1990). Effectiveness of visual imagery versus rule-based strategies in teaching spelling to learning disabled students. *Research in Rural Education, 7,* 61–70.

Golly, A., Sprague, J., Walker, H., Beard, K., & Gorham, G. (2000). The first step to success program: An analysis of outcomes with identical twins across multiple baselines. *Behavioral Disorders, 25,* 170–182.

Kame'enui, E., & Simmons, D. (1997). *Designing instructional strategies: The prevention of academic learning problems* (2nd ed.). Upper Saddle River, NJ: Merrill/Prentice Hall.

Kerr, M., & Nelson, M. (1998). *Strategies for managing behavior problems in the classroom* (3rd ed.). Upper Saddle River, NJ: Merrill/Prentice Hall.

Kozma, R., & Croninger, R. (1992). Technology and the fate of at-risk students. *Education and Urban Society, 24,* 440–453.

Maehr, M. L. (1991). The "psychological environment" of the school: A focus for school leadership. In P. Thurston & P. Zodhiates (Eds.), *School leadership: Vol. 2. Advances in educational administration* (pp. 51–81). Greenwich, CT: JAI.

Martin, A., Linfoot, K., & Stephenson, J. (1999). How teachers respond to concerns about misbehavior in their classrooms. *Psychology in the Schools, 36,* 347–358.

Martin, G., & Pear, J. (1996). *Behavior modification: What it is and how to do it*. Upper Saddle River, NJ: Prentice Hall.

Rabren, K., Darch, C., & Eaves, R. (1999). Teaching character motives to students with learning disabilities. *Journal of Learning Disabilities, 32,* 36–47.

Rusch, F., Rose, T., & Greenwood, C. (1988). *Introduction to behavior analysis in special education*. Engelwood Cliffs, NJ: Prentice Hall.

Sprick, R., Garrison, M., & Howard, L. (1998). *CHAMPS: A proactive and positive approach to classroom management*. Longmont, CO: Sopris West.

Chapter 7

Social Skills Instruction in the Classroom

George Sugai
University of Oregon

Timothy J. Lewis
University of Missouri-Columbia

OVERVIEW

- What Are Social Skills?

- Why Teach Social Skills?

- What Is Social Skills Instruction?

- How Should Social Skills Be Taught?
  What Social Skills Should Be Taught?
  What Would a Social Skills Lesson Plan Look Like?

- How Is Student Learning of Social Skills Determined?

- How Effective Is the Instruction?

- How Effective Is the Skill for Students?

- How Can Social Skills Instruction Be Enhanced and Supported?

- Summary

- Chapter Activities

Classrooms are exciting and busy places. Not only are teachers teaching and students learning, but every minute is filled with a variety of social exchanges. Greetings and stories are shared, games are played, directions are given and followed, arguments are escalating and being settled, conflicts are and are not being resolved, and praise and criticism are given and received. Sometimes these social engagements are appropriate to the situation and other times they are not. But in all situations, students and teachers are engaged in social exchanges that enable communication of information, achievement of important outcomes, and effective movements and negotiations through the social environment.

When we acknowledge that social skill competence is an important ingredient for success at school, a number of difficult questions must be addressed. For example,

- What social skills do students need to be considered socially competent by relevant adults and/or to be accepted by their peers?
- How do students acquire and become fluent with these important social skills?
- Why do some students display socially unacceptable rather than acceptable behaviors?
- Who is responsible for seeing that students learn and become fluent with social skills for success at school?
- Can and should social skills be taught at school? If yes, what social skills should be taught?
- Why do students display social skills in some settings but not others?
- Do students need social skills to benefit from academic instruction?
- What does social skills instruction have to do with behavior and classroom management?

Answering these questions can be difficult because they are rooted in personal attitudes, values, and perceptions about the role, limits, and responsibilities of schools. However, the fact that social exchanges occur in every classroom and in every student-to-student and student-to-teacher interaction suggests that the role of social skills instruction in the classroom cannot be ignored. The purpose of this chapter is to describe the importance of social skills instruction in establishing and sustaining positive classroom environments, maximizing teaching and learning, and discouraging displays of problem behaviors. To achieve this purpose, five questions are addressed: (a) What are social skills? (b) Why teach social skills? (c) What is social skills instruction? (d) How should social skills be taught? and (e) How can social skills instruction be enhanced and supported?

WHAT ARE SOCIAL SKILLS?

Although a variety of definitions exists, we define social skills as those behaviors individuals display within a given situation that predict and are associated with important social outcomes (Gresham, 1986; Gresham, Sugai, & Horner, 2001; Sugai & Lewis, 1996). We focus on "behavior" because it provides a measurable and confirmable indicator of what students and teachers do when interacting with each other and moving through the environment. Although larger constructs, like *respect, responsibility,* and *perseverance* have been used to represent social skills, we find these terms too broad by themselves to define, teach, and assess. In addition, these constructs typically represent a social agent's (e.g., teacher, parent) label for a collection of observable behaviors that have been displayed by a student. For example, when she needs help completing a difficult work assignment, Kikui raises her hand and waits until the teacher can assist her. If Kikui sees that the teacher is busy, she puts her hand down, tries a different problem, and raises her hand later. Based on these behavioral observations and indicators, her teacher reports that Kikui is respectful of other students and teachers, and has perseverance. Behaviors serve as the basis for social labels or character traits that others assign to the individual.

Second, we focus on *situation specificity* because social skills are defined and affected by the context in which they are and are not displayed. Behaviors rarely occur in a vacuum; they occur in social and instructional situations that can be described and recreated. Student behaviors are triggered by a myriad of learned antecedent events. For example, objects (e.g., books, whiteboards, play equipment), meaning-filled symbols (e.g., written letters and words, clocks), verbal statements (e.g., directions, instructions), and behaviors of others (e.g., teasing, compliments, threats) occasion or trigger student behavior.

Similarly, consequence events (i.e., what happens after) affect the likelihood that a social behavior will occur (if behavior is socially reinforced) or not occur (if behavior is socially punished) again in the future. Students learn social skill variations appropriate for a range of social and learning contexts and apply these skills based on the saliency of environmental cues and the impact or effect their behaviors have on the environment. For example, raising one's hand may be an acceptable way of getting attention or assistance in the classroom, but is usually inappropriate at the dinner table at home. Walking away, for example, may be an appropriate way for a student to address a volatile situation with a peer on the playground or in the hallway, but is usually unacceptable when the student is being corrected by the principal, teacher, or parent.

Social skills, in and of themselves, are not appropriate or inappropriate. Similarly, because schools do not operate in a vacuum, the larger societal context also affects whether a behavior is appropriate or not. While the emphasis of this chapter is on school-based social skills, educators must take into account each student's prior learning history that may have been shaped by a culture, language, or customs and may be different from the learning histories of educators within the school. For example, everyone agrees that students should be respectful, but respect is shown in many ways. The real task is to identify a range of behaviors that represents respect and acknowledge that some behaviors may not be acceptable or familiar to the dominant culture of the school, but may reflect what the student has been taught.

Finally, the effective use of a social skill is associated with two important social outcomes. First, when students display situation-appropriate social skills, peer acceptance and relationships are improved. Second, adult descriptions of the student are positive. For instance, because Roosevelt shares items, initiates friendly conversation, plays cooperatively, and handles disagreements peacefully, he has many friends who refer to him as a popular leader and buddy. In fact, his friends have nicknamed him "peacemaker." His teachers describe him as socially competent, well-liked, a good self-starter and manager, and pleasure to have in their classes. In contrast, Wanda steals items, boasts about personal qualities that make her better than others, and makes false statements about her peers. As a result, Wanda spends most of her time alone and has few lasting friendships, and adults describe her as "troubled," "untrustworthy," and "unapproachable."

This social validation characterization of social skills helps us to improve teachers' ability to assess, teach, monitor, and evaluate the social competence of students and the extent to which instruction is effective. In conclusion, social skills can be characterized in the following ways:

1. Social skills may be appropriate or inappropriate depending on the immediate school or larger societal context in which they are used and observed.
2. Social skills are defined by observed behaviors and the contexts in which they are used and observed.
3. Peers and adults (teachers, parents, and so on) validate the extent to which students are socially competent.
4. Social skills are learned behaviors that can be taught.
5. The likelihood that a social behavior is displayed is related to the extent to which antecedent (triggers) and consequence (reinforcers and punishers) events are present.
6. Social skills instruction emphasizes teaching and encouraging the use of behaviors that are more acceptable within school than current problem behaviors.

WHY TEACH SOCIAL SKILLS?

The ability to negotiate the many social demands and conditions of classroom and nonclassroom settings is a formidable challenge. In interactions with peers, students initiate conversations, play cooperatively, attempt to solve disagreements, establish and discontinue friendships, and engage in a myriad of other simple and complex exchanges. Additional skills are required for successful adult interactions, such as following classroom routines, expectations, and rules; conversing and communicating about academic and nonacademic topics; or obtaining adult attention or assistance. When working independently, students engage in a range of self-management skills. They assess the quality of their actions, instruct themselves about future actions, arrange their physical and social environment to occasion certain behaviors or actions, and manipulate consequences for their actions (acknowledge and/or correct).

The underlying question is how do students acquire and become fluent with these skills? Although we would like to assume that students acquire these skills from home, by watching others, or figuring out what to do (experience), social skills learning opportunities are haphazard at best, and more often random than systematic. For some students, exposure to examples of unacceptable behavior occurs at a much higher rate than exposure to socially appropriate behavior. Simply telling or showing acceptable behavior is no guarantee that students will display appropriate behavior at the correct time and place. For some students, the cues and incentives for engaging in the undesirable behavior are more powerful than those for engaging in the desired behavior. For example, when adults are present, Tom is a systematic, positive, and objective peer conflict manager. However, when no adults are around, he is more likely to resort to solutions that are aggressive and uncompromising. Some students are taught social behaviors by significant individuals (e.g., parents, relatives, peers) that conflict with the social expectations of others (e.g., school staff, neighbors). For example, although Manuela's parents have taught her to "stand your ground at all costs if you think you are right," her teachers expect her to "work toward an agreeable solution if there is a disagreement." How is Manuela to resolve these conflicting strategies?

Clearly, schools cannot assume that students have been exposed to, learned, and are fluent with any particular set of social skills. In addition, leaving social skills instruction to others is a risky proposition that could foster the acquisition of rule-violating, inappropriate behaviors. Social skills must be taught directly and to fluency to ensure that all students are successful in a variety of learning and social situations.

Students with learning and behavior problems often need to be taught how to successfully learn in a group.

To summarize, we believe that social skills instruction is important in schools for the following reasons:

1. Students need a variety of social skills to be successful in their social exchanges with others in a variety of learning, teaching, and social situations in and out of school.
2. Students need basic social readiness skills (e.g., asking for assistance, securing attention, making transitions) that enable them to benefit from the learning opportunities provided by teachers.
3. Students who have learned and display problem behaviors need to learn and become fluent with more socially or situation-appropriate alternative behaviors that also meet their individual social needs.

WHAT IS SOCIAL SKILLS INSTRUCTION?

Without a doubt, social skills are acquired in a variety of ways. At one level, social skills are acquired through informal and daily social encounters and interactions with others. From this perspective, it is assumed that by experiencing the effects of their actions, students will learn to discriminate which social skills are more appropriate and acceptable, and when and where they should be used. Given the range of informal social skills learning opportunities that students experience, this incidental method of social skills instruction is likely to be random and inefficient.

For this chapter, we approach social skills instruction as a necessary and formal function of schools. Given that social competence has an important role in supporting academic success, orderly classroom organizations and routines, and successful student functioning in a variety of situations, we define social skills instruction as direct and planned activities designed to teach specific social behaviors that, when displayed, result in positive judgments of social competence from peers and adults (Fuller, Lewis, & Sugai, 1995; Sugai & Lewis, 1996).

This conceptualization of social skills instruction is useful for a number of reasons. First, it aligns with our notions of social competence and social validation in which the importance of positive peer and adult social validation is emphasized (Gresham, 1986; Gresham et al. 2001). Second, the importance of teaching overt behaviors, rather than generalized character concepts, is emphasized. Third, like academic instruction, social skills instruction is planned and led deliberately and directly by the teacher. Finally, students are active participants in the learning process.

HOW SHOULD SOCIAL SKILLS BE TAUGHT?

The development of instructional plans for teaching social skills is facilitated when (a) social skills are viewed as situation-specific, observable behaviors and (b) the approach to social skills instruction is similar to teaching academic skills. However, when considering how social skills are actually taught, teachers must consider three general questions: (a) What social skills should be taught (assessment)? (b) What would a social skills lesson plan look like (instruction and curriculum)? and (c) How is student learning of social skills determined (evaluation)?

What Social Skills Should Be Taught?

Although social skills are important and needed in many contexts outside of school (e.g., work, family, community), in this chapter we focus on those social skills that are required for social and academic success with peers and adults in classroom and nonclassroom settings at school. To improve assessments of what social skills should be taught, teachers should consider (a) a general case approach, (b) phases of learning, and (c) contextually appropriate assessment techniques.

General case approach. A general case approach is a useful way of conceptualizing what social skills should be taught (Becker & Engelmann, 1978; Becker, Engelmann, & Thomas, 1975; Engelmann & Carnine, 1982; Engelmann & Colvin, 1983; Horner, Sugai, Lewis-Palmer, & Todd, 2001; Wolery, Bailey, & Sugai, 1988). At the general level, broad labels can be applied to sets of behaviors related by a common purpose or communicative function, such as respect, responsibility, perseverance, safety, or independence. Each label has a definition or *general case rule* that defines what it means and how and when it is applied. Perseverance might be defined as "maintaining a course of action" or "working until complete," or the rule for being responsible might be "following through with what is expected" or "being accountable for one's actions."

At a more specific level, groups or classes of behaviors are described that represent the broad label and general case rule. For example, Rudi is described as having perseverance because he (a) works on his projects until they are completed, (b) practices a new basketball skill until mastery, and (c) helps his friends with their homework until they can do it on their own. Similarly, Anamaria shows respect in the cafeteria by speaking quietly and picking up her trash before the next students sit at her table. When in the classroom, respect means raising her hand to answer a question or saying "thank you" when another student or the teacher helps her. In addition, some behaviors could be inappropriate in some situations yet appropriate in another. For instance, Bruce is respectful to his teachers by looking at them when they talk to him, but at home, looking at his father while he is speaking would not be respectful.

To determine the general case, identify broad skills that everyone in the school can agree are important (e.g., respect, responsibility). Once key skills are determined, identify specific examples of each that reflect (a) students' age and developmental level, (b) specific setting or activity variations (e.g., hallways, common areas, transitions, small group activities), and (c) students' language and cultural learning experiences outside of school.

Phases of learning. In addition to knowing what skills and behaviors need to be taught, teachers also should consider the phase of learning for a given social skill and student: (a) acquisition, (b) fluency, (c) generalization, (d) maintenance, and (e) adaptation. Haring and White (1980) offer a useful guide for matching instruction to the student's phase of social skill learning. Assessing for the phase of learning enables teachers to increase efficiency by emphasizing specific aspects of their instruction. The instructional emphasis for each of their five phases of learning is summarized in Table 7.1.

Most published social skills curricula assume that students display social skill deficits and offer lessons that assume no or limited prior knowledge. Determining

TABLE 7.1   Instructional Emphasis for the Five Phases of Learning

Phase	Description	Instructional Emphasis
Acquisition	Accurate performance (shape, order, content, etc.) of the social skill behaviors.	1. Show, tell, model, and describe the behavior. 2. Guide, lead, and coach the student through the behaviors. 3. Give high rates of positive reinforcement for correct displays of behaviors. 4. Give informative corrections when errors occur.
Fluency	Accurate, smooth, even performance of social skill at situation-appropriate rates or speeds.	1. Provide multiple opportunities to practice (e.g., role play). 2. Give high rates of positive reinforcement for fluent performance.
Generalization	Accurate and fluent performance of the social skill beyond the classroom or instructional setting.	1. Teach with multiple representative examples from the universe of situations in which the skill will and will not be required. 2. Teach in the settings in which the social skill will be required. 3. Incorporate relevant features from the required settings as instructional prompts (e.g., people, materials, activities). 4. Use forms of positive reinforcement found in noninstructional settings.
Maintenance	Continued performance of the social skill when instruction has been discontinued in the instructional setting.	1. Use systematic fading or removal of instructional prompts or assists. 2. Decrease amounts and rates of instructional positive reinforcement. 3. Increase use of naturally occurring types and rates of positive reinforcement.
Adaptation	Use of social skill variations that have not been taught but are required in noninstructional and/or novel situations.	1. Teach representative multiple variations of the social skill behaviors. 2. Teach and link behavior variations to the defining features of the required setting.

Source: From *Exceptional Teaching*, by N. Haring and O. White, 1980, Columbus, OH: Merrill.

the phase of learning prior to instruction is important to avoiding wasted instructional time. In our experience, most students, especially students without developmental disabilities, display social skill problems related to fluency and generalization. That is, they know what to do and can tell you what they should do, but an inappropriate social skill is more efficient (fluency) and meets their needs across multiple settings (generalization). Considering this type of assessment information can help teachers shape instruction that will lead to better student outcomes.

Contextually appropriate assessment techniques.   The first step in developing a social skills lesson is determining what social skills need to be taught and to whom. A variety of techniques can be employed to facilitate these assessments. A

TABLE 7.2 The Most Commonly Described Assessment Methods

Assessment Type	Description	Example
Rating Scale and Interview	Perceptions, judgments, reports, nominations, rankings, etc. by teacher, parent, peers, or student about relative and general status of student social skill competence (*indirect method*).	• Teacher lists students from most to least on their ability to_____. • Students indicate who they would most/least like to play with. • Teacher, parents, and others rate student's ability to converse with others. • Teacher, parents, and others report the concerns they have about the child's ability to maintain friendships.
Role Plays and Situation Problem Solving	Analogue situations in which students demonstrate how they might behave (*indirect method*).	• You and your friends are in a situation in which _____. Show how you would solve this problem. • Show me what you might do if _____.
Archival Review	Review of student's behavioral history, previous social skills instruction attempts, or prior assessment information (*indirect method*).	• Office discipline-referral data. • Behavior intervention plans and individual education plans.
Direct Observation	Direct observations of behavioral events (frequency, duration, intensity) and the contexts (triggering and maintaining events, people, activities, etc.) in which they occur (*direct method*).	• Counts in the classroom the number of times anger is managed appropriately and inappropriately. • Functional behavioral assessments (antecedents, behaviors, and consequences) to determine why student uses inappropriate skills.

summary of the most commonly described assessment methods is provided in Table 7.2. We recommend that both direct and indirect assessment techniques be used. Indirect methods (ratings, interviews, and archival review) are useful sources of social validation information about how others (peers and adults) view a student's social competence. Direct methods (observation) provide information of what the student actually does, where the behavior occurs (context), what type of social skills problem exists (e.g., phase of learning), and why the student continues to use inappropriate skills. For instance, observation data indicate that when presented with a difficult academic task or activity, Shakulla shakes her head, pushes the task away, and puts her head down on her desk until the instructional period is over. If teachers give her individualized assistance on how to complete the task, she is more likely to complete the task (direct observation). Her teachers report that Shakulla knows how to ask for assistance on difficult work (interview), but has not demonstrated the skill this school year (fluency and generalization phase of learning).

In general, we recommend that teachers assess student social skills competence against four levels of contextual information that are accessible in their schools: (a) school-wide and classroom rules, (b) essential social skills for classroom success, (c) behavior incident patterns, and (d) individual student social skills problems.

TABLE 7.3   General Case School Rules and Specific Classroom Applications

School Rule	Classroom Wide	Group Instruction	Independent Study	Transitions	Free Time
Respect others	Use inside voice. Wait until others are finished before speaking.	Wait your turn to answer or speak. Raise your hand to ask a question.	When done, find a quiet activity. Work quietly. Stay in seat or work area.	Hands and feet to self. Use inside voice.	Hands and feet to self. Inside voice. Involve others.
Respect property	Recycle paper. Return textbooks.	Have materials ready before instruction starts. Return materials immediately (< 1 minute) after lesson.	Use your own supplies. Keep school property clean.	Hands and feet to self. Pick up litter. Return materials to storage places.	Return environment to state better than before.
Respect self	Do your best. Ask for assistance.	Do your own work. Follow along with teacher.	Do your own work. Use your time wisely.	Go directly to next activity. Decide where you want to go first.	Have a plan.
Respect learning	Do assignments first. Read instructions before starting.	Ask teacher for help with difficult work. Give other students a chance to answer.	Have a back-up activity. Check your work.	Collect materials for next activity. Be on time for next activity.	Have a backup activity. Read a book. Do homework.

1. *School-wide and classroom rules.* All students should be provided direct instruction on the general school and classroom rules, provided the rules are positively stated. If rules focus on the absence of behavior (e.g., "don't run," "no fighting"), emphasis should be shifted to replacement behaviors that allow students to comply with the larger school rules (e.g., "walk in the hallway," "use peer mediators to resolve conflicts"). Procedures for teaching school-wide expectations (e.g., *Be Respectful, Be Responsible, Be Prepared, Be Safe*) are described in the chapter on school-wide discipline and can be applied at the classroom level. Classroom expectations should be (a) taught directly, (b) full of multiple positive and negative examples, (c) monitored continuously and actively, and (d) acknowledged frequently and corrected positively in natural classroom contexts. Examples of the general case school rules and specific classroom applications is illustrated in Table 7.3.

2. *Essential social skills for classroom success.* All students should be directly taught those social skills important to general classroom success. In Ms. Tomoko's

Skill Name
Managing Conflicts with Peers (How to handle disagreements with peers.) Essential steps to managing conflict: **1.** Let it go or use words to reach a solution. **2.** If words don't work, walk away and ask an adult for assistance.
Teaching Examples
1. You are playing a game and have a disagreement over a rule. You and your friends agree to let it go and replay the game. **2.** You and some friends are walking down the hallway and another student calls you an inappropriate name. You say "I don't like it when you talk that way," and you walk on with your friends. **3.** Only one history textbook is available. You and a friend want to use it at the same time. When you can't come to an agreement, you ask your teacher to help you figure out a solution.
Kid Activity
1. Ask 2 to 3 students to give and describe an *example of a situation* in which they had a conflict and resolved it by developing an agreement. **2.** Ask students to *indicate or show* what they would do if they could not agree upon a solution. **3.** *Encourage* and support appropriate discussion/responses. Minimize attention for inappropriate responses.
After the Lesson (During the day)
1. Just before students transition into an activity where conflicts and disagreements are likely, ask them to tell you how they could manage conflicts that might occur (*precorrection*). **2.** If conflicts occur during an activity, stop the activity and review steps for managing conflicts appropriately, using the problem situation (*reminder*). **3.** Whenever students manage a conflict successfully and appropriately, provide *specific praise*.

FIGURE 7.1   A lesson plan for teaching conflict resolution.

classroom, all students are taught (a) how to be ready and prepared to learn, (b) how and when to ask for assistance, (c) how to solve problems and manage conflicts, and (d) how to manage homework. Many published social skills curricula contain multiple lessons and related activities. However, because these lessons tend to be written to accommodate a broad range of situations and students, they need to be adapted to reflect the unique language, classroom rules, and social contexts of the school in which students learn and interact. To simplify teaching these skills, Ms. Tomoko developed one-page lesson plans to teach each skill (see Figure 7.1; for more information see Langland, Lewis-Palmer, & Sugai, 1998). To support lesson plans for teaching important classroom-wide social skills for success, regular practice, active supervision, and high rates of positive reinforcement are important ongoing and follow-up strategies.

3. *Behavior incident patterns.* A useful and available source of information about school and classroom climate is behavior incident data. Schools typically

record major behavior incidents, such as fights, harassment, insubordination/non-compliance, tardiness, and these events are often linked to locations (e.g., classroom, playground, hallways), time of day, and staff members. From a classroom perspective, behavior management problems are social skills problems. When students use aggression to settle disagreements, the social skills problem is anger and conflict management. When students are frequently late to class, lessons must be developed and taught about being to class on time. We recommend classroom teachers regularly (at least monthly) review the patterns of behavior incidents and develop social skills lessons that target problem behavior and skill deficit areas.

4. *Individual student social skill problems.* When individual students present problem behavior, a "get tough" response (i.e., more restrictions, more verbal reprimands, more exclusion [e.g., detention, suspensions]) is typical. However, a proactive, function-based approach is recommended (Alberto & Troutman, 1999; Repp & Horner, 1999; Sugai & Tindal, 1993). (For a detailed discussion of individual student behavior support planning, see Horner, Sugai, Todd, and Lewis-Palmer, 1999–2000; Horner and Sugai, 2000; Nelson, Roberts, and Smith, 1998; O'Neill, Horner, Albin, Storey, and Sprague, 1996; Sugai and Horner, 1999–2000; Sugai, Horner, Dunlap et al., 2000; Sugai, Lewis-Palmer, and Hagan, 1998; Sugai, Lewis-Palmer, and Hagen-Burke, 1999–2000; Todd, Horner, Sugai, and Colvin, 1999.) A central feature of this approach is identifying and teaching acceptable alternative behaviors (social skills) that have a similar behavior function (purpose or motivation) to the student's problem behavior but are more efficient, effective, and relevant than the problem behavior. In particular, alternative behaviors need to be taught (social skills instruction). We know problem behavior typically serves a specific purpose (i.e., is associated with a learned outcome) for students (Dunlap et al., 1993; Hendrickson, Gable, Novak, & Peck, 1996; Iwata, Vollmer, & Zarcone, 1990). For example, some students disrupt games to gain peer attention. Others use profanity to be removed or "kicked out" of class and avoid completing the assigned work. Identification of the "function" or reason why students use an inappropriate social skill is important to determine before teaching appropriate alternatives. If students find an appropriate social skill fails to achieve the same outcome as an inappropriate behavior, they will abandon the appropriate behavior and continue the inappropriate one. A summary of the necessary steps of a function-based approach to individual student behavior support is given in Figure 7.2.

The basic message is that the decision of what must be taught should consider the social skills necessary to support a successful classroom environment for all students. In addition, knowing the function of inappropriate social skills for students is important to enhance the effectiveness of social skills instruction. This approach emphasizes general classroom social competencies (e.g., respect), typical classroom expectations and routines (e.g., making transitions), recurring problem behaviors (e.g., repeated office discipline referrals), and individual student problem behavior (e.g., getting adult attention). Considering what to teach also requires attention to the context in which targeted social skills are required, that is, where, when, with whom, and under what conditions. In addition, cultural and language variations should be considered.

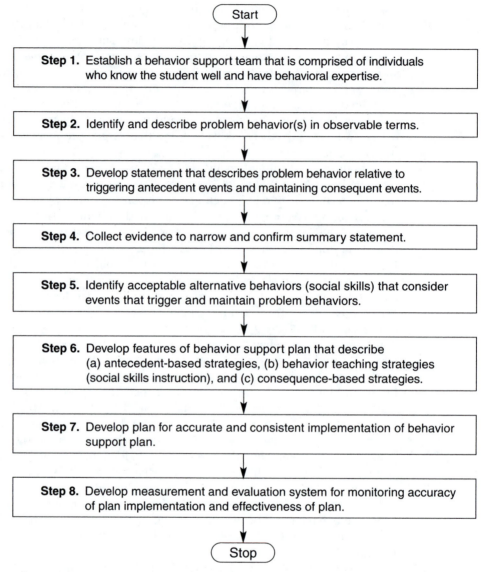

FIGURE 7.2 Steps of a function-based approach to individual student behavior support.

What Would a Social Skills Lesson Plan Look Like?

Although instructional emphases vary based on phase of learning (see Table 7.1), the features of a social skills and academic skill lesson plan are basically the same. Basic elements include (a) a model or demonstration, (b) a lead or practice opportunity, and (c) test or assessment of learning.

Model or demonstration. The purpose of demonstrations is to give students opportunities to see the defining features and behaviors of the social skill. Depend-

Role-playing, along with careful teacher monitoring, is an effective method to teach social skills.

ing on the developmental level and learning histories of the student, a model could be a verbal or written description, a graphic or symbolic representation, a video presentation, a scripted role play presented by other students or adults, or an observation of naturally occurring events. However, because models or demonstrations provide learners with both relevant and irrelevant information, teachers should supplement with instructional descriptions or activities that highlight essential elements and behaviors that define the appropriate social skill.

Lead and practice.   In most cases, models or demonstrations are accompanied by opportunities for the student to practice the social skill. The purpose of practice activities is to give learners opportunities to engage in the behaviors that comprise a social skill. As students participate in practice activities, teachers have occasion to lead students through the skill by giving reminders or prompts about what they should do, corrections about errors, and positive reinforcers for accurate behaviors. As with models or demonstrations, lead and practice activities vary based on developmental levels and learning histories of students and are used with instructional activities to underscore essential and generalizable features of a social skill.

Test or assessment.   To ensure that students are learning social skills, regular assessment of student learning should be scheduled during instructional activities. The assessment activity should assess students' phase of social skill learning and functional outcome of problem behavior. More importantly, the assessments should be based on examples and situations that have not been used in the instructional demonstrations, because the goal is to determine how well students can use a newly learned social skill in relevant but new situations. Assessment tasks could require students to demonstrate use of a social skill in a variety of ways: verbal or written descriptions, role plays, or demonstrations.

Across these three elements, an important consideration is the selection and use of teaching examples. Work by Engelmann and Carnine (1982) and Kame'enui and Simmons (1997) suggests that three guidelines be followed when developing demonstrations, role plays, and other instructional activities (Sugai & Lewis, 1996, p. 9):

1. Use both positive and negative examples of a social skill and the contexts in which the skill should or should not be applied.
2. Use a full range of positive and negative examples to represent social skill variations and the contexts in which the skill variations should and should not be used.
3. Sequence positive and negative examples that are minimally different to maximize discriminations about when and where a social skill should be used.

A basic social skill lesson has eight components (Sugai & Lewis, 1996) (see Table 7.4 for example). How each component looks, how much emphasis is placed on each, and how active the student is depends on developmental level and learning history of the student, and the phase of learning.

1. **Skill name.** A simple, descriptive name that serves as a communication label for students, school staff, and family members.
2. **Critical rule.** A brief phrase (general case) that operationalizes or specifies how and when the social skill should be used in natural contexts.
3. **Description of the skill and its components.** An operational (measurable, observable) description of the essential behaviors or steps (task analysis) that comprise the social skill and a representative collection of examples and nonexamples of (a) what the skill does and does not look like (range of response variations) and (b) where and when the skill should and should not be used. See above guidelines for example selection and use.
4. **Modeling and demonstration activities.** A set of instructional activities in which students have opportunities to see what the social skill and its variations look like and to learn about the naturally occurring situations in which it should and should not be used.
5. **Role play and behavioral rehearsal activities.** A set of instructional activities for students to practice a social skill, see their peers perform the skill, and receive positive reinforcement or corrective feedback for their use of a skill in a relevant, naturally occurring context.
6. **Review.** Frequent opportunities during and after lessons to reexamine and be reminded about a social skill name, general case rule, and behavioral components, especially in natural contexts and situations.
7. **Test.** Regular but unpredictable opportunities for students to demonstrate what they have learned (a) under new (untaught) situations and conditions and (b) without instructional prompts or assistance.
8. **Homework assignments.** Regular and structured opportunities for students to practice social skills independently, successfully, and outside the formal context of a lesson.

TABLE 7.4   Eight Components of a Social Skill Lesson

Lesson Component	Example
Skill Name	Talk-Walk-Squawk
Skill Rule	When you are teased, harassed, or being bothered, talk-walk-squawk
Skill Components	1. When you are teased/harassed, use your words. 2. If the teasing continues, walk away. 3. If the teasing continues, ask an adult for assistance.
Model/Demonstrations	Watch me as I show you what Talk-Walk-Squawk looks like: *Example 1: Playground* 1. I'm a student on the playground and a student teases me about my clothes. I say, "I don't like it when you say that about my clothes." 2. The student continues to make comments about my clothes, so I turn away from the student and walk to where one of my friends is playing. 3. The student continues to tease me and follows me across the playground, so I ask the playground supervisor to help me solve a problem. *Example 2: Cafeteria* *Example 3: During Science Lab*
Role Play/Behavioral Rehearsal	Now you try it. *Example 4: On the Bus* You and a friend are sitting together on the bus, and the student sitting in front of you turns and makes rude comments about your friend. Show me what you would do when the student makes the rude comments the first, second, and third times. [1. Say "Your comments are rude and unfriendly." 2. Move to another seat at the next bus stop. 3. Tell the bus driver that you need some help to solve a problem.] *Example 5: During Computer Exploration* *Example 6: In Line for Lunch*
Review	Ask students to tell, write, and/or show how to Talk-Walk-Squawk 1. Just before major classroom transitions. 2. Before beginning large-group instruction. 3. As they leave the room at the end of the day. 4. When they begin independent study time.
Test	Ask students to demonstrate how they would deal with teasing in the following situations: 1. Although you said *no* the first time, a student continues to ask you for money for the vending machine. 2. After a controversial decision, you win the ball game, but your opponent calls you a cheater. 3. Although you deny taking it, your close friend accuses you of stealing an expensive ballpoint pen.
Homework	Ask students to be prepared to discuss one or more of the following situations during Monday morning class meeting: 1. Watch a television show and describe how it did or did not manage teasing or harassment the correct way. 2. Teach your mom or dad what Talk-Walk-Squawk looks like and when it would be good to use. 3. Teach a student in another class what Talk-Walk-Squawk looks like and when it would be good to use.

Source: From "Preferred and Promising Practices for Social Skills Instruction" by G. Sugai and T. Lewis, 1996, *Focus on Exceptional Children, 29*(4), pp.1–16.

HOW IS STUDENT LEARNING OF SOCIAL SKILLS DETERMINED?

Determining how to assess students' social skills learning requires consideration of two basic questions: (a) How effective is the instruction and (b) how effective is the skill for the student?

How Effective Is the Instruction?

To answer this question, teachers should ask what behaviors are required in which settings or conditions at what level of accuracy/fluency. Answers to these questions serve as benchmarks or standards for evaluating student performance. As described previously, "Respecting others" will look different on the playground, in the cafeteria, and in small group instruction. Standards might be obtained by watching peers perform the same social skill, asking adults what they consider acceptable levels of behavior, or determining the skills necessary to meet specific expectations.

Next, information about student learning must be collected. Depending upon the phase of learning, performance information is collected through (a) written or verbal tests or direct observations of role plays or demonstrations (acquisition, fluency), (b) observations in natural settings and situations where the skill might be expected (fluency, maintenance, generalization, adaptation), or (c) interviews with peers and adults about student use of social skills (generalization, maintenance, adaptation).

Finally, the effectiveness of instruction is judged by comparing and evaluating the extent to which collected information about student behavior corresponds to specified standards or benchmarks. Based on the level of correspondence and the next criteria for success, instruction might be continued, lessened or intensified, or discontinued.

How Effective Is the Skill for Students?

Learning a social skill is clearly important, but it is insufficient if the student is not accepted more favorably by peers or judged to be more socially competent by significant adults. Thus, social validations of student learning are also required to evaluate the effectiveness of social skills instruction. This information can be obtained in a variety of ways: (a) interviews with students who are learning the skills, (b) interviews with members of the students' peer group, (c) direct observations of interactions between students and their peers, and (d) rating scales and interviews with significant adults (e.g., teachers, parents) who interact with and/or observe students and their peers. Assessment of the effectiveness, efficiency, and relevance of a social skill for students may be the most important indicator of the success of social skills instruction.

HOW CAN SOCIAL SKILLS INSTRUCTION BE ENHANCED AND SUPPORTED?

In this chapter, we have addressed the importance of social skills instruction within the context of instructional programming in classroom and nonclassroom environments of schools. Enhancing and supporting social skills instruction involves integrating it into the everyday activities, settings, and experiences of students and teachers. Social skills instruction cannot be an isolated event that happens between 10:15 and 10:45 on the second and third Tuesdays of each month. Similarly, social skills instruction cannot be trial-and-error or opportunistic; it must be direct, active, and engaging.

SUMMARY

To summarize this chapter and to review key concepts, we offer the following additional guidelines for enhancing and supporting classroom social skills instructional efforts:

1. Teach social skills directly and daily, much like academic skills, using: (a) examples and nonexamples that sample the range of acceptable skills, (b) practice opportunities for students to display skills, (c) guided opportunities to practice skills, and (d) initial high rates of corrective and positive reinforcement feedback to maximize student learning. Instructional activities should also be based on the phase of learning.

2. Select and teach social skills that are validated socially by students and significant peers and adults, are required for successful movement through the social environment, and enhance student social competence. Unrealistic, ineffective, and irrelevant skills will not be maintained and generalized by students.

3. Always teach for generalized responding by (a) developing generalizable social skill concepts that define a set or class of related social skills, (b) involving a range of other individuals, (c) teaching in settings in which social skills are required and expected, (d) teaching students self-management skills that can support social skills, and (e) establishing control through naturally available prompts, cues, and positive reinforcers. The real indicator of social skills success is when students accurately use social skills at the right times and places and adapt them to meet immediate requirements.

4. Precorrect for problem behavior situations by (a) identifying situations and settings in which social skill errors or competing problem behaviors are likely, (b) provide instructional prompts for desired social skills just before social skill errors are likely to occur, (c) assist the student to use or display the desired social skill, and (d) positively reinforce occurrences of the social skill. If students are not firm on a newly learned social skill, they are more likely to use previously effective, but inappropriate social behaviors that have worked in the past and in which they are already fluent.

5. Provide high rates of positive reinforcement that can be (a) presented immediately and contingently, (b) found and are available in the natural environment, (c) more effective for students than what currently maintains problem behavior, (d) faded to rates similar to naturally occurring levels, and (d) eventually self-administered and manipulated by students.

6. Work as a team to develop an action plan for school-wide and classroom-wide social skills instruction. A team should be comprised of teaching,

supervisory, and administrative staff; parents and students; classified staff (e.g., bus drivers, cafeteria workers, maintenance and security personnel) to increase input, commitments, and agreements and to enhance comprehensive implementation.

7. Integrate social skills instruction into academic programming and classroom/behavior management to enhance outcomes. Social behaviors are more likely to occur and be maintained where they are needed if instruction is incorporated into naturally occurring events and in common academic and nonacademic contexts.

8. Actively supervise use of social skills across classroom and nonclassroom settings. If students learn that staff members move, scan, and interact with them across multiple school settings, they are more likely to display desired social behaviors and inhibit their use of rule- and norm-violating problem behaviors.

9. Maximize rates of academic engagement and opportunities for successful responding to increase the likelihood that students will display desired social behaviors. Successful and effective instructional management is an excellent behavior management strategy that also gives students opportunities to experience success and the confidence to try new or difficult social skills.

10. Collect information or data to assess the effectiveness, efficiency, and relevance of social skills instruction. Many sources of accessible data (e.g., office discipline referrals, behavioral incident reports, attendance rates) can be used to enhance a social skills instructional strategy and to guide school teams to identify what social skills need to be taught and/or strengthened. Ultimately, educators must observe students within the settings where social skill problems are of concern to determine (a) appropriate skills are used, (b) adults in those environments are encouraging use of skills (e.g., reinforcement), and (c) the skills taught are becoming embedded in natural activities and routines of each setting.

A team approach is the most successful method to determine what social skills need to be taught in the classroom.

CHAPTER ACTIVITIES

1. Identify a social skill to be taught and then develop a detailed lesson plan that includes all aspects of teaching (e.g., instruction and curriculum).
2. Develop a set of school-wide behavior rules. Write a justification for the rules you selected.
3. Identify three examples of how support staff (e.g., paraprofessionals) can enhance and support effective social skills instruction.

REFERENCES

Alberto, P., & Troutman, A. (1999). *Applied behavior analysis for teachers* (5th ed.). Upper Saddle River, NJ: Merrill/Prentice Hall.

Becker, W. C., & Engelmann, S. E. (1978). Systems for basic instruction: Theory and applications. In A. Catania & T. Brigham (Eds.), *Handbook of applied behavior analysis: Social and instructional processes* (pp. 75–92). Chicago: Science Research Associates.

Becker, W. C., Engelmann, S., & Thomas, D. R. (1975). *Teaching 2: Cognitive learning and instruction*. Chicago: Science Research Associates.

Dunlap, G., Kern, L., dePerczel, M., Clarke, S., Wilson, D., Childs, K. E., White, R., & Falk, G. D. (1993). Functional analysis of classroom variables for students with emotional and behavioral disorders. *Behavioral Disorders, 18,* 275–291.

Engelmann, S., & Carnine, D. (1982). *Theory of instruction: Principles and applications*. New York: Irvington.

Engelmann, S., & Colvin, G. (1983). *Generalized compliance training: A direct instruction program for managing severe problem behaviors*. Austin, TX: Pro-Ed.

Fuller, M., Lewis, T. J., & Sugai, G. (1995). *Social skills instruction in schools: A survey of teachers in Oregon public schools*. (Behavior Disorders Research Report No. 4). Eugene, OR: University of Oregon, Behavior Disorders Program.

Gresham, F. M. (1986). Conceptual issues in the assessment of social competence in children. In P. Strain, M. Guralnick, & H. Walker (Eds.), *Children's social behavior: Development, assessment, and modification* (pp. 143–179). New York: Academic Press.

Gresham, F. M., Sugai, G., & Horner, R. H. (2001). Social competence of students with high-incidence disabilities: Conceptual and methodological issues in interpreting outcomes of social skills training. *Exceptional Children, 67,* 331–344.

Haring, N., & White, O. (1980). *Exceptional teaching*. Columbus, OH: Merrill.

Hendrickson, J. M., Gable, R. A., Novak, C., & Peck, S. (1996). Functional assessment for teaching academics. *Education and Treatment of Children, 19,* 257–271.

Horner, R. H., & Sugai, G. (2000). School-wide behavior support: An emerging initiative (special issue). *Journal of Positive Behavioral Interventions, 2,* 231–233.

Horner, R. H., Sugai, G., Lewis-Palmer, T., & Todd, A. W. (2001). Teaching school-wide behavioral expectations. *Report on Emotional and Behavioral Disorders in Youth, 1*(4), 77–79, 93–96.

Horner, R. H., Sugai, G., Todd, A. W., & Lewis-Palmer, T., (1999–2000). Elements of behavior support plans: A technical brief. *Exceptionality, 8,* 205–216.

Iwata, B. A., Vollmer, T. R., & Zarcone, J. R. (1990). The experimental (functional) analysis of behavior disorders: Methodology, applications, and limitations. In

A. C. Repp & N. N. Sigh (Eds.), *Perspectives on the use of nonaversive and aversive interventions for persons with developmental disabilities* (pp. 301–330). Sycamore, IL: Sycamore Publishing.

Kame'enui, E., & Simmons, D. (1997). *Designing instructional strategies: The prevention of academic learning problems.* Upper Saddle River, NJ: Merrill/Prentice Hall.

Langland, S., Lewis-Palmer, T., & Sugai, G. (1998). Teaching respect in the classroom: An instructional approach. *Journal of Behavioral Education, 8,* 245–262.

Nelson, J. R., Roberts, M. L., & Smith, D. J. (1998). *Conducting functional behavioral assessments.* Longmont, CO: Sopris West.

O'Neill, R. E., Horner, R. H., Albin, R. W., Storey, K., & Sprague, J. R. (1996). *Functional analysis of problem behavior: A practical assessment guide* (2nd ed.). Sycamore, IL: Sycamore Publishing.

Repp, A. C., & Horner, R. H. (Eds.). (1999). *Functional analysis of problem behavior: From effective assessment to effective support.* Belmont, CA: Wadsworth Publishing.

Sugai, G., & Horner, R. H. (1999–2000). Including the functional behavioral assessment technology in schools (invited special issue). *Exceptionality, 8,* 145–148.

Sugai, G., Horner, R. H., Dunlap, G., Hieneman, M., Lewis, T. J., Nelson, C. M., Scott, T., Liaupsin, C., Sailor, W., Turnbull, A. P., Turnbull, H. R., III, Wickham, D., Reuf, M., & Wilcox, B. (2000). Applying positive behavioral support and functional behavioral assessment in schools. *Journal of Positive Behavioral Interventions, 2,* 131–143.

Sugai, G., & Lewis, T. (1996). Preferred and promising practices for social skills instruction. *Focus on Exceptional Children, 29*(4), 1–16.

Sugai, G., Lewis-Palmer, T., & Hagan, S. (1998). Using functional assessments to develop behavior support plans. *Preventing School Failure, 43*(1), 6–13.

Sugai, G., Lewis-Palmer, T., & Hagan-Burke, S. (1999–2000). Overview of the functional behavioral assessment process. *Exceptionality, 8,* 149–160.

Sugai, G. M., & Tindal, G. (1993). *Effective school consultation: An interactive approach.* Pacific Grove, CA: Brooks/Cole.

Todd, A., Horner, R., Sugai, G., & Colvin, G. (1999). Individualizing school-wide discipline for students with chronic problem behaviors: A team approach. *Effective School Practices, 17*(4), 72–82.

Wolery, M. R., Bailey, D. P., & Sugai, G. (1988). *Effective teaching: Applied behavior analysis with exceptional students.* Boston: Allyn & Bacon.

Chapter

8

Punishment:
A Transition Tool Only

OVERVIEW

Punishment plays a significant role in instructional classroom management, but only as a transition tool. Punishment is used as a temporary and transitional intervention that enables the teacher to stop an inappropriate behavior and reestablish instructional control so that reinforcement strategies can be continued. In instructional classroom management, punishment always sets the stage for reestablishing instruction as the primary focus of the teacher. To accomplish this, teachers must have a complete understanding of what punishment is, the limited role it plays in classroom management, and how to implement different punishment strategies effectively with students who pose difficult management problems.

More often than not, punishment is associated with negative connotations. First, many teachers consider punishment an end in itself. For example, once a teacher uses punishment to decrease disruptive behavior of a student, she/he may think other interventions are not necessary. When people think of punishment, the harshest images come to mind, for people assume punishment is always severe. This negative interpretation of punishment is "far removed from the definition of punishment" (Kame'enui & Simmons, 1997, p. 481) and even further removed from the role we have prescribed in instructional classroom management.

In the first part of this chapter, we define punishment and describe its role as a transition tool. Punishment is a tool teachers can use to gain control quickly so that instructional interventions can be applied. Next, we discuss several misconceptions professionals have about punishment and its use in the classroom. We present a list of guidelines teachers should follow when implementing punishment procedures. In the last section of this chapter, we list and discuss specific punishment strategies for use in instructional classroom management.

DEFINITION OF PUNISHMENT

Punishment is the application of an aversive consequence that weakens the future occurrence of the behavior it follows (Sprick, Garrison, & Howard, 1998). Just as reinforcement is defined by increasing the probability of occurrence of a targeted behavior, punishment is defined by its effect on behavior. It is a mistake to assume certain consequences (e.g., verbal reprimand, sending a student to the office, requiring students to stay after school) will serve automatically as punishers for all students. A teacher may require a student to go to the principal's office as a consequence for fighting in class, but unless this consequence decreases the frequency of fighting, sending this student to the principal's office is not punishment. In fact, in one study, Darch and Thorpe (1977) reported the practice of sending disruptive students to the school office often increased their disruptive behavior in elementary grades. Madsen, Becker, Thomas, Koser, and Plager (1968) showed that consequences expected to decrease behavior can actually function as reinforcers. These authors showed that the use of a teacher's "sit down" command actually increased the number of times students were out of their seats. While most people assume "sit down" is an effective punisher, it often is not. When teachers use punishment strategies, it is important the behavior to be decreased is monitored closely to determine the effect of the consequence. Teachers must ask, "Is the frequency of the behavior decreasing because of the consequence?" If not, the consequence is not an effective punisher.

PUNISHMENT USED AS A TRANSITION TOOL

Punishment in instructional classroom management is used primarily as a transition tool. Figure 8.1, adapted from Kame'enui and Simmons (1997), illustrates how punishment can serve as a temporary transition strategy. As noted in Figure 8.1, punishment serves as a bridge between the implementation of two stages of instructional strategies. In this conceptualization of punishment, it is used only after a comprehensive instructional program is designed and implemented and alternatives to punishment are considered when behavior problems first occur. If a student's behavior

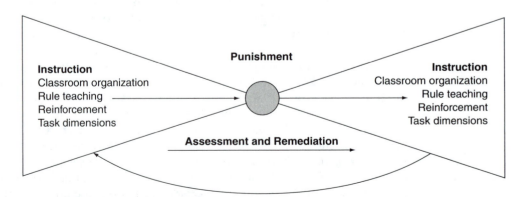

FIGURE 8.1 Punishment: A transition tool.

suggests punishment is warranted, it is then applied, but only temporarily and only as a transition to instruction. If a teacher doesn't quickly shift to positive, instructional interventions once a student's inappropriate behavior is controlled, the teacher's instructional program can be negatively influenced. For example, Knapp et al. (1991) evaluated the relationship between classroom management and the quality of instruction and concluded: "Ultimately choices about management approach affect the kind of academic learning experience available to children. On the whole we were struck by how often the academic learning environment was set by management choices made with little thought to academics" (p. 41). As punishment strategies are applied, we recommend the teacher quickly assess the instructional program and make modifications in areas that establish instructional control. As soon as students are responding and cooperative, punishment should be withdrawn. Then it is appropriate for the teacher to emphasize instruction, verbal reward, or tangible rewards like gold stars or points. This transition must be done as quick as possible as reinforcement enhances students' intrinsic motivation in learning (Cameron & Pierce, 1996).

Advantages of punishment can only be achieved with short-term use. Punishment helps eliminate behavior problems while giving the teacher time to modify the instructional program, giving the teacher greater opportunities for reinforcement. Reynolds (1992) suggests, "classroom management goes beyond the problems of misbehavior or student engagement" (p. 11). Once disruptive behavior is under control, a teacher must actively engage students in content and the learning process. If a teacher uses punishment indiscriminately over an extended period of time, the potential for abuse is greatly increased. Research shows that students with disabilities are sometimes victims of improper punishment procedures. Teachers who use punishment frequently usually focus on aversive procedures and rarely consider instructional-program modification as part of the intervention model. Thinking of punishment as a transition tool only helps teachers use primarily positive management strategies.

Alternatives to Punishment

Punishment has several disadvantages in the classroom. When used in the absence of reinforcement, it is not an instructional procedure for it does not teach, it only stops behavior (Sprick et al., 1998). Teachers who use punishment as their primary intervention strategy do not teach students alternative forms of behavior. While appropriate use of punishment may provide opportunities for teaching, instruction is required for students to learn alternative, socially acceptable behavior or academic skills. Using punishment frequently in the classroom can create a hostile learning environment for all students in the classroom. When punishment is overused by a teacher the students figure out ways to avoid punishment. Punishment does not eliminate the desire of students to engage in misbehavior.

Because of the disadvantages of punishment we recommend teachers consider alternative strategies to decrease disruptive behavior. We discuss alternative strategies that are relatively easy to use and do not require lengthy implementation. Five strategies we recommend are discussed in the next few pages.

Discuss the problem with the student or the class.   As Sprick et al. (1998) point out, it is possible that disruptive students are unaware that behavior is a problem. This may be the case with young children who exhibit both learning and behavior problems. Tulley and Chiu (1995) report discussing correct or desired behavior with a student or entire class is an effective intervention strategy for most types of disruptive behaviors. As the first alternative to punishment, we recommend teachers discuss the problem behavior with the student during a neutral time when the student is more likely to listen. The best time to discuss the problem with the student is when the student is not engaged in a demanding and frustrating learning activity. By choosing a time when the student is relaxed and cooperative, it is more likely he or she will listen and constructively discuss the problem. Discussing the problem is most appropriate for mild forms of disruptive behavior, and the teacher should provide the student the following information:

1. A clear description of the behavior in question
2. An example of the behavior and when it occurred in the class
3. A description of when the problem behavior seems to occur
4. An explanation of why the student's behavior is unacceptable

By discussing why the behavior is unacceptable, the student is more likely to take responsibility for trying to change the behavior. After talking with the student, the teacher should monitor the problem behavior and decide if another intervention is required. The Learning Activity that follows guides you in interviewing students to understand why they misbehave and why teachers punish during class.

Reinforce the behavior of other students.   An alternative to punishment is to reinforce the appropriate behavior of other students, especially in the presence of the behavior problem. Considerable evidence suggests this strategy is effective in decreasing mild forms of disruptive behavior such as talking during class and other forms of inattentiveness (Corno, 1992). Reinforcement to the students engaged in appropriate behavior should be delivered frequently and intensively. When reinforcing students who are near the disruptive student, the teacher should be very precise in

Discussing a behavior problem with a student is one alternative to punishment.

Interviewing Students About Why Students Misbehave and Teachers Punish

Purpose of Activity

To gain an understanding of the causes of behavior problems and why teachers punish during class.

Step 1: Gain permission to interview three students with different ability levels. Students can come from different classrooms and grade levels.

Step 2: Set up an interview time of approximately 15 minutes for each student.

Step 3: Tape record each interview if students are comfortable with this arrangement. The recording will be used to complete a post-interview analysis. If it is not possible to record the interview, take notes during questioning period.

Step 4: Complete with each of the students the following interview format. Add other questions to the interview if you would like.

Section 1: Causes of Behavior Problems

1. Why do some students cause behavior problems in class?
2. Do you think your class is well behaved?
3. Do you ever misbehave in class? Give an example.
4. Why did you cause problems in class?

Section 2: How and Why Teachers Punish Students

1. What kind of discipline strategies does your teacher use in class?
2. Does the teacher discipline fairly in your class?
3. Do you know exactly what behaviors will be punished in your class?
4. Do you think the discipline procedures used are effective?

Step 5: Listen to the interview and develop a summary to present to class. Be prepared to lead a class discussion about the students' responses.

identifying the appropriate behavior (see Chapter 6). This method works effectively to decrease mild forms of disruptive behavior: (a) if the student has learned to earn the teacher's attention by following classroom rules, (b) if the student's behavior problem has been drawing considerable attention from the teacher and other students, and (c) if it is paired with ignoring the problem behavior. This strategy will not work quickly, and it is most appropriate with students who are not exhibiting severe forms of disruptive behavior and who are properly placed in the instructional program so as to experience success.

Use differential reinforcement of other behavior.   Differential reinforcement of other behavior (DRO) is defined as "the contingent presentation of a reinforcer for any behavior more appropriate than the response to be reduced" (Wolery, Bailey, &

Sugai, 1988, p. 384). For example, to decrease the frequency of a student's arguing with classmates, the teacher reinforces any appropriate interaction this student has with others. This increases the frequency of the student's appropriate interactions while decreasing arguing. DRO is an attractive alternative to punishment because it emphasizes positive reinforcement and provides the basis for teaching the student alternative, appropriate behavior. DRO is an important alternative to help teachers increase their positive interactions with students with learning and behavior problems. Shores, Gunter, Denny, and Jack (1993) report teachers infrequently give positive responses to appropriate behavior of students with histories of aggressive behavior.

DRO is not as effective and would have to be combined with other strategies if: (a) the student is engaging in many types of disruptive behaviors, (b) the reinforcers maintaining the behavior are not controlled by the teacher, and (c) the reinforcers used by the teacher are not as powerful as those that are maintaining the inappropriate behavior.

Ignore the behavior problem.   Ignoring is the process of withholding rewards (e.g., teacher attention) following a behavior that has been rewarded previously. For example, if a student frequently talks to another student during class, the teacher may react by saying, "Tonya, remember there is no talking during class. Please finish your work quietly." If this strategy does not decrease the student's talking, the teacher's attention may actually encourage the student's behavior. Ignoring the behavior may be an effective strategy to decrease the student's talking.

One misconception about ignoring inappropriate behavior is that it is sometimes equated with tolerating and accepting the behavior problem. Some teachers feel an ignoring strategy is too passive, but we disagree. Ignoring inappropriate behavior can be effective if the teacher follows three implementation guidelines. First, the teacher must define the behavior to be ignored and monitor its frequency to determine if ignoring is effective. Second, the teacher must use the ignoring strategy consistently each time the target behavior occurs. For example, if the teacher decides to ignore a student's persistent negative comments about himself or herself (e.g., "I'm no good at school and will never be able to finish this work"), it is important the teacher ignore these comments every time they are made. If the teacher ignores them only on occasion (e.g., "Come on Sid, this work is easy for you"), then the ignoring strategy will not be effective. In fact, if ignoring is applied incorrectly, the frequency of the student's negative comments will increase and strengthen over time. Third, if the ignoring strategy is to be effective, the reinforcer for the disruptive behavior must be the teacher's attention (i.e., the student must desire the teacher's attention). Finally, ignoring is an appropriate alternative to punishment for behavior problems that occur infrequently and are not severe. These behaviors are minor rule violations, negative comments about school (e.g., "I hate reading class"), and other forms of inappropriate verbal behavior (e.g., talking during class). The ignoring strategy is also effective with mild problem behaviors that occur at the beginning of the school year, like tattling or physical complaints. Teachers who carefully ignore these comments and reinforce successful work and play activities should be able to manage mild student complaints. The ignoring strategy can be effective with students of all ages and ability levels who engage in inappropriate behaviors to gain attention from students or the teacher.

Modify the instructional program. As Figure 8.1 indicates, it is possible to eliminate behavior problems with instructional methods and strategies designed to help students be successful. Many behavior problems occur because students are either bored by an activity that is too easy or frustrated by one that is too difficult. Keel, Dangel, and Owens (1999) suggest modifying instructional materials for students with disabilities to promote "learning that can be applied regardless of the setting in which the student is served" (p. 3). Christenson and Ysseldyke (1989) identify instructional factors necessary for students with learning and behavior problems to be successful. Several are listed below:

1. Clearly stated teaching goals and expectations
2. Lessons that are clear with specific teaching procedures
3. Many opportunities for students to respond and participate
4. Sufficient academic allocated teaching time for students to learn
5. Active monitoring of student progress
6. Evaluation that is frequent and appropriate

GUIDELINES FOR USING PUNISHMENT AS A TRANSITION TOOL

In order to use punishment correctly as a transition tool, it is important that teachers follow several administrative and implementation guidelines.

Administrative Guidelines

Develop a list of punishment strategies. We recommend teachers develop a list of punishment strategies from least intrusive to most intrusive at the beginning of the school year. Teachers should choose only those strategies they are comfortable using. We present specific punishment strategies and advantages and disadvantages for each technique in the latter part of this chapter.

Inform parents about punishment strategies. Teachers should inform parents about what they plan to do before applying punishment strategies and tell parents about the general causes of behavior problems. Parents will be more supportive if they understand more severe forms of discipline will be used only after an array of positive, instructional solutions have been tried. We recommend that teachers apprise parents of their overall management plan, including an explanation of the instructional philosophy and an explanation of punishment strategies. Teachers should always discuss classroom discipline with parents in the larger context of teaching and learning in the classroom. Teachers should discuss their instructional goals and objectives and how punishment will be used as a transition tool. Researchers (Scott-Little & Holloway, 1992) have demonstrated that parents often are not aware that environmental factors such as curriculum design and instruction influence behavior.

Communication about instruction and management can be accomplished by sending parents a letter at the beginning of the school year or through an oral presentation at a school open house. Informing parents of punishment strategies will ensure they are

Parents should be informed about the punishment strategies used in the classroom.

not surprised by disciplinary procedures used during the school year. Informing parents about the instructional program increases the likelihood that they will play an effective and positive role in their child's instructional program. For some strategies, such as time-out from positive reinforcement, it is advisable to obtain parental consent as well.

Inform students about punishment strategies.   The teacher should discuss punishment strategies at the beginning of the school year so that students will not feel the teacher is unfairly singling them out for punishment. This discussion will communicate to students that the teacher is organized and thoughtful in all aspects of the instructional program. We recommend teachers discuss expectations, class-room procedures, and rules when students are introduced to the punishment strategies in the classroom.

Implementation Guidelines

Use punishment in conjunction with reinforcement.   Punishment is most effective if it is used in conjunction with reinforcement. If used without reinforcement, punishment can have destructive long-term effects. Shores et al. (1993) found that teachers have difficulty using reinforcement with punishment: "Our experience has been that teachers often have a difficult time responding positively to students if the students recently have been engaged in inappropriate behavior" (p. 4). The authors recommend teachers follow the adage "catch the student being good" as a prompt to use reinforcement frequently. Punishment used in isolation will create a negative classroom, characterized by sullen and unhappy students, critical parents, and disil-lusioned or cynical teachers. Punishment used alone is not an instructional interven-tion, because it does not teach students alternatives. Grossman (1992) has also commented on the importance of taking a broad view of classroom management. "For better or worse, classroom management and instruction are eternally married. How teachers manage their classrooms enables or constrains the possibilities of teaching, classroom discourse, and student learning" (p. 174).

Implement punishment strategies calmly. Implementing punishment aggressively and angrily does not increase its effectiveness. Rather, punishment strategies are most effective when implemented calmly with as little emotion as possible and with great consistency. Teachers are better able to use punishment procedures consistently if they are not angry. If teachers are not calm when they punish, students may feel the teacher has a personal vendetta against them.

Apply strategy consistently. Once a teacher decides upon a punishment strategy, it must be applied consistently in the presence of the behavior problem. The strategy will not be effective if a teacher applies it occasionally or if the consequence is not applied the same way each time it is used. Many students, particularly those with behavior problems, will not alter their behavior unless punishment is applied consistently over a period of time.

Withdraw punishment strategies as soon as possible. We recommend punishment be used as a transition tool only. Once the behavior problem is under instructional control, it is important that teachers change their focus and concentrate efforts on developing instructional modifications and reinforcement.

PUNISHMENT STRATEGIES

Five punishment procedures can be considered for decreasing behavior problems after alternative procedures are attempted. These are verbal reprimands, quiet-time, owing-time, response-cost, and time-out from positive reinforcement.

Verbal Reprimands

A verbal reprimand or warning gives students a signal that if inappropriate behavior continues, they will receive a specified consequence. Research evidence suggests that a teacher's verbal reprimands decrease the frequency of a limited number of behavior problems (Walker, Colvin, & Ramsey, 1995), especially mild ones. For example, reprimands might be an effective way to decrease students' inappropriate talking during study time, but reprimands will not eliminate fighting. Reprimands are effective with only recent behavior problems. The teacher must use this strategy the first few times the student engages in the inappropriate behavior, and it will not be effective with persistent behavior problems. In fact, some research evidence suggests that using verbal reprimands may actually increase the frequency of persistent behavior problems (Walker et al., 1995).

We recommend the teacher follow four specific guidelines to decrease the behavior problems when using verbal reprimands:

When reprimanding a student, tell the student what behavior is inappropriate and why. To make sure the communication between teacher and student is unambiguous, it is important the teacher tell the student what the problem behavior is and why it is a problem. For example, if a student is taking too much time and purposely stalling when moving from a reading group to another activity, an incorrect verbal reprimand would be, "Antonio, let's go!" This reprimand may be clear to the teacher, but it may be ambiguous to the student. A more appropriate reprimand would be, "Antonio, it is taking you too long to get to your spelling group. You're wasting class time. If you waste more time, you will have to make it up after class!" This is a more appropriate reprimand, because it gives the student more information and links a specific consequence to future rule violations.

Always pair a verbal reprimand with a consequence. When giving a student a verbal reprimand, always specify consequences for continued rule violation. In the example, Antonio was told if he continued to dawdle, he would have to make up the time after school. The reprimand should be consistently backed up with consequences that are effective in decreasing the behavior problem. If reprimands are not linked with the consistent delivery of consequences, the reprimands will not work.

When delivering a verbal reprimand, position yourself close to the student and speak in a quiet but firm voice. Reprimands are less effective if the teacher is physically distant from the student. Reprimanding a student from across the room, for example, is less effective than the teacher calmly walking up to the student to deliver the reprimand. However, we are not suggesting the teacher confront the student in a menacing manner, but by getting reasonably close to the student, the teacher is more likely to gain the student's attention. Also, reprimands will be more effective if the teacher uses a calm, firm voice. Screaming the reprimand will render it ineffective, because the student hears the anger rather than the direction. In addition, the loud, emotional screaming may send the message, "I don't like you."

Follow verbal reprimands with reinforcement. Teachers must be prepared to use reinforcement following verbal reprimands. After a student is reprimanded for a rule violation, it is important for the teacher to reinforce the student for following instructions as soon as possible. For example, if the teacher reprimands a student for talking during independent work time, the teacher must reinforce the same student when he or she is working quietly. Verbal reprimands will only be effective if the teacher reinforces the student for appropriate behavior. Reinforcement teaches the student alternative ways of behaving in the classroom.

Advantages of verbal reprimands

Reprimands are easy to implement. As one of the easiest punishment strategies to implement, reprimands take little or no instructional time and do not require a considerable amount of planning.

Reprimands require no change in the instructional program. One significant advantage of reprimands is that teachers do not need to make adjustments to their instructional program. While reprimands are being used, teachers can continue their instructional program. In addition, reprimands can be effective in almost any instructional context, provided the teacher follows the prescribed guidelines properly.

Reprimands can be used with students of all ages and ability levels. Because reprimands can be effective in elementary and secondary school settings, they can be a versatile tool for teachers. However, reprimands are particularly effective with students who do not have academic problems and exhibit only mild behavior problems.

Disadvantages of verbal reprimands

Reprimands are not an effective long-term management strategy. For this reason, teachers should not rely on reprimands as a primary management strategy to decrease behavior problems.

It is possible for reprimands to become reinforcers for students. If teachers use reprimands exclusively without subsequent reinforcement, the verbal reprimand may serve as a reinforcer and actually strengthen and increase the frequency of the behavior problem. Some students find any attention from the teacher reinforcing, and this is more likely to happen if the teacher fails to link consequences with the verbal reprimand.

Reprimands are not effective in decreasing high-frequency behavior problems or problems that have occurred persistently over time. Even when used properly, this technique is not a powerful punishment procedure. Reprimands will only be effective in decreasing mild forms of inappropriate behavior. For behavior problems that occur frequently or are more severe, other punishment strategies are more appropriate.

Quiet-Time Strategy

Another punishment strategy to decrease the occurrence of behavior problems is quiet-time. Students are asked to stop all activities and remain quiet for a specified period of time. Once the teacher has reestablished control, the students are allowed to resume assigned activities. This strategy is most successful in decreasing the frequency of mild forms of disruptive behavior in elementary students (e.g., loud and boisterous behavior during group activities).

A teacher should follow five steps when implementing the quiet-time strategy:

Step 1: Require children to stop what they are doing immediately.
For example, if the entire class is too noisy during the completion of an art project, the teacher can initiate quiet-time by stating, "I want everyone to stop what they are doing right now!" If some students continue to talk, the teacher should present the same statement again and wait for the students to become quiet.

Step 2: Require children to remain absolutely quiet.
It is important that the teacher require students to be absolutely quiet. This means no talking, whispering, or questions by any students during quiet-time. In some rare cases, it may be appropriate to require the children to put their

heads down on their desks. If students are in the halls or on the playground, require them to stand against the wall or away from potentially distracting activities or equipment, if possible. The quicker the teacher can establish silence, the more effective the strategy will be.

Step 3: Maintain quiet-time for 1 or 2 minutes, but never longer than 2 minutes.

It is difficult and ineffective to require students to remain absolutely quiet for a longer period.

Step 4: Have students resume previous task.

The teacher should praise students who quickly get back to work. It is important to monitor all students and make sure everyone is working on the assigned activity. The teacher should not lecture or draw any attention to the quiet-time strategy but should remind students of appropriate behavior for working on the assigned task.

Step 5: Use reinforcement to maintain appropriate behavior.

Once all students are working quietly, the teacher should systematically and immediately reinforce them. The teacher does not discuss the quiet-time incident with children at this time, but the teacher should discuss it at the end of the school day or the beginning of the next day. We recommend rule teaching and preteaching of rules along with the teacher's expectations at the beginning of the next day's class.

Advantages of quiet-time strategy

It is effective with groups of students. The quiet-time strategy is effective during group activity and has many applications (e.g., recess, group learning) in the elementary school setting. Because of the group focus, quiet-time is an efficient intervention strategy.

It is efficient to implement. This strategy should not take more than 2 to 3 minutes to implement, and the teacher is not required to make any adjustments in the teaching plan.

An instructional component is included. In the quiet-time strategy, students are not only punished for engaging in inappropriate behavior but are also provided instruction on how to comply with rules through the teacher's review. This strategy teaches classroom rules and allows reinforcement.

Disadvantages of quiet-time strategy

It is not effective for severe disruptive behavior. Effectiveness of the quiet-time strategy is limited to mild forms of disruptive behavior that occur infrequently. It is not an effective intervention for more severe forms of disruptive behavior such as fighting, not following directions, and aggressive verbal behavior (e.g., "I don't have to finish my work if I don't want to."). For these types of inappropriate behaviors, punishment procedures designed to work with individuals are more appropriate (e.g., owing-time, time-out).

Using quiet-time can be unfair to some students. The quiet-time strategy is typically used with groups, and sometimes students who have not violated classroom rules are required to stop work and remain quiet with the class. We recommend this strategy, as with all punishment strategies, be used as a transition tool only. Repeated violations of classroom rules require teachers to make substantial changes in their instructional programs.

Owing-Time Strategy

The third punishment strategy is owing-time. In this intervention, the student who is disruptive during organized class activities is required to "pay back" instructional time that was wasted as a result of his or her disruptive behavior (Sprick et al., 1998). The student is also required to complete all unfinished work. Requiring the student to owe time can be applied to students of all ages and ability levels. One reason we recommend this strategy is that instructional time is not lost. This is a significant issue for teachers working with low-performing students who can ill afford to miss instructional time.

The owing-time strategy can be used in at least two situations. For example, when a problem behavior occurs frequently throughout the day (e.g., talk-outs, name calling, talking back to the teacher), the teacher records each incident and converts this to an amount of time the student is required to pay back. For inappropriate behaviors that last longer than 1 minute (e.g., out of seat, late for class), the teacher converts the number of minutes the behavior lasted to a payback of equal time.

The owing-time strategy is more intricate than other punishment procedures we have discussed. Its success is contingent upon a carefully implemented plan of several steps:

> **Step 1: The teacher should define precisely the behaviors that will result in owing-time and those that will not.**
> If a teacher has problems with a student talking back after an assignment is given, then examples of "talk-backs" that will result in owing-time must be identified and defined by the teacher. The teacher may decide to penalize any verbal behavior that challenges the assignment and the teacher's authority. Examples might include, "I don't have to do the math problems if I don't want to," or "That assignment is unfair, it's too long." The teacher should provide the student a list of acceptable comments so the student has a clear idea of what statements are acceptable and what ones are not. A statement that expresses concern but does not challenge the teacher's authority might be acceptable, as in, "Do I have to complete all of these before I go home?"
>
> **Step 2: The teacher should discuss the problem behavior with the student.**
> Before the owing-time procedure is implemented, the teacher discusses the problem behavior with the student by providing clear examples of the behavior during a neutral time.
>
> **Step 3: Determine how much time the student will owe in two ways.**
> The teacher can count the misbehaviors (e.g., talk-outs, fights, noncompliance) and determine how many minutes the student will owe for each misbehavior. For situations where the inappropriate behavior occurs frequently, each rule violation should translate into at least 1 minute of owed time. Sprick et al. (1998) recommend the following guidelines for determining the number of minutes owed by the student. Students should be informed about how the number of minutes to be owed is determined before this strategy is used.

Number of Misbehaviors	Number of Minutes Owed per Infraction
1–3	10
4–6	5
7–10	3
11+	1

According to this chart, if the student engages in four verbal arguments, he or she owes 20 minutes. The teacher should also consider more severe, low-frequency misbehaviors. Therefore, if students engage in three significant misbehaviors (e.g., noncompliance) each infraction would be assigned 10 minutes of owing-time for a total of 30 minutes. It is necessary to adjust the number of minutes owed to reflect the severity of the misbehavior.

Step 4: Determine when students will pay back the time they owe: after school, recess, free-time periods.

Students should not miss any instructional time when paying back owed time. When students are paying back time, we recommend the teacher require the students to sit quietly at their desks and complete any assignments missed as a result of their misbehavior. If students have no specific assignments to complete, they should be required to read or study. We also suggest the teacher not talk to students during this time period, so that this session does not become reinforcing for them.

Step 5: When informing a student he/she violated a rule and owes time, we recommend the teacher briefly state the misbehavior and amount of time owed.

The teacher should avoid lengthy explanations and not argue with the student about the amount of time owed or whether a rule was violated. Sprick et al. (1998) recommend the interaction with the student last no more than 5 seconds. If the student has concerns about how the owing-time strategy was implemented, the student can arrange to meet another time to discuss the situation. It is important to resume teaching as quickly as possible.

Advantages of owing-time strategy

Owing-time is effective with most forms of misbehavior. This strategy is particularly effective in controlling severe forms of inappropriate behavior such as fighting and noncompliance. The versatility of this punishment procedure makes it appropriate for both elementary and secondary classrooms.

Owing-time makes the student accountable. Students learn they are responsible for completing assignments and are accountable for making up time wasted as a result of misbehavior. The teacher must not assign additional academic work. We recommend academic work not be used as a punisher.

Disadvantages of owing-time strategy

The procedure is time-consuming for the teacher. Because the student must be monitored during the payback period, owing-time can take a significant amount of the teacher's time. This should be considered before this punishment strategy is selected.

Record keeping is cumbersome. This strategy requires the teacher to record and track the amount of time students owe, which adds to the teacher's workload.

Consequences are delayed. Another disadvantage of this strategy is that students receive delayed consequences, usually, paying back time long after they have violated classroom rules. Delayed consequences are less effective than consequences that are immediately delivered.

Response-Cost Strategy

Response-cost, a system similar to the owing-time strategy, is the loss of a specified amount of positive reinforcement contingent on inappropriate behavior. In this strategy, the teacher continues to apply the reinforcement strategy (e.g., points contingent upon appropriate behavior, free-time contingent upon correct responding), but when students misbehave, the teacher takes away a specified amount of the reinforcer. For example, if a student talks out during class, the teacher takes away points the student previously earned each time a talk-out occurs.

Teachers should follow five steps to implement response cost effectively.

Step 1: The teacher meets with student and discusses the behavior and why it is a problem.

This meeting takes place during the student's free-time and not during class time.

Step 2: The teacher identifies a reinforcer for the student by discussing reinforcement options.

For example, the student might earn free-time if he/she works quietly and productively during class. Points and free-time are examples of reinforcers that can be effectively used during response cost, as they can be easily given and taken away as fines.

Step 3: During discussion with the student, the teacher identifies the amount of fine for specific rule infractions, refraining from assigning too high a value to fines.

For example, the teacher suggests that each time the student talks out during class, he/she loses two points from the total earned for that class.

Step 4: The teacher must tell the student how fines will be determined and communicated.

The teacher should not give the student too much attention when fined so the process does not become reinforcing. Reid (1999) suggests, "put ten stars on the chalkboard. Each time the student is fined, erase one star. Or take a piece of paper and cut strips on one end. Tape the paper to the student's desk. Each time he or she in fined, simply tear off one strip" (p. 10). The fine should be communicated to the student in a matter-of-fact manner.

Step 5: A critical feature of response cost is to continue to positively reinforce the student frequently, for it is reinforcement that maintains appropriate behavior.

The teacher should frequently identify behavior to reinforce so that the student is earning points or free-time.

Advantages of response-cost strategy

Response-cost is an effective strategy for all forms of disruptive behavior. Because of its effectiveness, response cost is a strategy that can be used in the most difficult management circumstances.

Response-cost is an effective transition strategy. Because response cost combines reinforcement and punishment strategies, it is easy for the teacher to use as a transition tool. As soon as the teacher has successfully eliminated disruptive behavior, reinforcement can be used exclusively.

Disadvantages of response-cost strategy

Response-cost does not teach alternative behavior. Response cost is not a teaching intervention as students are not taught appropriate alternatives.

Response-cost is a complex procedure to implement correctly. Because response-cost requires the teacher to balance the application of reinforcement and fines (punishment), it can be difficult to apply correctly while teaching.

Time-Out From Positive Reinforcement

Time-out is a powerful punishment procedure that can be used to decrease the frequency of severe forms of misbehavior. There is a large body of research that has demonstrated that time-out, in its various forms, can be effective with most types of behavior problems in elementary and secondary classrooms. Time-out from positive reinforcement is defined by Wolery et al. (1988) as "a procedure where, contingent upon a target behavior, the student experiences a period of time when less reinforcement is available" (p. 416).

There are two types of time-out procedures. In the first, nonexclusionary time-out, the student remains in the environment where the problem behavior occurred. For example, if a young student hits another student during a group project, a nonexclusionary time-out procedure requires the disruptive student to put his or her head down on the desk for a specified period of time. The teacher and other students do not attend to the student in time-out. Two forms of nonexclusionary time-out are effective with young students:

1. **Time-out ribbon.** The student wears a ribbon or another marker (discriminative stimulus) to serve as cue for the teacher and others to reinforce at high rates when the student is behaving. When the student misbehaves, the ribbon is removed from the student, which signals everyone to withhold reinforcement during the time the ribbon is off. When the student begins to behave appropriately, the teacher gives back the ribbon, and the student again receives high levels of contingent reinforcement.
2. **Contingent observation.** For this time-out procedure, the student is removed from a group activity because he/she behaved badly. Once removed, the student is required to watch the activity from the side of the room. The contingent observation is for a fixed amount of time (maximum 1 minute), and the student does not receive reinforcement from the teacher or other students.

Exclusionary time-out requires the student to be completely removed from the setting where the problem occurred, either to a separate part of the classroom or a separate room. This seclusion ensures the student does not have access to reinforcers from the original setting. Exclusionary time-out is the most restrictive and controversial form of time-out. Teachers should document when time-out is used and record its effects. As Reid (1999) points out, "If time out is effective in reducing behavior, it should be used less frequently over time, because inappropriate behavior should decrease."

The procedure for using time-out from positive reinforcement has six steps:

Step 1: List and define the behaviors that will result in time-out.

Teachers should not only list the behaviors, but should include a detailed description of the behavior. This helps the teacher recognize the behavior to be punished with time-out and helps the students understand the inappropriate behaviors that will result in time-out. We recommend the teacher select the two or three most severe behaviors (e.g., fighting, refusal to follow critical classroom rules). Time-out will be a more effective strategy if used for a limited number of inappropriate behaviors.

Step 2: Choose location of the time-out area.

In nonexclusionary time-out, the student does not leave the instructional setting when the procedure is implemented. The teacher might have the student place his or her head on the desk for time-out from positive reinforcement. It is important during nonexclusionary time-out that the teacher have control over the classroom so that other students do not interact with the student in time-out. To accomplish this, the teacher must reinforce students for working and not attending to the disciplined student.

For exclusionary time-out, the teacher must find a location, preferably outside the classroom, where the student will go for the time-out. Teachers should select an area that is visible so the student can be monitored during the time-out procedure. The time-out area may also be placed in an area of the classroom where the student will not have contact with other students.

Step 3: Administer the time-out procedure calmly and without emotion.

The teacher should draw as little attention as possible to the student, so that the student will not find the time-out procedure reinforcing. When telling the student to go to the time-out area, the teacher should specify the inappropriate behavior and the consequence. For example, if a student hits another student, the teacher administers exclusionary time-out saying: "Jim, hitting others is not allowed in this room. Go to the time-out area." The teacher directs the student in a way that suggests time-out is not negotiable (e.g., the teacher should not say, "I would like you to go to the time-out area.").

Step 4: Determine the length of the time-out period.

When students are directed to the time-out area, the teacher should use a stop watch or kitchen timer to track the time, preferably no longer than 3 minutes. Time-out periods over 3 minutes are not generally more effective. Students should be told when they enter the time-out area they must remain quiet the entire time. If the student leaves the time-out area or engages in any other disruptive behavior, the teacher should reset the timer, and the time-out period should begin again. The cycle should continue until the student has remained quiet in the time-out area for the entire designated time.

Step 5: Require the student to make up any work missed during time-out.
Time-out should not become reinforcing by allowing the student to get out of completing assignments.

Step 6: When the student is out of the time-out area, reinforce appropriate behavior.
When the student is working well with the rest of the class, the teacher should immediately reinforce the behavior and not discuss the time-out incident with the student. As the teacher reinforces the student for getting back to work quietly and completing assigned work, the teacher demonstrates no grudge and that the "slate is wiped clean."

Advantages of time-out

Time-out from positive reinforcement can be a powerful transition tool. If used properly, time-out is a powerful transition tool for decreasing the frequency of difficult behavior problems. It is an effective punishment strategy to decrease serious behavior problems while students are taught to behave appropriately.

Time-out is a versatile punishment procedure. Time-out can be effective with students of all ages and in most instructional settings. It can also be an effective strategy with low-performing students.

Disadvantages of time-out

Loss of instructional time. One limitation of using time-out is that the student loses instructional time while he or she is placed in time-out. This is significant with low-performing students, who cannot afford to lose learning opportunities.

As soon as a student returns from time-out from positive reinforcement, he or she should begin the learning activity immediately and have opportunities to earn reinforcers.

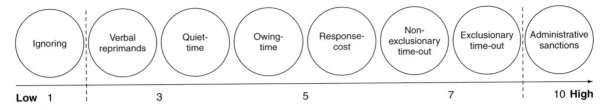

FIGURE 8.2   Continuum of complexity.

Time-out is a complex procedure to implement. Implementation of the time-out strategy is frequently done incorrectly. Teachers must have a complete understanding of time-out before using it in the classroom.

Time-out is easy to abuse. Time-out can be easily abused, because it is easy to remove a disruptive student from class. Time-out must be monitored closely and used under careful supervision.

PUNISHMENT STRATEGIES AND THE CONTINUUM OF COMPLEXITY

Before selecting any of the punishment strategies discussed in this chapter, teachers should consider the costs of each strategy, which include the legal and ethical considerations. Figure 8.2 illustrates a model of the relationship between specific punishment strategies and their degree of complexity. Punishment procedures lower on the continuum are easier to implement and have fewer administrative, ethical, and instructional costs associated with their use. The quiet-time strategy is easier to use than is exclusionary time-out. For example, before teachers use time-out, the principal should give approval and parents should be informed. In addition, legal and ethical concerns are greater with time-out than with the quiet-time procedure or any other punishment strategies, because the student is excluded from instruction in the classroom context. In general, punishment strategies higher on the continuum result in loss of instructional time. We recommend teachers use punishment strategies lower on the punishment continuum before using strategies that are more complex.

SUMMARY

In this chapter, we discussed how punishment serves as a transition tool in instructional classroom management. We also recommended that teachers consider using five alternative strategies before selecting punishment. If punishment must be administered, we offered guidelines for using five punishment strategies to decrease inappropriate behavior. The punishment strategies presented were verbal reprimands, quiet-time, owing-time, response-cost, and time-out from positive reinforcement. For each strategy, we recommended specific steps for implementation as well as advantages and disadvantages of the strategy.

CHAPTER ACTIVITIES

1. Discuss how the authors suggest using punishment as a transition tool.

2. Identify and discuss the five alternatives to punishment described in this chapter.

3. For each of the following punishment strategies, provide: (a) a definition and description, (b) the steps recommended for implementation, and (c) the advantages and disadvantages of using the strategy.
- Ignoring
- Verbal reprimand
- Quiet-time
- Owing-time
- Nonexclusionary time-out
- Exclusionary time-out

REFERENCES

Cameron, J., & Pierce, D. (1996). The debate about rewards and intrinsic motivation: Protest and accusations do not alter the results. *Review of Educational Research, 66,* 39–51.

Christenson, S., & Ysseldyke, J. (1989). Assessing student performance: An important change is needed. *Journal of School Psychology, 27,* 409–425.

Corno, L. (1992). Encouraging students to take responsibility for learning and performance. *Elementary School Journal, 93,* 69–83.

Darch, C., & Thorpe, H. (1977). The principal game: A group consequence procedure to increase on-task behavior. *Psychology in the Schools, 14,* 341–347.

Grossman, P. (1992). Why models matter: An alternative view on professional growth in teaching. *Review of Educational Research, 62,* 171–179.

Kame'enui, E., & Simmons, D. (1997). *Designing instructional strategies: The prevention of academic learning problems* (2nd ed.). Upper Saddle River, NJ: Merrill/Prentice Hall.

Keel, M., Dangel, H., & Owens, S. (1999). Selecting instructional interventions for students with mild disabilities in inclusive classrooms. *Focus on Exceptional Children, 31,* 1–16.

Knapp, M., Adelman, N., Marder, C., McCollum, H., Needles, M., Turnbull, B., & Zucker, A. (1991, October). *Teaching for meaning in schools that serve the children of poverty: Summary report.* Washington, DC: U.S. Dept. of Education.

Madsen, C., Becker, W., Thomas, D., Koser, L., & Plager, E. (1968). An analysis of the reinforcing function of sit down commands. In R. K. Parker (Ed.), *Readings in educational psychology* (pp. 27–35). Boston: Allyn & Bacon.

Reid, R. (1999). Attention deficit hyperactivity disorder: Effective methods for the classroom. *Focus on Exceptional Children, 31,* 1–20.

Reynolds, A. (1992). What is competent in beginning teaching? A review of the literature. *Review of Educational Research, 62,* 1–35.

Scott-Little, C., & Holloway, S. (1992). Child care providers' reasoning about misbehaviors: Relation to classroom control strategies and professional training. *Early Childhood Research Quarterly, 7,* 595–606.

Shores, R., Gunter, P., Denny, K., & Jack, S. (1993). Classroom influences on aggressive and disruptive behaviors of students with emotional and behavioral disorders. *Focus on Exceptional Children, 26,* 1–10.

Sprick, R., Garrison, M., & Howard, L. (1998). *CHAMPS: A proactive and positive approach to classroom management.* Longmont, CO: Sopris West.

Tulley, M., & Chiu, L. (1995). Student teachers and classroom discipline. *Journal of Educational Research, 88,* 164–171.

Walker, H., Colvin, G., & Ramsey, E. (1995). *Antisocial behavior in school: Strategies and best practices.* Pacific Grove, CA: Brooks/Cole.

Wolery, M., Bailey, D., & Sugai, G. (1988). *Effective teaching: Principles and procedures of applied behavior analysis with exceptional students.* Boston: Allyn & Bacon.

Chapter

9

Managing Persistent Behavior Problems: Strategies and Examples

OVERVIEW

Nothing tests the effectiveness of an instructional program more than persistent behavior problems. When chronic behavior problems plague a classroom, students and teachers alike gain little from the instructional process. How these problems are managed will determine how successful teachers are at meeting their professional objectives for the academic year. In order to manage persistent behavior problems effectively and humanely, teachers must have a predetermined plan for altering the instructional task, modifying the learning context, and using reinforcement and punishment. In essence, the teacher must have multiple options because persistent behavior problems are complex. No single approach is effective for every situation. For some types of problems, the task must be changed; for others, the learning context or the amount of reinforcement must be adjusted. Unfortunately, most teachers have no such plans. Regardless of the approach taken, it is important to gain control of persistent behavior problems, because chronic, disruptive behavior often leads to severe problems such as aggression or intimidation (Kamps & Tankersley, 1996). Coie (1994) found the existence of antisocial behaviors at ages 7 and 8 in school settings is strongly predictive of future aggressive behavior. Sugai and Lewis (1999) indicate that "early patterns of challenging behavior, coupled with limited or inappropriate parent supervision, set up children and youth for school failure, dropping out of school, and incarceration" (p. 3).

There is much evidence that teachers often do not respond to chronic and persistent behavior problems with well planned instructional interventions (Walker et al., 1996). Colvin and Sugai (1988) have described how teachers are typically punitive in their responses to persistent behavior problems: "If the student fails to terminate this troublesome social behavior, the typical approach is to escalate the level of negative consequence, usually in the form of detention, suspension, and expulsion" (p. 341). This approach is not instructional or positive. However, it is understandable why this punitive, noninstructional approach is often taken. Attempting to manage persistent behavior problems is a fatiguing and troubling experience for teachers. The emotional drain caused by students who are always challenging school rules can quickly wear a teacher down. Even if teachers are initially successful in curbing chronic behaviors, the exclusive use of punitive methods is destructive to the teaching mission. In the same vein, teachers who use spur-of-the-moment strategies will often find persistent behavior problems worsen.

In this chapter, we discuss a model and specific strategies for managing persistent behavior problems. We conclude this chapter with a series of vignettes that provide examples of how to manage persistent behavior problems more effectively.

A MODEL FOR MANAGING PERSISTENT BEHAVIOR PROBLEMS

Our model emphasizes developing instructional modifications to teaching under the guiding principle that *teachers must exhaust all instructional remedies in responding to persistent behavior problems,* as shown in Figure 9.1. If this approach does not result in successful management of the problem, we recommend more extensive program modifications. The model we recommend is useful because it (a) does not require much extra teacher time, (b) implementation procedures are straightforward, (c) there are no negative effects for other students in the classroom, and (d) the approach is primarily instructional (Keel, Dangel, & Owens, 1999).

As a first step in managing persistent behavior problems, we recommend teachers complete a quick assessment of classroom organization and the instructional context. After assessment, we recommend the teacher consider making adjustments in the organization of the program, as well as changes in the learning task. Reinforcement strategies should be adjusted, if necessary, to increase program effectiveness. For example, reinforcement might be increased to better maintain a student's attention during difficult learning activities. The final step of the model is implementation of other teaching and management strategies to eliminate persistent behavior problems. These include precorrection, developing neutral instructional tasks, and implementation of punishment procedures. Punishment is implemented only after exhausting all instructional remedies. The knowledge of a student's self-concept is important to understanding behavior and academic problems. Mehring and Colson (1990) report the negative experience caused by the inability to successfully respond during lessons only reinforces a student's belief about his or her ability. Our model is useful for teachers to improve instructional and management strategies with all students, not only those engaging in chronic disruptive behavior.

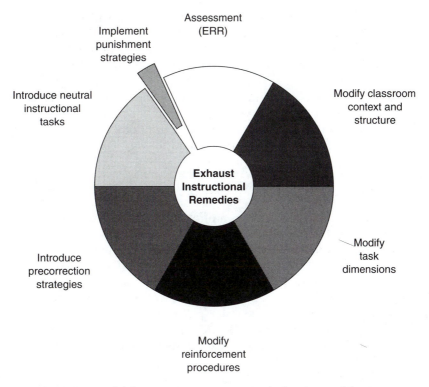

FIGURE 9.1   Model for managing persistent behavior problems.

Assessment

In the presence of persistent behavior problems, the purpose of assessment is to provide the teacher quick information on how to best modify the teaching program so the student's behavior can be brought under instructional control. We suggest teachers use a modified form of the assessment plan presented in Chapter 5 as a guide to determine the possible causes of persistent behavior problems. The ERR strategy (evaluate/revise/reconsider) is the basis for these assessment activities. The teacher should reassess all aspects of the instructional program (e.g., classroom organization, reinforcement procedures) to determine what factors are maintaining the persistent behavior problems. We recommend the teacher begin by asking the following 10 questions:

1. Can the student actually perform the social skill requested by the teacher?
2. Are persistent behavior problems fostered by the organization of the classroom?
3. Are the problem behaviors specific to a particular person or more than one person?
4. Are the problem behaviors specific to a particular time of day or setting?
5. Are the problem behaviors specific to a particular instructional task, response form, or problem type?

6. Are the problem behaviors specific to a particular sequence of events?
7. Are certain reinforcers or reinforcement schedules more effective than others in managing the persistent behavior problem?
8. What punishment procedures have been effective in the past in decreasing the occurrence of disruptive behavior?
9. Can this problem be solved by using school-wide management strategies? (See Chapter 10.)
10. Do I need to solicit help/input from others (e.g., teachers, parents, supervisors) to better manage the problem?

These questions provide the teacher an informal procedure to evaluate the instructional program. Question 2 asks the teacher to consider classroom organization: transitions between groups, adequacy of classroom rules, and teaching schedule. Many persistent behavior problems are related to these areas. Questions 3 and 4 focus on the setting and help the teacher determine if the problem occurs in the presence of more than one person or is related to a particular time of day. Questions 5 and 6 require the teacher to look at instructional tasks, while 7 evaluates reinforcement and 8 identifies effective punishment procedures. Questions 9 and 10 consider variables outside the classroom, including the school-wide management plan or factors from home that may contribute to behavior problems. A multidisciplinary approach may help solve persistent behavior problems. These questions help the teacher develop an appropriate instructional response to persistent behavior problems.

Modification of the Context and Structure of the Lesson

We recommend teachers modifying the instructional context in response to persistent behavior problems. As Lewis and Sugai (1996) point out, changes in the organization and the physical arrangement of a classroom can have dramatic effects on students' behavior. Teachers might modify seating assignments, sequence and types of learning activities, and physical arrangement of the classroom. Each of these modifications is described below.

Modify seating assignments. All teachers know the wrong seating assignment can foster disruptive behavior. Low-performing students who are seated at the back of the class will not feel connected to instructional activities or teacher guidance and reinforcement. Teachers also have a difficult time monitoring students' behavior and responses when they are seated in the back. We recommend disruptive students sit at the front of the class so the teacher can increase positive interactions, monitor the student's academic responses, and provide instructional support when necessary. Students engaged successfully in learning have fewer behavior problems.

Modify the sequence or type of learning activities. The sequence of learning activities within a lesson has an impact on learning and behavior, particularly for students at risk for learning and behavior problems. Many persistent learning and behavior problems are a result of students having difficulty at the beginning of a lesson. Students who are not successful at the beginning of a lesson often spend the

The classroom seating arrangement has a powerful influence on students' behavior and academic performance.

remainder of class time being disruptive to mask failure or gain the teacher's attention. The teacher can remedy this by selecting easily completed learning activities at the beginning of the lesson to help lower-performing students begin successfully. The teacher can use carefully placed "change-up" activities to gain the attention and interest of young students. A change-up activity has an academic focus but is structured as a learning game to increase student motivation. For example, when young students are learning letter-sound correspondence, the teacher can stop the teaching session and ask students if they would like to play a game. "Let's see who knows the sounds, the students or the teacher." The teacher races the students to see who can say the identified sound fastest. Whoever wins 10 points first, students or teacher, wins the race. Activities such as this may increase the motivation of students during learning activities associated with higher rates of disruptive behavior.

Modify the physical arrangement of the classroom.   Teachers can effectively accommodate students with persistent behavior problems by changing the arrangement of the classroom. The teacher might rearrange the seating of students from traditional rows to groups or pods, making it much easier to reinforce student groups. Group reinforcement is effective with students with persistent behavior problems and allows the teacher to increase the frequency of reinforcement during class, especially when teaching difficult information. Group seating arrangements make it easier for high-performing students to provide instructional support to less skillful students.

Modification of Task Dimensions

Persistent behavior problems, like any disruptive behavior, can be caused by improper task structure and selection. One indication that improper task structure is contributing to chronic behavior problems is if the student becomes disruptive at the same time a new task is introduced. This is more evident if the student had been performing adequately on similar instructional tasks.

If students have completed previously introduced tasks without exhibiting learning or behavioral problems, it is possible the new task is too difficult. Many low-performing students exhibit chronic behavior problems with new learning tasks. The task may require prerequisite skills the student hasn't mastered, or the structure of the task (i.e., multiple steps) may be too complex for the student. The student's frustration during instruction may fuel the disruptive behavior.

As discussed in Chapter 3, one way to decrease persistent behavior problems is to adjust the task requirements. For example, if the persistent behavior problem occurs in the context of teaching complex multiplication (e.g., 23 × 19), the teacher should withdraw the original task and reintroduce several of the critical prerequisite skills (e.g., multiplication facts, how to carry from the ones to the tens column). Each prerequisite skill should be reintroduced and taught to mastery before complex multiplication is reintroduced to the student. Because the student should perform more successfully on these component tasks, the teacher will have more opportunities for reinforcement. By increasing success, it is less likely the student will be disruptive. Once the student is again working on complex multiplication, the teacher can modify the response modality. Rather than have the student write answers independently, the teacher has the student complete several problems orally, with teacher guidance. Once the teacher is convinced the student can indeed complete the task, the student is required to complete the problems independently and in the original response form.

Modification of Reinforcement

The purpose of reinforcement in management of persistent behavior problems is to help the student perform successfully in an appropriate learning activity as quickly as possible. Once adjustments have been made in the task, and the student has been presented with the new learning activity, reinforcement procedures are used to keep the student responding and to decrease the probability that behavior problems will recur. One method is to replace the current reinforcer with one that is more powerful. Rather than using social reinforcers, the teacher might use tangible reinforcers in response to persistent behavior problems. In addition, the teacher can increase the frequency of reinforcement if the current schedule seems inadequate. Because the student should perform more successfully in the new learning activity, the teacher is provided an excellent opportunity to increase the frequency and intensity of the reinforcement program, which in turn increases the student's confidence and establishes positive instructional control.

We recommend the teacher increase the intensity of the reinforcer early in the learning activity so the student begins working with as much support as possible. Because many persistent behavior problems occur at the beginning of a new unit of instruction, we recommend the teacher reinforce the student on increases in *academic performance,* however incremental, to keep the focus in the classroom on academic activities. For example, if the persistent behavior problem typically occurs during oral reading of stories, the teacher should use an intensified reinforcement approach when the student is working on skills prerequisite to oral reading (e.g., sound-symbol relationships). Effectiveness of modification of task dimensions to manage chronic behavior problems must not be underestimated. Deutsch-Smith and Pedrotty-Rivera (1995) argue "many behavior problems occur because students are either bored with an activity that is too easy or frustrated because it is too difficult" (p. 3).

Strategic Use of Precorrection Strategies

Precorrection is a valuable technique for reducing the occurrence of persistent behavior problems. In precorrection, students are taught which behaviors are unacceptable and why. Students with chronic behavior problems are provided extensive practice on correct behavior skills. Precorrection has been shown to foster conflict resolution among students (Johnson & Johnson, 1996). Precorrection is a primary method to reduce persistent behavior problems. We recommend teachers design and implement precorrection interventions after they have reevaluated their classroom organization, task dimensions, teaching structures, and reinforcement procedures. If persistent problems continue, teachers should follow a six-step procedure to implement precorrection strategies (Colvin & Sugai, 1988):

> **Step 1: Determine the context that elicits the persistent behavior problem.**
> First, the teacher identifies the specific context in which the persistent behavior problem is most likely to occur to determine if there is a relationship between certain activities and the occurrence of persistent behavior problems. The goal is for the teacher to ascertain if classroom variables elicit the disruptive behavior. A teacher must observe the student's behavior carefully to determine a functional relationship between contextual variables and disruptive behavior.
> **Step 2: Communicate the expected behaviors to the student.**
> Once the learning context that precedes persistent behavior problems is identified, the teacher determines the behavior that is expected from the student. The question the teacher would ask himself or herself is, "What is the appropriate behavior that is incompatible with the persistent behavior problem?" The behavior requirements are then discussed with the student to make certain the student understands the teacher's expectations. It is important that the teacher explain the behavior requirements to the student, using clear and understandable terms (e.g., "Eric, if you have a question, you have to raise your hand and wait to be called on."). If the student does not understand the expected behaviors, then the precorrection strategy will not be successful. We recommend the behaviors discussed with the student be functional replacements for the persistent behavior problem. For example, the student understands that he or she can receive attention from the teacher by quietly completing assignments rather than talking to classmates.
> **Step 3: Modify learning context.**
> The purpose of this step in the precorrection strategy is to change the task requirements and the student response form so it is more likely the student will perform as expected and less probable that the student will become disruptive (Colvin, Sugai, Good, & Lee, 1997). For example, if a student is frequently

disruptive during math class, it may be necessary to teach the difficult parts of a lesson individually before presenting the entire lesson. By preteaching difficult material in a simplified context (i.e., one-to-one) and by allowing the student to practice the most difficult material with extensive teacher guidance, the student will perform more successfully and become less disruptive when he or she is placed in the group. This preteaching will help decrease the likelihood this student will be disruptive during group math lessons.

Step 4: Provide practice on the expected behaviors.

Even after the teacher discusses the expected behavior with the student, the inappropriate behavior may very well continue. Although discussing the appropriate behavior with the student is a necessary step in the precorrection strategy, it is not sufficient to eliminate persistent problem behaviors. The next step is to provide students with specific training on the expected behavior before they enter the original context. For example, if the behavior problem occurs during oral reading activities, the teacher should have the student practice the expected behaviors just before oral reading group. If a student tends to interrupt other students while they are reading out loud, the teacher should practice with the student on following along while others read and raising his or her hand to make a comment during an oral reading session. This behavior rehearsal can last 4 or 5 minutes and continue each day until there is improvement in the student's behavior.

Step 5: Strongly reinforce the expected behaviors.

When teaching students to replace inappropriate behavior with an acceptable alternative behavior, it is important that teachers use powerful reinforcement procedures. As Colvin and Sugai (1988) state, ". . . the new behavior will be in competition with the old inappropriate behavior, which has been reinforced intermittently over time. Therefore, to replace this behavior, strong reinforcement must be provided for the expected or replacement behaviors" (p. 12). We recommend the teacher reread Chapter 6, "Using Reinforcement to Increase Student Motivation," to gather ideas on how to increase the power of reinforcement procedures. No matter how a teacher decides to increase the power of reinforcement, it is important to use reinforcers early and frequently to help decrease recurrence of disruptive behavior.

Step 6: Prompting expected behaviors.

Teachers should expect to use extensive prompting procedures to elicit appropriate behavior during early stages of learning. Once placed back into the original learning context, students will have a tendency to fall back into old and inappropriate ways of behaving. Teachers must provide students assistance in behaving in new ways in old contexts. Sprick, Garrison, and Howard (1998) suggest a prompting strategy that has two parts. First, they recommend the teacher reinforce any occurrence of the expected behavior immediately and intensively. Next, they suggest the teacher periodically remind students about the expected behaviors. This reminder should occur throughout the lesson. For example, if the expected behavior is hand raising (as opposed to students calling out answers), the teacher could say, "Class, I'm going to ask you to discuss several important industries in the state of Oregon. Remember to raise your hand to discuss the industries I name."

Teachers must position themselves so they are able to prompt and reinforce difficult social behaviors.

Strategic Use of Neutral Tasks

A strategy to decrease the frequency of persistent behavior problems is to introduce neutral learning tasks in place of an activity that fosters disruptive behavior. Neutral learning activities are those activities not related to the current instructional activity that are moderately easy for the student to complete. Persistent behavior problems are frequently linked to difficult learning tasks. Once these high-risk learning activities are identified, the teacher is in a position to have a set of neutral learning activities available to use when disruptive behavior occurs. The purpose of introducing neutral tasks is to provide the student with an activity not associated with frustration and increase the opportunity for the teacher to establish instructional control.

For example, if a second-grade student becomes verbally noncompliant (e.g., "You can't make me do these problems, and I won't do them no matter what!"), the teacher can alter the sequence of instructional tasks by introducing an activity the student is likely to complete, rather than attempt to force the student to comply with the harder assignment. This approach defuses the situation and increases the probability the student will participate in a learning activity. Neutral tasks are used only as a temporary intervention and in conjunction with other management strategies.

EXAMPLE: USING NEUTRAL TASKS

TEACHER: Yolanda, I want you to read the list of words on the board. First, sound out each word and then say the word quickly. Get ready. [*The teacher points to the first word in the list.*]

STUDENT: [*The student sounds out the word* mast.] Mmmaaassst.

TEACHER: Say the word quickly.

> STUDENT: Mast.
>
> TEACHER: Good. Look at the next word. [*Teacher points to the word* with.]
>
> Get ready to sound it out. [*The teacher points to the word* with.] [*At this point, the student becomes inattentive and starts to talk to another student. The student disregards the teacher's request to read further.*]
>
> TEACHER: [*The teacher presents a neutral learning task, an activity she knows the student can complete successfully.*] Yolanda, listen, I want you to count by 5's to 25, Okay? Get ready. Count.
>
> STUDENT: [*After a brief pause, the student counts by 5's to 25.*]

This counting activity is a neutral task. The student is more likely to comply with the command to count by 5's, because she has been successful in this task before. The teacher should present another counting task before reintroducing the original reading task. If the student responds appropriately, the teacher should reinforce the good work intensively and frequently. An example of a sequence of neutral activities and new learning tasks is presented in Table 9.1.

In this sequence, neutral tasks of 1 minute or less are presented once disruptive behavior occurs. Once the disruptive behavior is eliminated, the original learning task is reintroduced (reading words from the board) with more likelihood of success. The reintroduction of neutral tasks throughout the lesson eases the level of difficulty of the original task for the student. The modified sequence increases the opportunity for the teacher to reinforce students during instruction. It is important to note that when reading is reintroduced, the student reads for about 1 minute. Immediately following that, another counting activity is presented, followed by the reading task for 2 minutes.

Strategic Use of Punishment Strategies

As Figure 9.1 illustrated (on p. 199), punishment strategies are used only after the teacher has exhausted all instructional interventions, careful assessment is completed, and students are taught appropriate alternative behaviors. Punishment can play a significant role in managing persistent behavior. If used properly, punishment will help the teacher regain instructional control while he or she makes further mod-

TABLE 9.1   Task Sequence for Responding to Persistent Problems

Task Sequence and Description	Task Level	Time
Reads words from board	new	3 minutes
Becomes noncompliant	mastered	30 seconds
Counts by 5's	mastered	30 seconds
Counts by 2's	new	1 minute
Reads words on board	mastered	1 minute
Counts by 10's	new	2 minutes
Reads words on board	new	2 minutes

ifications in instruction. We recommend teachers follow four steps when implementing punishment procedures to decrease persistent behavior problems:

Step 1: Is punishment used correctly?

If one or more punishment strategy discussed in Chapter 8 is currently being used, the teacher should evaluate the procedure to make sure it is implemented correctly according to the guidelines outlined in Chapter 8. For example, if verbal reprimands are used to decrease talk-outs, the teacher should use reprimands consistently. However, the teacher must tell the student what the consequence will be for talking-out if the reprimands are to be effective. The teacher must determine if the selected punishment strategy is being implemented in a systematic and consistent fashion.

Step 2: Select another punishment strategy.

The most powerful option a teacher has to eliminate persistent behavior problems is to substitute the current punishment strategy with one that is more powerful. For example, if the owing-time strategy has been used to eliminate student fighting and it has been ineffective, we recommend the teacher select either nonexclusionary or exclusionary time-out as a way to gain better control. As another example, if verbal reprimands are not decreasing out-of-seat behavior of elementary grade students, a more powerful strategy should be selected (e.g., quiet-time, owing-time).

Step 3: Give the new punishment strategy time to work.

It takes considerable time to eliminate persistent behavior problems completely. For example, if owing-time has been selected to decrease coming late to class, it may take a week or two before the student consistently arrives on time.

Step 4: Consider two other punishment strategies.

MANAGING PERSISTENT BEHAVIOR PROBLEMS: FOUR EXAMPLES

In this section, we present four examples of persistent behavior problems teachers often face. Each example is followed by an analysis that describes potential causes of the behavior problem and concludes with several instructional strategies to eliminate the persistent behavior problem.

EXAMPLE: PERSISTENT PROBLEM 1

Setting:	Regular third-grade classroom of 32 children
Context:	Small-group reading instruction
Time:	Friday, 8:30 A.M.
Phase:	Winter (January)
Activity:	Individual oral reading in basal readers

Mr. Coddens is listening to Jewel read. Sitting next to Jewel is Andy, who is following along with his finger and paying attention to every word Jewel is reading. While reading, Jewel makes a decoding error, and before she has a chance to correct her error, Andy
tells Jewel the correct word. Jewel does not like Andy correcting her reading mistake and
starts an argument with Andy, telling him to mind his own business. This problem has
occurred for a couple of weeks and is escalating in frequency and intensity. Mr. Coddens
has ignored Andy and Jewel's arguments in the past, but today he tells Andy to leave the
room and go into the hall until he can behave properly in reading group. Andy stays in
the hallway until reading class is over.

Instructional Analysis of Problem 1

The problem Mr. Coddens faces is not unusual; instead, it's representative of the
kinds of problems that surface in the day-to-day routine of instruction. In this case,
the problem is the result of three general management responses:

1. **Failure to specify and teach rules before instruction.** Mr. Coddens
   failed to clarify the rules and expectations for student correction of errors
   during oral reading. This ambiguity resulted in Andy correcting Jewel's
   reading errors, which is contrary to what Mr. Coddens wants to happen.
2. **Failure to understand and implement a punishment procedure.** Mr.
   Coddens chose to ignore Andy's corrections the first two times they
   occurred but decided to attend to them on the third occasion. In a sense,
   Mr. Coddens gave up on his punishment procedure and attended to the
   problem when it was most intense.
3. **Inappropriate use of punishment procedure.** Mr. Coddens' response
   was his use of exclusionary time-out. The use of time-out appeared excessive for a problem that Mr. Coddens initially chose to ignore.

Instructional Strategies for Prevention of Problem 1

Mr. Coddens could have avoided the problem by applying an instructional classroom
management approach. The following strategies might have been implemented:

1. **Identify and teach rules and instructional routines.** Develop and
   teach a rule for responding to errors during oral reading. For example,
   "When you're following along and you hear an error, raise your hand quietly. Do not yell out, but raise your hand quietly [teacher demonstrates by
   raising his hand] and keep your eyes on the reading. Let's practice following that rule." The teacher demonstrates the rule by role-playing positive
   and negative examples of following the rule.
2. **Determine if task requirements are clear and appropriate.** There are
   two sets of task requirements in this situation. For the reader, the task
   requires the oral reading of words in the basal passage. It is important to
   determine if the oral reading task is too difficult or too easy. If the task is
   too difficult, then oral reading errors will abound and the reader will be
   greatly frustrated. If the task is too easy, the reader may become sloppy

from an eagerness to rush through the reading. For students who are following along, the task requirement is to point to each word and raise a hand when an error is noted. The teacher would then stop at the end of each sentence and ask students to identify any errors that the reader made.

3. **Utilize a precorrection strategy before instruction.** In order to prevent the problem, the teacher should employ a precorrection strategy in which the teacher reviews the rules and expectations for responding to errors during oral reading before the oral reading group is called. The precorrection strategy would have prepared Andy for the oral reading lesson by reviewing the correct way to respond to Jewel's reading errors. This precorrection procedure is easily conducted immediately before the oral reading lesson and requires less than a minute of instruction.

4. **If necessary, change the task requirements.** In some cases, it may be necessary to change the task requirements. In this particular situation, the teacher is requiring students to focus on something negative (i.e., oral reading errors). If the history between Jewel and Andy is such that a negative cycle of interactions is being maintained, then it may be necessary to change the context of their interactions. Instead of requiring Andy to note Jewel's oral reading errors, the teacher would require Andy to note the most difficult word Jewel read correctly. The change in task requirements now reinforces both Andy and Jewel.

EXAMPLE: PERSISTENT PROBLEM 2

Setting: Regular seventh-grade classroom of 25 students

Context: Hallways

Time: Friday, 11:00 A.M.

Phase: Fall (October)

Activity: Transition from one class to the next

Ms. Walton's seventh-grade English class ends with a bell at 11:00 A.M. Ms. Walton always gives her students about 5 minutes before the bell to prepare for the end of class. During this time, students collect their materials, put things away, and, unfortunately, talk and argue. By the time the bell rings, most of the students are overly boisterous. When the noise and disruption start to get out of hand, Ms. Walton verbally reprimands the students. The students usually respond to the bell by running into the hall to continue their talking and arguing. Ms. Walton uses the time between classes to prepare for her next class, but this is difficult, as students are usually noisy, uncooperative, and disruptive. Several of Ms. Walton's students are frequently late to the next class because of chaos in the halls. When students are late, the teacher usually tells the students not to be late again. Ms. Walton's students are considered the worst offenders at the 11:00 a.m. break. The situation has gotten so disruptive that the principal met with Ms. Walton and asked her to eliminate the hallway disruption. Prior to the meeting, Ms. Walton spoke with her class several times about the problems they were creating in the hallway and told them to "stop acting like a bunch of third graders." Ms. Walton even required several students to stay after school for disruptive hallway behavior. However, none of these interventions has eliminated the persistent disruptive behavior.

Instructional Analysis of Problem 2

Many junior and senior high schools face the problem of disruptive behavior in hallways between classes. This management problem is often persistent and escalates as the school year progresses. Casual approaches to its management are almost always ineffective. The problem is the result of three instructional/management decisions made by Ms. Walton and the school principal:

1. **Failure to structure the last 5 minutes of class and failure to teach transition behavior in the hallways.** One of Ms. Walton's critical mistakes was how she organized the last 5 minutes of class. Students were already disruptive before they left the classroom, and the disruptive behavior escalated once the students were in the hallway going to the next class. In addition, students were running from the classroom immediately after the bell. Ms. Walton should have established better instructional control by requiring students to wait for her to dismiss them. Ms. Walton could withhold dismissal until students were in control. Exercising control and order during the initial stages of transition prevents disruptive behavior, which is easier than stopping it.

2. **Failure to articulate clearly to the students the expected behavior in the hallways.** The feedback students received was erratic and reactive. Students were never provided a clear explanation of what was expected of them when they passed from class to class. Neither Ms. Walton nor the principal provided clear and consistent rules for behaving in the hallways. When students were fooling around in the hallway and late for class, there was no consistent reprimand made from anyone.

3. **Use of reactive approaches to management.** The entire management system was reactive and punitive. Ms. Walton failed to provide consistent reinforcement when students behaved properly in the hallway. Without a school-wide discipline plan for all teachers to discuss with students, there was no consistent response to disruptive behavior throughout the school. (See Chapter 10 for a complete discussion of a school-wide management plan.)

Instructional Strategies for Prevention of Problem 2

This problem could have been avoided if Ms. Walton had instituted a proactive management strategy in her classroom and if the principal had instituted a school-wide plan for monitoring hallways between classes:

1. **Structure the last 5 minutes of class.** One of the major problems was that students in Ms. Walton's class were disruptive before they left her class. One strategy for preventing the hallway problem is to use the last 5 minutes for an activity that can be better managed to make sure all students were following classroom rules at the bell. It would then be much easier for Ms. Walton to ensure that her students would leave her room and enter the hallway quietly.

Effective use of instructional classroom management extends into the hallways of the school.

2. **Identify specific rules for behavior in the hallways and have students practice transition behavior.** Ms. Walton should discuss with her students the problems they are causing in the hallways between classes. Next, she should identify a clear list of acceptable behaviors in the hallways and a list of unacceptable ones. Ms. Walton should then use class time to have students practice passing from class to class until they can do it appropriately.

3. **Use a precorrection strategy immediately preceding the end of each class.** Once students have had an opportunity to practice passing classes, Ms. Walton should use part of the last 5 minutes of class to review what is expected of them in the hall. She should be very specific about behaviors that are acceptable while passing classes (e.g., quiet talking) and those that are not (e.g., running, pushing, shoving). Also, Ms. Walton should present clearly articulated consequences for disruptive behavior and for arriving late to the next class. This precorrection strategy can be completed in less than a minute and should be implemented each day until students begin to follow the established rules. Ms. Walton should review the precorrection strategy about once a week, so that students do not fall back into bad habits.

4. **Monitor behavior closely and increase reinforcement for following rules.** Two important aspects of managing hallway behavior are to monitor the behavior of students while they are passing between classes and deliver reinforcement as they improve their performance. Unless the hallway behavior is monitored, reinforcement contingent on performance can't be reliably delivered. Ms. Walton should expect to leave her classroom during the 11:00 A.M. break and monitor her students as best she can. Other teachers must be willing to take positions in the hallway to help monitor students to guard against escalation of disruptive behavior. Teachers must also increase the level and intensity of reinforcement for

students who follow the rules while going from one class to the next. In fact, Ms. Walton should start the reinforcement process as soon as she dismisses students and they are leaving the classroom. She should position herself at the door to praise students who walk to the door in a quiet and orderly fashion and to monitor their behavior in the hallways. This reinforcement strategy should be used each day and should become part of the teacher's instructional routine.

5. **Establish consistent use of discipline procedures.** Ms. Walton, along with the other teachers in the school, should institute specific consequences for hallway misbehavior. In Chapter 10, we provide the details of how to conceptualize and implement school-wide discipline policies.

EXAMPLE: PERSISTENT PROBLEM 3

Setting:	Resource room for students with mild learning/behavior problems
Context:	Spelling class, 8 students
Time:	Monday, 9:00 A.M.
Phase:	Fall (October)
Activity:	Students are completing independent spelling exercises

Juan is a fifth grader who has been receiving special education services in a resource room for students with mild learning and behavior problems. Juan has academic problems in reading (i.e., he still has difficulty sounding out phonetically regular words). His performance is lowest and his behavior is most unmanageable during spelling. Ms. Wang, his resource room teacher, organized her spelling lesson so that students would practice writing the assigned spelling words each day (usually four new words per day) and complete spelling exercises from a spelling book used in the regular fifth-grade classroom.

Ms. Wang, as part of her management routine, allows students to go to a free-time area and choose an activity once they have completed their work. This routine is followed daily except Friday, when students are required to take a spelling test in the regular classroom. During spelling class, Juan does not pay attention to directions and rarely finishes his assignment. He wanders around the room when other students are in the free-time area, and he picks fights with other students.

Juan is under the care of a pediatrician who has placed him on Ritalin to control aggressive behavior and hyperactivity. Ms. Wang had recommended to Juan's parents that he needed help to control his social and academic behavior. Ms. Wang has several classroom strategies to respond to Juan's inappropriate behaviors, including ignoring his daydreaming. She does not call on Juan or attend to his inactivity. Once Juan attends to his spelling work, Ms. Wang tries to get him involved in the lesson by calling on him to answer a question. To manage his wandering behavior, Ms. Wang reprimands Juan when he gets out of his seat without permission (e.g., "Juan, get back to your desk. You know the rules!"). Juan gets into frequent fights when he wanders around the room, and Ms. Wang sometimes has him stay after school for 30 minutes. Ms. Wang spends this 30 minutes talking to Juan about the importance of getting along with other students and not fighting. During these discussions, Juan is responsive to Ms. Wang's concern. However, Ms. Wang is discouraged by Juan's continuing problems in class, and she is not sure what to do next.

Instructional Analysis of Problem 3

The persistent problems described in this example—inattention, failure to follow rules, and fighting—are typical of students who are placed in instructional programs that are too difficult and in classrooms with loosely defined rules. When students have several persistent behavior problems, the teacher should: (a) establish a plan to control the behavior that is most disruptive and potentially destructive (e.g., fighting), (b) determine the sources of the disruptive behavior by assessing the instructional context quickly, and (c) modify the instructional program to prevent problems. In spite of the fact that Juan presents multiple problems, Ms. Wang must consider instructional solutions for managing his learning and behavior problems effectively. She could not control Juan's disruptive behavior for the following reasons:

1. **Failure to place Juan in the appropriate spelling activity and provide instructional support.** A likely cause of Juan's inattention during spelling is that the assigned tasks are too difficult. Requiring students to copy and memorize four new spelling words per day is a daunting task for low-performing students. In addition, Juan's reading problems should have alerted Ms. Wang that Juan needs spelling instruction that teaches him phonetically regular words first. In addition, Ms. Wang's decision to ignore Juan's inattentiveness is inappropriate, because it is likely other more powerful reinforcers (e.g., getting out of the assignment, other students attending to his inattentive behavior) are maintaining his inappropriate behavior. Students who are inattentive are often unaware they are daydreaming and not tracking the lesson. In Juan's case, the teacher's ignoring provides no instruction in how to attend to the spelling lesson.

2. **Failure to monitor student behavior consistently and with a plan.** Ms. Wang has organized her classroom to allow students to get out of their seats without permission when they complete their spelling assignments. She rarely monitors the work of all students to ensure they have completed their work. Consequently, Juan is receiving mixed messages. He is learning that students don't have to follow the rules, because the teacher does not monitor student behavior.

3. **Failure to provide clear expectations about rules and routines during the spelling session.** Because students are not taught spelling skills and are not monitored carefully when they are practicing these skills independently, students' interactions in the classroom often occur randomly. In these situations, Juan often acts impulsively, which sometimes causes a fight with another student.

4. **Failure to manage Juan's fighting proactively and provide specific and consistent consequences.** Ms. Wang has not dealt consistently with Juan's frequent fighting. Although she has a consequence in place (30 minutes after school), it is not immediate and is used infrequently. Juan is learning that he can create a major disruption with few consequences. Because Juan is poorly equipped to perform in the spelling class, he is perhaps insecure during class. Inconsistent use of punishment is nearly always ineffective with students like Juan. In addition, Ms. Wang should not use the after-school time as a discussion session, for this may reinforce Juan's behavior.

Instructional Strategies for Prevention of Problem 3

The problems described in this example are typical of those teachers have with students who are performing well below grade level in several areas. The fact that Juan's spelling problems are related to his reading problem should not be ignored. Problems ensue when a student is placed in a lesson where he or she cannot compete and learn, as evidenced by Juan's behavior in spelling class. An outline of one approach to manage Juan's persistent behavior problems is provided below.

1. **Develop a plan to control Juan's fighting.** Ms. Wang should choose a punishment strategy to eliminate Juan's fighting immediately. The owing-time strategy or time-out from positive reinforcement are acceptable alternatives to her present approach. It is critical that all students are told the consequences for fighting and that a consequence is administered *each* time a fight occurs. In addition, Ms. Wang should reorganize her spelling lesson to increase her positive interactions with Juan. Increasing the reinforcement frequency is as important as using the punishment strategy consistently.

2. **Place students appropriately and reorganize the spelling lesson to increase success of students.** The spelling session, as it is presently organized, is not conducive to successful learning. Once Ms. Wang places the students in the proper level of the spelling program, she should break the 25-minute lesson into three parts: (a) group instruction on critical spelling skills (10 minutes), (b) independent written spelling assignment carefully monitored by the teacher (10 minutes), and (c) a structured group activity to check written assignments or quiz new spelling words orally (5 minutes). This lesson structure allows for increased positive interactions and increases teacher feedback.

3. **Structure teaching activities to increase Juan's attention.** Once Juan and other students are placed in the spelling program appropriately, Juan can be taught to increase his attention to the task. Ms. Wang should first teach Juan to attend to an easy or neutral task, rather than spelling, because this is too difficult for him. Ms. Wang might use a math task that is easy for Juan, such as number identification or skip counting. As Juan responds, Ms. Wang should reinforce him for *attending*. In the process, Juan is being taught to manage his time and complete sections of a task before moving on. In addition, Ms. Wang should choose a powerful reinforcer for Juan for attending to his work and completing spelling activities.

EXAMPLE: PERSISTENT PROBLEM 4

Setting: Elementary school

Context: All unmonitored areas (e.g., hallways, playground, bathrooms)

Time: Throughout the entire day

Phase: Spring (April)

Activity: All unmonitored activities (e.g., hall passing, free-time, boarding buses)

A day does not go by without fights, arguments, and general disruptive behavior in an unsupervised area in Monroe Elementary School. Fighting occurs most frequently in hallways, restrooms, and the bus boarding area. Teachers have no standard school policy for handling these problems, and each teacher handles student disputes in unsupervised areas differently. After breaking up a fight, one teacher might verbally reprimand the students, another requires the students to stay after school, and another has the offending students report to the principal. Each teacher simply chooses a consequence for the disruption on the spur of the moment. The frequency of fighting and other forms of disruptive behavior have increased throughout the year at Monroe Elementary School.

Instructional Analysis of Problem 4

The problem at Monroe Elementary School is one that occurs frequently in schools that do not have a coordinated policy and approach for monitoring and managing student behavior in all areas of the school. In this section, we identify three problems that contribute to persistent fighting at Monroe Elementary School:

1. **Inadequate monitoring of unsupervised areas in the school.** Persistent fighting and disruptions at Monroe are most frequent in unsupervised areas. Although every area in the building can't be monitored at all times, it is clear that certain areas (e.g., hallways, bathrooms) elicit most of the problems and require immediate adult supervision.
2. **Lack of consequences for disruptive behavior.** Because of the lack of consistent monitoring, many incidents of disruptive behavior were not handled at all by the staff. Discipline was not administered quickly and fairly at Monroe School, and students learned if they fought in unsupervised areas, they would not be caught.
3. **Failure to establish a school-wide management program for Monroe Elementary School.** The most significant shortcoming of the school's response to fighting and disruptive behavior was the lack of a school-wide discipline policy. This fostered inconsistent management of unsupervised areas.

Instructional Strategies for Prevention of Problem 4

A school-wide policy provides a coordinated approach for managing students in all areas of the school. An effective policy defines the behaviors that are prohibited at school, provides a plan for how unsupervised areas of the school will be monitored, and establishes a set of consequences for fighting and other forms of disruptive behavior. This policy would also include parents in the management of students with more severe forms of disruptive behavior. Chapter 10, which includes examples of school-wide discipline policies, provides a complete discussion on how to establish procedures for managing the behavior of students throughout the school, including: (a) details of how a school can develop a mission statement, (b) policies for consistent discipline of students, and (c) the roles that teachers, parents, and principals play in a school-wide management program.

The Learning Activity presented here involves developing an example of and providing an instructional analysis of a persistent behavior problem.

Learning Activity

Develop an Example of a Persistent Problem and Provide an Instructional Analysis

Purpose of Activity

To understand the factors that contribute to persistent behavior problems:

Step 1: Following the format in this chapter, develop an example of a persistent behavior problem in a classroom. Include a complete description of the problem by indicating the frequency, when it typically occurs, how the teacher has attempted to manage it, and the school context of the behavior problem.

Step 2: Provide an instructional analysis of the problem. Identify and discuss three to five instructional and classroom-based factors that may be contributing to the behavior problem. Explain how each factor contributes to the behavior of the student.

Step 3: Develop three to five instructional solutions for the behavior problem and discuss why each solution should be effective in managing the persistent problem. Identify and discuss any disadvantages of the instructional solution.

Step 4: Present your persistent behavior problem to the class and ask students to develop their own instructional analysis. Compare analyses and discuss effective ways the teacher can manage this behavior problem.

SUMMARY

In this chapter, we presented a model for teachers in designing proactive management for persistent behavior problems. The model includes procedures for assessment of persistent behavior problems, as well as ideas for modifying classroom organization, evaluating task dimensions, and reinforcing positive student performance. We also presented precorrection strategies, presentation of neutral tasks, and use of punishment procedures. We provided an instructional analysis and instructional strategies for prevention of four different behavior problems.

CHAPTER ACTIVITIES

1. Discuss the model for managing persistent behavior problems that was presented in this chapter. Be sure to list each component of the model and discuss the role each plays in managing persistent behavior problems.
2. Ask a teacher to describe a persistent behavior problem that he or she is having in the classroom. From this description, list and discuss the instructional strategies that would be used to prevent this type of behavior problem.
3. Following the format used in this chapter, develop an example of a persistent behavior problem. Include a complete description of the problem, an

instructional analysis, and a list of instructional strategies for prevention. Have other students develop their own instructional analysis and instructional strategies for prevention for your persistent behavior problem.

REFERENCES

Coie, J. (1994). Early adolescent disorder from childhood aggression and peer rejection. *Journal of Consulting & Clinical Psychology, 60,* 783–792.

Colvin, G., & Sugai, G. (1988). Proactive strategies for managing social behavior problems: An instructional approach. *Education and Treatment of Children, 11,* 341–348.

Colvin, G., Sugai, G., Good, R., & Lee, Y. (1997). Using active supervision and pre-correction to improve transition behaviors in an elementary school. *School Psychology Quarterly, 12,* 344–363.

Deutsch-Smith, D., & Pedrotty-Rivera, D. (1995). Discipline in special education and general education settings. *Focus on Exceptional Children, 27,* 1–14.

Johnson, D. W., & Johnson, R. T. (1996). Peacemakers: Teaching students to resolve their own and schoolmates' conflicts. *Focus on Exceptional Children, 28,* 1–11.

Kamps, D., & Tankersley, M. (1996). Prevention of behavioral and conduct disorders: Trends and research issues. *Behavioral Disorders, 22,* 41–48.

Keel, M., Dangel, H., & Owens, S. (1999). Selecting instructional interventions for students with mild disabilities in inclusive classrooms. *Focus on Exceptional Children, 31,* 1–16.

Lewis, T. J., & Sugai, G. (1996). Functional assessment of problem behavior: A pilot investigation of the comparative and interactive effects of teacher and peer social attention on students in general education settings. *School Psychology Quarterly, 11,* 1–19.

Mehring, T., & Colson, S. (1990). Motivation and mildly handicapped learners. *Focus on Exceptional Learners, 22,* 1–14.

Sprick, R., Garrison, M., & Howard, L. (1998). *CHAMPS: A proactive and positive approach to classroom management.* Longmont, CO: Sopris West.

Sugai, G., & Lewis, T. (1999). Effective behavior support: A systems approach to proactive school wide management. *Focus on Exceptional Children, 31,* 1–24.

Walker, H., Horner, R. H., Sugai, G., Bullis, M., Sprague, J. R., Bricker, D., Kaufman, M. J. (1996). Integrated approaches to preventing antisocial behavior patterns among school-age children and youth. *Journal of Emotional and Behavioral Disorders, 4,* 193–256.

School-Wide Discipline and Instructional Classroom Management: A Systems Approach

George Sugai • Shanna Hagan-Burke • Teri Lewis-Palmer
University of Oregon

OVERVIEW

- An Instructional Approach to School-Wide Discipline
  Continuum of Behavior Support
  Systems Approach to School-Wide Discipline
  Establishing Effective, Efficient, and Relevant Host Environments

- Components of a School-Wide Discipline System
  School Purpose Statement
  School-Wide Behavior Expectations
  Teaching Behavioral Expectations
  Continuum of Procedures for Encouraging Expectations
  Continuum of Procedures for Discouraging Rule Violations
  Procedures for Monitoring the Effectiveness of the School-Wide Discipline Plan

- Implementation of School-Wide Discipline System Within the 180-Day Plan
  Before Implementation
  During Implementation
  After Implementation

- Summary

- Chapter Activities

For teachers to be successful in their sustained use of effective classroom instructional and behavior management practices, school-wide supports must be considered. Events between students and staff members, on the bus and playground, and in the restrooms, hallways, cafeteria, and library have significant impact on school climate and the effectiveness of instructional management in the classroom. Expectations about appropriate conduct, routines for accomplishing school-wide tasks and activities, procedures for handling major rule violations, and active supervision in nonclassroom areas must be taught, practiced, encouraged, and monitored, even within the classroom setting.

Most schools implement some sort of school-wide discipline program to enable staff members to respond to rule-violating behavior. However, this minimum level of discipline may be insufficient at both the school-wide and classroom levels; a more appropriate approach focuses on the school-wide prevention of problem behavior and the provision of support for instructional and behavior management in the classroom. Discipline is a collection of overt procedures and routines designed and implemented to enhance and support students' academic and social success. School-wide discipline has multiple functions: (a) teach and promote positive behavioral expectations, (b) inhibit or discourage rule-violating behavior, and (c) create a culture of competence in which communications and expectations are effective, efficient, and relevant.

In this chapter, we describe elements of an effective school-wide discipline system and highlight the important relationship between school-wide and classroom management. We underscore the need for an instructional approach (as described throughout this book) to school-wide management and describe the necessary components and implementation features of successful school-wide discipline systems.

AN INSTRUCTIONAL APPROACH TO SCHOOL-WIDE DISCIPLINE

Schools have clear and specific procedures and consequences for dealing with displays of student problem behavior. When problem behavior occurs, the response consists of a range of actions and consequences. On the first infraction, students are reminded of what is expected, their parents are contacted, future consequences are emphasized, and verbal reprimands are given. When problem behavior continues or escalates, schools respond by increasing the intensity of disciplinary consequences. Loss of privileges shifts to in-school detention that escalates to out-of-school suspension if the behavior recurs. Reacting to problem behavior is a natural response because it produces an immediate decrease (relief) in problem behavior (Gunter, Denny, Jack, Shores, & Nelson, 1993; Gunter, Jack, DePaepe, Reed, & Harrison, 1994; Gunter, Jack, Shores, Carrel, & Flowers, 1993; Jack et al., 1996; Shores et al., 1993; Wehby, Dodge, Valente, & Conduct Problems Prevention Research Group, 1993; Wehby, Symons, & Canale, 1998; Wehby, Symons, & Shores, 1995). When discipline measures are used alone in response to chronic problem behaviors, decreases in the behaviors are often temporary, and in some cases problem behaviors increase in intensity and frequency (Alberto & Troutman, 1999; Mayer, Butterworth, Nafpaktitis, & Sulzer-Azaroff, 1983; Skiba & Peterson, 1999; Wolery, Bailey, & Sugai, 1988).

A less natural but more effective response is to emphasize an instructional approach that stresses prevention of problem behavior: (a) primary prevention of the acquisition of problem behavior, (b) secondary prevention of the recurrence of problem behavior, and (c) tertiary prevention of the worsening of problem behavior (Walker et al., 1996). This instructional approach is characterized by formal efforts to identify, develop, teach, and encourage prosocial behavioral expectations for all students and all staff and in all school settings (Colvin, Kame'enui, & Sugai, 1993; Lewis & Sugai, 1999; Lewis, Sugai, & Colvin, 1998; Mayer, 1998; Nelson & Colvin, 1996; Nelson, Martella, & Galand, 1998; Sprick, Sprick, & Garrison, 1992; Sugai & Horner, 1999).

Features and procedures of an instructional approach to school-wide discipline are characterized in this chapter. In this approach, a balanced integration of four important elements of school-wide discipline must be emphasized. First, schools must specify clear and measurable outcomes that give priority and meaning to academic achievement and social competence. The development of interventions and the evaluation of progress are difficult if specific outcomes are not indicated. Second, schools must use data to guide decision making relative to the (a) selection and modification of curricula and practices, (b) evaluation of student progress, and (c) enhancement of systems fidelity of implementation. Third, evidence-based prac-

FIGURE 10.1 Four elements of an instructional approach to school-wide discipline.

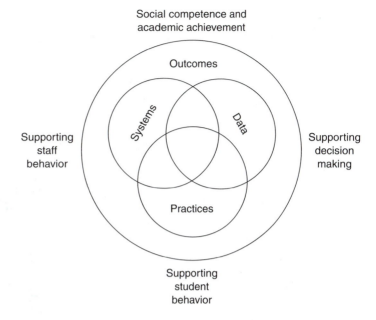

tices that have a high probability of achieving desired student outcomes must be identified, adopted, and implemented. Finally, systems must be established that support adult adoption, high fidelity implementation, and sustained use of effective practices. Figure 10.1 illustrates these four elements and their relationship to one another.

Continuum of Behavior Support

An instructional approach to school-wide discipline also emphasizes the importance of matching the intensity of the intervention or instructional programming to the intensity of the problem behavior. Schools sometimes make the mistake of developing general, low-level interventions (e.g., posting and reading of school rules) to control serious vandalism, truancy, and violence. The result is no change in these high-intensity behaviors and an abandonment of the intervention. The intervention may be a sound choice for preventing new students from engaging in those behaviors, but more intensive interventions (e.g., individualized contracts, increased adult active supervision) are needed for the students who are engaging in the problem behaviors.

An effective school-wide discipline program can and should benefit a broad range of students with varying behavioral needs within a variety of contexts, including classrooms. Sugai and Horner (1999) described a continuum of positive behavior support to demonstrate how schools can match the intensity of their intervention efforts with the intensity of students' problem behaviors (see Figure 10.2). This continuum of support is comprised of the three levels of prevention and intervention described previously.

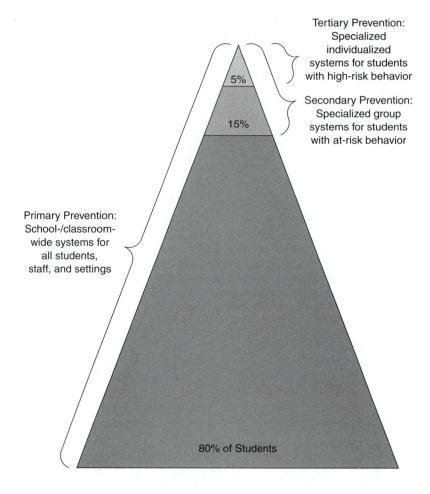

FIGURE 10.2 A continuum of behavioral support.

Tertiary Prevention:
Specialized
individualized
systems for students
with high-risk behavior

Secondary Prevention:
Specialized group
systems for students
with at-risk behavior

Primary Prevention:
School-/classroom-
wide systems for
all students,
staff, and settings

5%

15%

80% of Students

Primary or universal interventions. Universal interventions include general school-wide discipline and classroom management practices that prevent the development of inappropriate social behavior and promote the development of prosocial skills. Because universal interventions function to prevent problem behaviors, they are positive and proactive and utilize an instructional approach to the management of student behaviors. This instructional focus allows schools to avoid an overreliance on reactive and punitive responses to problem behaviors. Universal interventions target all students and are typically effective with approximately 80% of a school's student population (Colvin, Kame'enui, & Sugai, 1993; Colvin, Sugai, Good, & Lee, 1997; Gresham, Sugai, & Horner, 2001; Langland, Lewis-Palmer, & Sugai, 1998; Lewis et al., 1998; Taylor-Green et al., 1997).

Secondary prevention or group-based interventions. Some students (about 15%) require more than universal school-wide and classroom interventions because they present risk factors (e.g., disability, poverty, dysfunctional family) associated with school failure. These students need interventions that (a) are function based (communicative purpose of problem behavior), (b) increase adult monitoring and supervision, (c) provide greater numbers of opportunities to receive positive reinforcement, (d) enhance academic engagement and social behavior success, and (e) remove opportunities to engage in problem behavior. These interventions can be administered uniformly to all at-risk students, increasing efficiency and relevance of the intervention programming. Logically, effective universal interventions must be in place for a school to accurately identify those students who require more intensive and specialized secondary prevention efforts.

Tertiary or individualized interventions.   Often, a relatively small proportion of students (about 5%) account for the majority of behavior problems within a school (Colvin, Kame'enui, & Sugai, 1993; Gottfredson, Gottfredson, & Hybl, 1993; Nelson, 1996; Sugai & Horner, 1994; Tobin, Sugai, & Colvin, 1996). These students present intensive problem behavior challenges that are largely unresponsive to primary and secondary prevention efforts and require individually designed and implemented behavior interventions and support plans. Tobin and her colleagues (1996) examined 5 years of school discipline referral data and identified a small number of students (n = 18) that exhibited chronic problem behaviors and were referred at least once during each term of 3 years of middle school. Likewise, Gottfredson et al., (1993) found that 10% of the students in one school were responsible for 45% of the office referrals generated in one school year. By utilizing a school-wide systems approach to behavior management and providing a continuum of behavior support, students who require more intensive, individualized interventions are identified more readily. The continuum allows schools to be more efficient with their time and increases the likelihood their efforts will be effective.

Schools quickly discover that having an effective school-wide discipline system and continuum of behavior support in place supports classroom management efforts designed to address a range of student needs. Many aspects of general classroom management systems are designed to affect all students within that setting, but more intensive classroom-based interventions are needed for students who display behaviors unresponsive to secondary and tertiary prevention interventions. Schools must understand that school-wide discipline systems are important elements of a continuum of behavior supports. School-wide discipline procedures are universal prevention interventions that are presented to all students to (a) foster prosocial behavior, (b) maximize opportunities for teaching and academic achievement, and (c) inhibit occurrences of problem behavior.

A relatively small number of students (1–15%) have learning histories that cause general school-wide interventions to be ineffective for them, and these students require additional specialized and individualized interventions (Sugai & Horner, 1999–2000). School-wide discipline systems should not be abandoned because these students are unresponsive, but schools should instead think of school-wide discipline systems as being important foundations for (a) supporting the majority of students, (b) preventing development of chronic problem behavior for students with high-risk backgrounds and learning histories, and (c) identifying and providing more specialized and individualized behavior supports for students with high-intensity problem behaviors.

Systems Approach to School-Wide Discipline

An instructional approach and a continuum of behavior support are necessary but insufficient. Schools must also consider multisystem implementation efforts. All students and staff should be involved in school-wide efforts to improve school climate and implement an instructional approach to discipline in all school settings. This effort is the foundation for discipline-related activities in the classroom, in nonclassroom settings, and with individual student behavior-support programming. For example, staff members know that peer conflicts in the hallway carry over into classrooms, that academic failure or frustration during instruction affects the quality of transitions onto the playground, and that serious behavior of one student can disrupt the teaching and learning of an entire classroom. A multisystem effort (see Figure 10.3) applies classroom management practices and procedures to school-wide discipline processes and emphasizes appropriate behavior on the playground and in hallways, as well as in the classroom.

School-wide system.   A school-wide support system consists of "those structures and procedures that involve and affect all students, all settings, and all staff" (Sugai & Horner, 1999, p. 15). Universal interventions are implemented on a school-wide basis. Sugai and Horner (1999) suggested that when a large proportion of a school's students is unsuccessful across a range of behavioral contexts, it is an indication that the school-wide system is not functioning correctly. The authors indicated that when the school-wide system is functioning properly: (a) students can describe acceptable and unacceptable forms of behavior, (b) teachers and administrators agree on definitions of common school rules, and (c) rules and expectations are enforced consistently.

FIGURE 10.3   Systems of school-wide discipline.

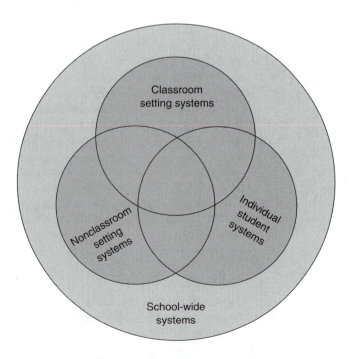

Nonclassroom system. A nonclassroom system of behavioral support is comprised of procedures and structures that address unique noninstructional contexts and involve all students and staff (e.g., hallways, cafeterias, playground). Interventions for nonclassroom settings are designed to address the unique features of a specific setting/context within a school and often emphasize active supervision practices. These interventions address architectural features that create frustrating barriers or demands or a lack of clearly specified routines for students and staff in those contexts (Colvin et al., 1997; DePry & Sugai, 2002; Kartub, Taylor-Greene, March, & Horner, 2000; Lewis & Garrison-Harrell, 1999; Nelson, Colvin, & Smith, 1996; Todd, Horner, Sugai, & Sprague, 1999). Nonclassroom interventions may be universal by focusing on prevention on the part of all students. On the other hand, nonclassroom interventions may be targeted toward groups of a few students who fail to benefit from universal interventions and are in need of more support in nonclassroom settings.

Individual student system. A relatively small number (1–5%) of students are unresponsive to universal and targeted group interventions and experience difficulties across a range of school-wide, nonclassroom, and classroom contexts. These students have intensive needs that require individualized and specialized support. Individualized student systems focus on gathering information about the contexts in which a student's problem behaviors occur and the purpose these behaviors serve with respect to outcomes (functional-based behavior support planning) (O'Neill, Horner, Albin, Storey, & Sprague, 1997; Sugai & Horner, 1999–2000; Sugai, Lewis-Palmer, & Hagan-Burke, 1999–2000). That information is used to develop an individualized behavioral intervention plan to address a student's ability to succeed across a variety of school settings and situations.

Classroom system. The classroom system is comprised of procedures and interventions designed to affect student behaviors within classrooms (Colvin & Lazar, 1997; Paine, Radicchi, Rosellini, Deutchman, & Darch, 1983). Most of this book is designed to enhance a school's classroom system of behavioral support, and as such, instructional classroom management is often the vehicle for (a) *universal interventions* directed toward all students in the class, (b) *target group interventions* that are focused on supporting students "at risk" for social and academic failure, and (c) *individual student interventions* that emphasize specialized and high-intensity efforts for students who failed to benefit from universal and group-based approaches.

This chapter presents the role of instructional classroom management within the context of a school-wide discipline system. This systems approach allows teachers to access a school's continuum of behavior support and provides different systems to channel intervention efforts toward implementation efficiency and high likelihood of student success.

Establishing Effective, Efficient, and Relevant Host Environments

Taken together, a prevention focus, a continuum of behavior supports, and a multi-system approach contribute to the development of an effective, efficient, and relevant school-wide system of discipline or positive behavior support. However, essential to achieving this outcome is establishment of a clearly developed supportive or "host environment" (Zins & Ponti, 1990). Sugai and colleagues have argued that the problem isn't that we don't have a documented technology to respond to the challenges of student problem behavior; the problem is that we haven't been able to "fit" the technology to the unique problem context that characterized each school (Lewis & Sugai, 1999; Sugai & Horner, 1999; Sugai, et al., 2000).

To achieve effective host environments that support adoption and sustained use of evidence-based practices, a number of important system features should be considered: active administrative support, overt staff agreements and participation, local behavioral competence within the school, and team-based action planning and implementation.

Administrative support.   Endorsement and active support of a school administrator is essential to a systems approach to discipline and positive behavior support. Sugai and Horner explain, "Although a team of teachers can accomplish many tasks, someone must have the capacity to make important decisions related to funding, schedules, personnel roles and functions, resource allocations, and so on. These kinds of decisions usually rest with a building administrator (i.e., principal or assistant principal)" (1999, p. 17). Colvin and Sprick (1999) examined the role of administrators in the development and implementation of comprehensive school-wide discipline planning and identified 10 "critical activities" required of administrators to effect change in school, and concluded that administrators are critical to:

1. Maintaining policy (i.e., carefully leading staff toward innovations that have a high probability of creating a positive effect). "The principal serves as a gatekeeper for establishing, administering, and maintaining standards" (p. 67).
2. Making public statements of support for the school-wide discipline effort.
3. Establishing a leadership team to lead the process.

Administrative support is a key feature of a school-wide behavior plan.

4. Supporting team members by acknowledging their efforts, being sensitive to their workload, and allocating time for their meetings and tasks.
5. Guiding decision making by having clear and agreed-upon processes for staff to reach decisions.
6. Taking a leadership role in problem solving, which doesn't mean taking over but rather stepping in and leading a group to a workable solution.
7. Supporting team meetings with regular attendance.
8. Recognizing staff members and the team for their progress.
9. Providing ongoing information to key school groups (e.g., site council, student council, parent organizations) about the school-wide discipline effort.
10. Monitoring implementation activities and providing feedback.

Collegial agreements and commitments. Unless staff members as a group agree to acknowledge and participate in a school-wide effort, fidelity of implementation often suffers and outcomes are lessened. Colvin, Kame'enui, and Sugai (1993) explained that collegial commitment to change and participation is a fundamental feature of a proactive school-wide discipline program. When all staff members are committed to an active and accurate implementation of school-wide discipline policies, practices, and processes, a predictable and consistent school climate (host environment) is established for students, staff, and family members. Nelson and Colvin (1996) argued that the type of school environment that promotes the social development of children is relatively easy to identify. "The worst outcomes are achieved in environments that are either harsh and punitive in nature, or inconsistent in their expectations of child behavior and its consequences. The best outcomes are achieved when the environment is predictable, consistent, well-organized, and safe" (Nelson & Colvin, 1996, p. 172).

Local behavioral competence. Practices, routines, and procedures of school-wide discipline are for naught if individuals within the school lack the conceptual knowledge and technical skills to implement them. Schools can ask outside consultants or specialists to provide this competence, but lack of access, limited availability, and poor response times are significant drawbacks. Schools should cultivate overt behavioral competence inside the school and within the staff. At least two individuals should have this behavioral competence in order to ensure sustainability when staff members join and leave the school.

Consistent with this book, behavioral competence also encompasses skills related to (a) selecting, adopting, and modifying evidence-based practices and curricula; (b) assessing the strengths and limitations of the school-wide discipline system; (c) arranging for the most efficient implementation of school discipline practices and processes; (d) collecting and evaluating progress data to determine adequacy of progress; (e) establishing and facilitating implementation of behavior support systems for students who are unresponsive to universal interventions; and (f) reinforcing linkages of school-wide discipline, classroom management, active supervision in nonclassroom settings, and specialized behavior supports for individual students.

Team-based approach. The last fundamental feature of a competent host environment is a team-based approach to action planning and implementation (Todd,

Horner, Sugai, & Colvin, 1999; Todd, Horner, Sugai, & Sprague, 1999). Promoting and sustaining appropriate student discipline is too large a task for any one person in a school, regardless of his or her role. A "team" of staff members must be assembled to lead school-wide discipline efforts. This does not mean school-wide discipline comes only from or is implemented by the team. All staff must actively support and participate in the process to promote meaningful and sustained change in student behavior. As Nelson and Colvin (1996) explained, while the committee directs and guides the school-wide discipline process, it needs to be a combined effort with staff at all levels working together.

Membership of a team should be considered carefully and should be representative of the larger staff. Many schools accomplish this with representation of at least one team member from each grade level. In addition to classroom teachers, team members might be counselors, school psychologists, teaching assistants, special educators, hall monitors, security officers, parents, and janitors. High schools organized by department may find departmental representation (e.g., science, language arts, physical education) more functional than grade-level representation. Administrative representation is again essential, and someone (e.g., principal or vice-principal) with authority to make administrative decisions must be on the team. Other aspects of a school environment can and should be represented. For example, team members may not understand fully all factors associated with problem behaviors in the gymnasium (or cafeteria) without input from a staff member directly involved with that setting. The main idea is that school-wide discipline teams should be comprised of individuals who, as a group, are familiar with a broad range of situations in which students are expected to display appropriate behaviors.

COMPONENTS OF A SCHOOL-WIDE DISCIPLINE SYSTEM

A school-wide discipline system provides a necessary structure for supporting increased appropriate social behaviors and inhibiting displays of rule-violating behaviors. The overall goal is to establish a positive school climate that supports and maximizes teaching and learning outcomes for all students, staff, and family members in all school settings, including individual classrooms. A school-wide discipline system is more than reacting to problem behavior. Building a school-wide discipline system requires careful attention to six components: (a) purpose statement, (b) school-wide behavior expectations, (c) procedures for teaching those school-wide behavior expectations, (d) continuum of procedures for encouraging expectations, (e) continuum of procedures for discouraging rule-violating behavior, and (f) progress-monitoring system (Colvin, Kame'enui, & Sugai, 1993; Mayer, 1998; Sprick et al., 1992; Sugai & Horner, 1999; Taylor-Greene et al., 1997).

School Purpose Statement

Every school should have a statement that communicates its primary behavioral and academic purpose and values. The statement of purpose describes the explicit focus, values, and outcomes of the school's discipline system and serves as the central theme of the overall school-wide discipline system and operation. A statement of purpose should (a) be stated positively and succinctly; (b) focus on all staff, all students, and all settings; and (c) focus on academic and behavioral outcomes. For example, the purpose statement at Ikuma Elementary School follows:

Purpose Statement
At Ikuma Elementary School, we are a community of learners. We are here to learn, grow, and become good citizens.

School-Wide Behavior Expectations

Schools should establish clearly defined and positively stated behavioral expectations that operationalize the school's statement of purpose and communicate what students should do to be successful across the range of contexts at school. Behavioral expectations are verbal rule statements that provide a focus for consistent communications between all students, staff, and family members. These rule statements support a community in which all members have clear understandings of what is expected of themselves and others in all school settings.

Expectations should be stated positively (i.e., communicate what students should do rather than what they should not do). No more than five rules should be specified, and each expectation should be comprised of a few common words (e.g., "Respect the Environment") so students and staff members can remember them easily. All staff and students should be familiar with school-wide expectations, which should be part of the language used to provide students feedback about meeting those expectations.

Taylor-Greene et al. (1997) provided an example of one middle school's school-wide behavior expectations called the "high five." These expectations served as the foundation for student discipline at school: (a) Be Respectful, (b) Be Responsible, (c) Be There—Be Ready, (d) Follow Directions, and (e) Keep Hands and Feet to Self. At Ikuma Elementary School, four school-wide behavioral expectations were developed by the leadership team and centered upon the theme of "respect":

Ikuma Elementary School Behavioral Expectations
1. Respect Ourselves
2. Respect Property
3. Respect Others
4. Respect Learning

Teaching Behavioral Expectations

Simply developing, stating, and posting school-wide behavior expectations are unlikely to have an effect on student or staff behavior. School-wide expectations must be taught explicitly to all students across a range of situations, including classroom settings. Teaching school-wide behavior expectations promotes a positive school climate that sets the stage for effective classroom management.

School-wide behavioral expectations are taught in the same manner as academic skills: show/tell/model, guided practice, and monitor and positively reinforce in natural

School-wide expectations must be taught to all students for a range of settings, including the playground.

context. Lesson plans should be developed to assist staff members by providing (a) positively stated behavioral definitions for each behavioral expectation; (b) specific observable behavior examples for each expectation in typical school settings; (c) contrasts between positive and negative examples; (d) opportunities for teaching to occur in natural settings; (e) opportunities for students to practice the expectation in controlled and natural settings; (f) prompts (reminders and precorrections) on displays of behaviors in natural settings and contexts; (g) feedback (corrections and positive acknowledgments) on displays of behaviors in natural contexts and settings; and (h) continuous evaluation of the effectiveness, efficiency, and relevance of the design and delivery of the instruction. At Ikuma Elementary School, the teaching matrix illustrated in Table 10.1 illustrates how examples were used to teach behavioral expectations across multiple school contexts.

Continuum of Procedures for Encouraging Expectations

If newly taught behavioral expectations are to be acquired with high accuracy, occur more often in the future, and maintain over time without adult assistance, students must receive positive feedback/acknowledgments (i.e., positive reinforcement) for behaviors that reflect school-wide expectations. At the school-wide level, a range or con-

TABLE 10.1   Behavior Expectation Teaching Matrix at Ikuma School

	Classroom	Lunchroom	Bus	Hallway	Playground
Respect Others	Use inside voice Wait until others are finished	Eat your own food Clean up your area	Stay in your seat Use inside voice	Stay to the right Use inside voice	Wait your turn Follow game rules
Respect Property	Recycle paper Return textbooks	Return trays and utensils	Keep feet on floor Sit appropriately	Put trash in can Stay on walkways	Return equipment at the bell
Respect Self	Do your best Ask for assistance	Wash your hands Take lunch box home	Be on time	Use your words	Have a plan
Respect Learning	Do assignments first Read instructions before starting	——	——	——	——

tinuum of strategies should be established to encourage behavior expectations. When formalized, this continuum of strategies (a) encourages prosocial interactions between students and staff members, (b) contributes to establishment of a positive school climate, (c) serves as a reminder to staff members to shift attention from negative to positive behavior, and (d) communicates to students that prosocial behaviors are valued.

Students and staff and family members should define the operating features of this continuum of strategies. In some cases, verbal praise and other social acknowledgments are sufficient and appropriate. In many situations, tangible objects (e.g., paper tokens, tickets, certificates) are used symbolically to acknowledge a student's rule-following behaviors. The object should be chronologically, contextually, and culturally appropriate; however, the actual object itself is relatively unimportant. What is important is the event itself in which a positive student-staff member interaction occurs. The goal is to follow displays of appropriate behavior with positive social acknowledgments to increase the likelihood that the behaviors will occur again in the future.

After positive reinforcers or acknowledgments are determined, school staff should specify (a) when reinforcers should be delivered, (b) who should deliver them, (c) how often they should be used, (d) how many should be given, and (e) where they should be delivered. Table 10.2 illustrates how staff at Ikuma School operationalized their continuum of procedures for strengthening rule following behavior.

It is important to remember that reinforcers not only represent a symbolic acknowledgment for the student, but they also serve as a reminder to staff members to acknowledge rule-following behavior at least as often as they do rule-violating behavior. Effective and prosocial learning environments tend to be characterized by rates of positive interactions four to eight times higher than rates of negative interactions between

TABLE 10.2 Positive Reinforcement Procedures for Encouraging Rule-Following Behaviors at Ikuma School

What	When	By Whom	How Often	How Many	Where
Positive Office Referrals (see form)	Whenever a student provides an exemplary display of a school-wide behavioral expectation	All staff	Each occurrence	5–6 per day per teacher	Anywhere at school
Verbal praise	Continuously and contingently whenever a student displays behavior related to school-wide behavioral expectations	All staff	As often as possible	No maximum number per teacher	Anywhere at school
"Gotchas" (see slip)	Continuously and contingently whenever a student displays behavior related to school-wide expectations in *nonclassroom settings*	All staff, but especially supervisors, teaching assistants, cafeteria workers, bus drivers, and administrators	As often as possible	No maximum per teacher	Nonclassroom settings: hallways, bus loading areas, playgrounds, common areas, cafeteria
Classroom acknowledgments (see individual classroom management plans)	Continuously and contingently whenever a student displays behavior related to school-wide expectations in *classroom settings*	All classroom teachers, teaching assistants	At least hourly	No maximum per classroom	Classroom settings during instruction, transitions, unstructured activities
"Substitute Specials" (see slip)	Whenever a substitute teacher observes a student engaged in a behavior related to school-wide expectations	All substitute teachers	At any time	At least 3 every hour	Anywhere at school, especially in classrooms
"Office Specials" (bumper sticker, school pencil, store discount coupons, lunch with principal)	Whenever office staff recognize students for especially noteworthy behavioral growth, progress, or displays	Office staff: principal, assistant principal, counselor, secretaries, office assistants	At any time	At least one per grade level per day	Anywhere at school

students and staff members (Latham, 1992; Paine et al., 1983). The following guidelines are useful as procedures are developed and implemented:

1. Shift systematically from (a) other- to self-delivered reinforcers, (b) frequent to infrequent delivery, (c) predictable to unpredictable delivery, and (d) tangible to social reinforcers.
2. Individualize as much as possible to accommodate individual differences and diversity.
3. Focus on building person-to-person relationships, especially around displays of rule-following behaviors.
4. Strive for six to eight positive acknowledgments and interactions for every single negative interaction.
5. Label the behavior for which the positive acknowledgment is intended.

Continuum of Procedures for Discouraging Rule Violations

In many schools, giving high priority to establishing and implementing procedures to discourage rule-violating behaviors is easy, because problem behaviors interfere with teaching and learning and draw teacher and student attention. In fact, most students in schools are quite responsive to simple and universal procedures designed to inhibit problem behaviors because they (a) are fluent with rule-following behaviors, (b) have received positive acknowledgments in the past for rule following, and (c) find typical school negative consequences sufficiently aversive. Therefore, simply telling and occasionally reminding these students of the rules and the consequences if they violate the rules is sufficient.

However, approaches that rely solely on the use of procedures to discourage rule-violating behaviors tend to be associated with short-term control and situation-specific inhibition of problem behaviors. In these situations, school environment and climate are perceived as controlling and negative. These approaches are insufficient, because they do not teach and encourage appropriate alternatives to problem behaviors. In some cases, occurrences of problem behavior increase in frequency and intensity when schools emphasize a punishment-based approach, especially for students who are at-risk for problem behavior or who already have emotional and behavioral disorders.

Given the above concerns, the following guidelines should be considered when establishing procedures to discourage rule-violating problem behavior:

1. Establish a clear sequence of consequences for repeated or intensifying rule-violating behavior. In particular, establish a clear distinction between those problem behaviors handled by classroom and supervisory staff and those referred to the administrative staff. Table 10.3 illustrates how Ikuma School distinguished between different types of problem behavior.
2. Use the least aversive but most effective consequence. No consequence should cause personal humiliation or emotional or physical pain or harm. Consequences should help the student discriminate between acceptable

TABLE 10.3 Procedure for Discouraging Rule Violations at Ikuma School

Level	Examples	Sample Consequences	Procedural Guidelines
I: Minor Behaviors that require immediate response and no follow-up	• Running • Unsafe/rough play • Littering • Unexcused tardy • Classroom disruption • Nondirected profanity • Chewing gum • Play fighting • Not following staff directions	• Verbal correction • Loss of privileges • In-classroom detention • 1–3 minute timeout	• Inform parent(s) and counselor after second occurrence • Go to Major on third occurrence of minor
II: Major Behaviors that increase in frequency and/or intensity, require immediate follow-up	• 3-peat Minor • Cheating • Unexcused absence • Overt noncompliance	• Verbal correction • Loss of privileges • Detention • Behavior contract • 1–5 minute timeout • In-school detention	• Complete Major Incident Report for each occurrence • Inform parent, counselor, and office staff on each occurrence • Request Student Assistance Team meeting on third occurrence and develop individualized behavior support plan • Request parent meeting on second occurrence
III: Administrative Behaviors that are chronic, disrupt teaching and learning process, and violate dignity, well-being, and safety of others	• Stealing • Fighting/assault/physical aggression • Vandalism • Weapon possession • Illegal substance possession/use • Intimidation/verbal threats • Harassment • Directed profanity • Repeated noncompliance	• In-school suspension • Out-of-school suspension • Restitution • Behavior contract	• Contact local law enforcement agency if civic/state laws violated • Document event and complete Major Incident Report for each occurrence • Develop individualized behavior support plan

and unacceptable behavior and be associated with decreases in future displays of the behavior.

3. Adopt a function-based approach to intervention development and implementation. When displays of problem behavior (or any behavior, for that matter) recur, they often serve a communicative function or purpose for the student. For example, the student may wish to gain access or get something (peer or adult attention, activities, tangible objects) or to escape or avoid something (peer or adult attention, tasks/activities). Intervention

selection should be based on assessment information that narrows the possible function of the problem behavior.

4. Collect data and use clear decision rules to assess the effectiveness of a given consequence. If a specific consequence is not associated with an acceptable decrease or elimination of the behavior, then a different consequence should be considered. A simple "3-peat rule" (third occurrence) should bring about a team-based problem-solving meeting in which a more individualized behavior support plan is considered.

5. Teach, emphasize, and encourage more acceptable alternative behaviors whenever problem behaviors occur. Students must learn about more acceptable ways of behaving, and displays of acceptable behaviors should be associated with immediate and meaningful positive acknowledgments or reinforcement.

6. Utilize team-based behavior support approaches for problem behaviors that are chronic and/or intense. This team should be comprised of the student, family members, teachers, and individuals with behavioral expertise. In some cases, more specialized resources (e.g., mental health) may be required to develop and implement effective and comprehensive behavior support plans.

Procedures for Monitoring the Effectiveness of the School-Wide Discipline Plan

Information about the effect of implementing a school-wide discipline plan is needed to answer a number of important questions (Lewis-Palmer, Sugai, & Larson, 1999; Sugai, Sprague, Horner, & Walker, 2000; Tobin et al., 1996; Todd, Horner, Sugai, & Sprague, 1999): (a) Is the school-wide discipline system working? (b) What modifications (additions, deletions, enhancements) are needed to improve the effectiveness and efficiency of the school-wide discipline system? (c) What particular problems (e.g., behaviors, settings, groups of students) need to be addressed?

A naturally occurring and available source of information is discipline data (e.g., behavioral incident reports, office discipline referrals). For these data to be useful, three important conditions must be met. First, all aspects of the school-wide system should be clearly defined, taught, and implemented. When descriptions of rule violations, consequences, and procedures are clearly defined and consistently implemented, the data are more trustworthy for decision making. Second, procedures for collecting, storing, and summarizing data must be efficient and relevant. If a data collection system takes more than 5% of a staff member's time, it is not likely to be maintained. Third, structures and routines should be in place for reviewing and interpreting the data and for developing meaningful recommendations from the data.

Although office discipline referrals can serve as general indicators of the status of school-wide discipline, referrals have limitations. First, each referral involves three individuals: (a) student, (b) teacher, and (c) office administrator. Each office discipline referral may be affected by whether the student engages (and gets caught!) in a problem behavior, whether a staff member observes the behavior and elects to process it, and whether an office administrator processes it. Because all three of these individuals contribute to the processing and recording of a behavioral incident, any one of them can also inhibit or halt the process.

Second, most school-wide discipline systems focus on students who violate school-wide rules by engaging in behaviors that are visibly disruptive and overtly infringe upon activities of others (i.e., externalizing behaviors). Behavior support teams are formed to develop and implement positive behavior support plans for these students. Some students do not violate school rules but are equally in need of behavior supports. Office discipline referral systems tend not to identify students who avoid social interactions or fail to develop relationships (e.g., social withdrawal, depression), spend excessive amounts of time alone, engage in situation-inappropriate behaviors (e.g., verbal/visual hallucinations), display behaviors that are personally dangerous (e.g., suicide attempts, self-injury). Schools must establish monitoring systems that screen for students who internalize as well as externalize problems.

Because of the limitations of office referrals, staff members are advised to collect multiple types of data (e.g., attendance, tardies, bus citations) from multiple sources (e.g., teachers, playground monitors, parents, students). Students who experience academic failure should also be monitored, because academic failure can be associated with occurrences of behavior problems.

At Ikuma School, office discipline referral data are shared at monthly faculty meetings and are used by the school-climate committee to judge the status of school-wide discipline efforts, identify problem situations that might require attention, and screen for individuals who require more intensive behavior supports. A sample of Ikuma School graphs is shown in Figure 10.4.

IMPLEMENTATION OF SCHOOL-WIDE DISCIPLINE SYSTEMS WITHIN THE 180–DAY PLAN

In this chapter we have stressed the value of creating and sustaining school-wide discipline systems, and these systems serve as foundations for behavior and classroom management for all students and staff in all settings. This approach has emphasized the importance of (a) interactions between instructional and behavioral programming, (b) systems that support the adoption and sustained use of evidence-based practices, (c) data-based and team-oriented decision-making routines and procedures, (d) a continuum of behavior support that is based on a three-tiered prevention model, and (e) direct teaching and encouraging (positive reinforcement) school-wide behavioral expectations. Clearly, many similarities exist between classroom instructional management and school-wide discipline systems.

In this section, we describe how establishment and implementation of a school-wide discipline system fits the 180-day plan approach. Six distinct stages should be considered: (a) establish a need and give priority to development of a school-wide discipline system, (b) establish structures for developing the discipline system, (c) identify and modify evidence-based practices that operationalize and directly address the school's outcome objectives and establish the basic components of a school-wide discipline system, (d) develop an action plan for the high fidelity implementation of the action plan and system over the school year, (e) implement the action

Average Number of Referrals per Day per Month

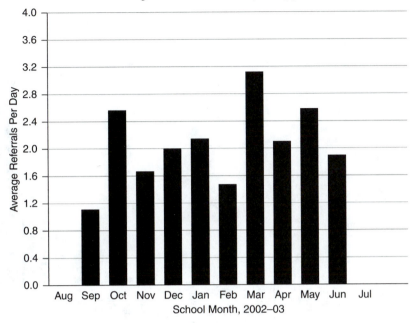

Number of Referrals by Problem Behavior Type

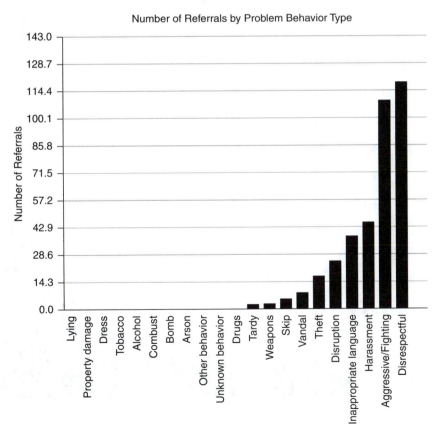

FIGURE 10.4 Samples of office discipline referral graphs from Ikuma School. Continued.

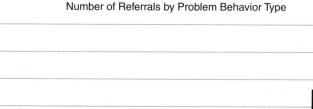

Number of Referrals by Problem Behavior Type

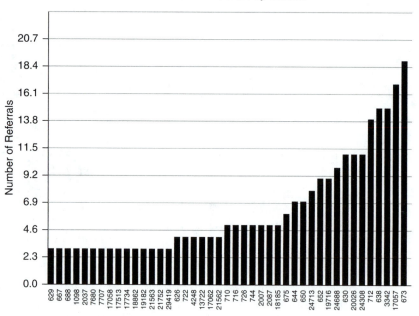

Number of Referrals by Student

FIGURE 10.4 Samples of office discipline referral graphs from Ikuma School. Continued.

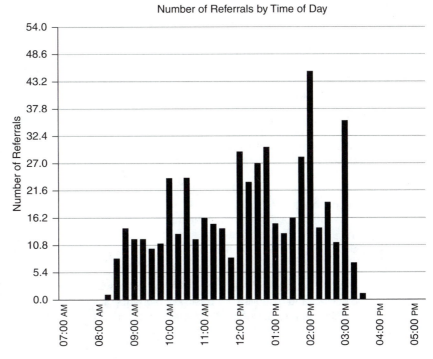

FIGURE 10.4 Continued.

plan for establishing the school-wide discipline system, and (f) develop monitoring systems to track and evaluate the implementation of the school-wide discipline system. The following checklist provides a summary of the key features of this developmental process (see Figure 10.5).

Though some of the activities occur at multiple times (e.g., collecting information), the six stages can generally be organized into the same chronological model used with instructional management: (a) before implementation, (b) during implementation, and (c) after implementation.

Before Implementation

A mistake that schools and classroom teachers make is adoption and implementation of a practice without considering if (a) a need exists for the practice, (b) the practice should be modified to enhance the fit between the problem context and the main features of the practice, or (c) the practice is accepted by staff members. To maximize the impact, efficiency, and relevance of implementation efforts, schools must invest in a structured period of careful development and planning before engaging in actual implementation of school-wide discipline systems. This planning focuses on establishing the organizational structures to guide implementation, specifying the need and priority for implementation, identifying and modifying evidence-based practices, and securing staff agreements to go forward with a given action plan.

1. Establish structures for developing a school-wide discipline system.
   a. _____ Establish a team with school-wide representation (e.g., administrator, grade-level representative, counselor, parent, student, cafeteria worker, playground supervisor).
   b. _____ Collect school-climate and behavior-related data (e.g., office discipline referrals, attendance, tardies, behavioral incidence reports, students failing classes/grades).
   c. _____ Secure administrator participation and support.

2. Establish a need and give priority to the development of a school-wide discipline system.
   a. _____ Review school-climate and behavior data to determine the status of school-wide discipline and areas of strengths and weaknesses.
   b. _____ Develop statements that indicate nature of need and level of priority (high, medium, low).
   c. _____ Specify activity and outcome objectives relative to enhancing school-wide discipline (i.e., components and processes).
   d. _____ Present data and recommendations to school faculty and secure participation, agreement, and support of at least 80% of staff.
   e. _____ Secure agreement and support by administrator and administrative team (e.g., site council, faculty senate).

3. Identify and modify evidence-based practices that operationalize and directly address the school's objectives and establish the basic components of a school-wide discipline system.
   a. _____ Identify, screen, and select research-validated practices that directly address the school's objectives on school-wide discipline.
   b. _____ Modify, if necessary, practices to fit the unique features of the school and its students, families, and staff members.

4. Develop an action plan for the high fidelity implementation of the school-wide discipline system over the school year.
   a. _____ Identify existing initiatives, activities, committees, practices, resources that could be utilized, modified, and/or integrated into the action plan.
   b. _____ List steps and requirements for actual implementation of the practice.
   c. _____ Develop timeline for preparing and implementing the practice.
   d. _____ Consider changes to and/or continuation of implementation efforts based on school calendar (i.e., beginning, during, end of school year) and natural change points (e.g., grading periods, holidays, breaks).
   e. _____ Provide training opportunities that maximize staff fluency with practice.
   f. _____ Secure and organize resources (e.g., time, personnel, materials) needed to support implementation steps.
   g. _____ Develop supporting implementation materials (e.g., scripts, checklists).
   h. _____ Implement training activities.
   i. _____ Develop mechanism for weekly review of implementation outcomes and modification of implementation strategies based on review.

5. Implement action plan for the school-wide discipline system.
   a. _____ Monitor fidelity/accuracy of implementation by staff members.
   b. _____ Collect and review school-climate data to track impact of implementation efforts.
   c. _____ Provide weekly positive and constructive feedback to staff on implementation efforts.

FIGURE 10.5 Checklist for developing a school-wide discipline system. Continued.

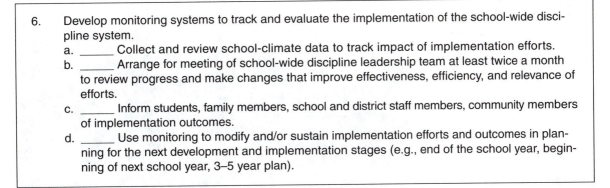

6. Develop monitoring systems to track and evaluate the implementation of the school-wide discipline system.
   a. _____ Collect and review school-climate data to track impact of implementation efforts.
   b. _____ Arrange for meeting of school-wide discipline leadership team at least twice a month to review progress and make changes that improve effectiveness, efficiency, and relevance of efforts.
   c. _____ Inform students, family members, school and district staff members, community members of implementation outcomes.
   d. _____ Use monitoring to modify and/or sustain implementation efforts and outcomes in planning for the next development and implementation stages (e.g., end of the school year, beginning of next school year, 3–5 year plan).

FIGURE 10.5 Continued.

The notion of "before implementation" should be conceptualized temporally and organizationally in three ways. First, schools engaging in a new or major renovation of a school-wide discipline system should invest in planning and set-up activities in the spring of the school year, during the summer months, and the week just before school begins. In this process, administrative structures and procedures are established; materials are identified, assessed, and modified; school staff are trained to high levels of fluency; implementation scripts and prompts are prepared; data systems are developed, and data are collected and analyzed.

Second, within school-wide discipline systems, new procedures are developed, modifications are made, and natural transition points are identified (e.g., ending of grading periods, just before holiday breaks). Structured planning activities are valuable investments for maximizing efficacy of initial implementation efforts and the quality and quantity of outcomes. For example, at Ikuma School, anticipation of spring vacation in March and the beginning of a new grading period have been associated with increases in student-to-student conflicts in nonclassroom settings. To prepare for these challenges, school staff plan for the reinstatement of regular hallway "sweeps" in which more adults are present and provide higher numbers of positive acknowledgments for displays of expectation-following behaviors.

Third, when schools identify predictable or longstanding problem situations or "hot spots," "precorrections" (Colvin, Sugai, & Patching, 1993; Lewis, Colvin, & Sugai, in press) should be provided. A precorrection is presented just before entering a situation in which problem behaviors or rule violations are highly probable. For example, entering the school building when the first bell rings has been a trouble spot at Ikuma School. The problem is that too many students and parents enter the common area of the school through one set of double doors. To precorrect for this, three staff members regularly situate themselves outside the doors and increase their social contacts and greetings before the first bell rings. The number of staff members is doubled the week before holidays and at the end of the school year. The effect is that movement through the doors is more orderly, slower, friendlier, and safer.

Students must be proactively taught appropriate behavior in "hot spots," where behavior problems occur frequently.

During Implementation

Many problems can be avoided with careful planning. However, to maximize success, schools must establish structures and engage in strategies that emphasize ongoing efficient implementation. A number of basic strategies should be considered. First, data on student outcomes and staff implementation should begin immediately upon initiation of a practice and continue throughout the use of the practice. Initially, these data may be collected daily, then weekly or monthly as implementation stability and maximum outcomes are achieved. For example, at Ikuma School, behavior incident reports are collected, summarized, and analyzed daily during the first month of school. After school-wide expectations have been taught and procedures for encouraging and acknowledging related behaviors have become consistent, weekly summarization and analysis activities are scheduled.

Second, opportunities to evaluate the accuracy and fluency of implementation efforts should be scheduled early and regularly. Implementation glitches and misrules can usually be identified within the first 2 or 3 days of implementation. If these inaccuracies are not corrected early, they become habits that are difficult to change, and they minimize positive outcomes. We recommend schools schedule reviews of implementation accuracy daily for the first 3 days of implementation and then weekly and eventually monthly thereafter until data on student performance suggest that maximum outcomes are being realized.

Third, staff members should receive feedback on a regular basis about the impact and quality of their implementation efforts. This feedback should be based on outcome data (e.g., behavior incident reports, attendance, tardies) and should address two areas. Feedback should be positively "corrective" (i.e., based on outcome data and focused on ways to improve implementation). Most importantly, feedback should positively acknowledge staff activities, contributions, participation, and outcomes. These positive acknowledgments (a) can originate from team members, administrators, families, and/or students; (b) should be appropriate to the school culture and context; and (c) should be provided on a regular basis (daily, monthly, quarterly). Positive feedback is especially important to increase the likelihood effective practices are sustained with high accuracy over time, places, and individuals. At Ikuma School, for example, the school climate team provides a monthly report on behavior incident reports at the faculty meeting and solicits suggestions on how outcomes might be improved. The team celebrates successes and accomplishments of students (individual, classroom, grade level) and staff (individual, grade level, specialty area). Team members and administrators provide daily and weekly positive social recognition to staff members engaging in school-wide discipline procedures, making significant contributions toward improving the school climate, or who need a "boost" to continue involvement.

After Implementation

Maximizing the efficiency and impact of school-wide discipline efforts also involves a planned review of the outcomes. Like "before implementation," information collection and review can happen at naturally occurring times (e.g., grading periods), at the end of major implementation efforts (e.g., teaching school-wide expectations), and at the end of smaller units of time (e.g., daily, weekly) or activities (e.g., after an assembly, after a lesson). The goal is to collect and review information that addresses the following implementation questions:

1. Are we making adequate progress toward our short- and long-term outcome goals?
2. What information and data should we continue to collect, stop collecting, and/or begin collecting?
3. What changes or adjustments need to be made in the short- and long-term outcomes of our action plan?
4. What modifications in practice, support, and procedure are needed to improve the effectiveness of our current efforts?
5. Can we improve the efficiency (e.g., time, resources, personnel, materials) of our current efforts?
6. What can we eliminate and still maintain a satisfactory rate of progress?
7. Who is being affected by implementation efforts and outcomes (students, families, staff, others)?
8. Who should be informed about our progress and successes (students, families, staff, district administrators)?
9. How should the school celebrate progress and accomplishments to date?

Based on answers to these questions, decisions to continue, modify, or discontinue can be made. In addition, positive acknowledgments and reinforcers can be provided to increase the likelihood of efficient, high quality, and sustained implementation efforts. For example, at Ikuma School, the school climate committee discovered that behavioral incidents in the common area next to the cafeteria and gymnasium were increasing in intensity and frequency and that the number of students engaging in major rule violations was doubling each week. They also found that fewer staff members were supervising actively, and staff members present were having twice as many negative interactions with students as positive. Over half the students reported they had been harassed verbally by a peer in the previous week. By projecting current rates of problem behaviors, the school team predicted it would not achieve the year-end goal. In fact, behavior rates would be similar to the beginning of the school year. Based on this information, the school team revised its approach to active supervision, changed the nature of acknowledgments given to students in the common area, and developed staff teams to increase accuracy and consistency of implementation.

SUMMARY

The purpose of this chapter is to describe essential elements of an effective school-wide discipline system and highlight the important role a discipline system serves in supporting classroom instruction and behavior management. We have underscored the need for an instructional approach to school-wide management and described the necessary components and implementation features of successful school-wide discipline systems. In summary, careful attention should be focused on the following major concepts and themes:

1. Establish a system and continuum of school-wide behavior support to enable effective adoption and sustained implementation of evidence-based practices of instructional, behavior, and classroom management.
2. Build school-wide discipline systems for all students and staff across all school settings.
3. Integrate school-wide, nonclassroom, and classroom behavior management practices into a common approach.
4. Emphasize an instructional approach in which behavioral expectations are defined clearly, taught directly, monitored continuously, and encouraged regularly and overtly.
5. Balance procedures for discouraging rule violations with a continuum of procedures for encouraging prosocial behavioral expectations.
6. Provide positive school-wide discipline practices and systems to all students, but intensify and specialize behavior support for individual students who are unresponsive.
7. Collect and use data to guide decision making.
8. Emphasize the prevention of problem behavior by teaching prosocial skills to all students, attempting to neutralize risk factors and precorrecting for predictable problem behaviors.
9. Attend to training and support needs of staff members who put into operation school-wide discipline and behavior support systems.
10. Work as a team to establish and maintain an effective, efficient, and relevant host environment.
11. Work smarter by investing minutes and effort into a small number of practices and initiatives that are outcome driven, have a high likelihood of working, and are implementable with a high level of accuracy.

CHAPTER ACTIVITIES

1. Visit a local school and ask for their student/parent handbook and school-wide discipline plan and critique their approach using (a) components of a school wide-system and (b) implementation using the 180-day plan discussed in the chapter.

2. Develop a separate set of school behavior expectations for an elementary, middle, and high school. Discuss how you determined each of the behavior expectations and the merits of your selections.

3. Define and discuss the concept "continuum of behavior support" as it is used by the authors. Give specific examples of behavior supports that reflect the continuum of intervention.

REFERENCES

Alberto, P., & Troutman, A. (1999). *Applied behavior analysis for teachers* (5th ed.). Upper Saddle River, NJ: Merrill/Prentice Hall.

Colvin, G., Kame'enui, E. J., & Sugai, G. (1993). School-wide and classroom management: Reconceptualizing the integration and management of students with behavior problems in general education. *Education and Treatment of Children, 16,* 361–381.

Colvin, G., & Lazar, M. (1997). *The effective elementary classroom: Managing for success.* Longmont, CO: Sopris West.

Colvin, G., & Sprick, R. (1999). Providing administrative leadership for effective behavior support: Ten strategies for principals. *Effective School Practices, 17*(4), 65–71.

Colvin, G., Sugai, G., Good, R. H., III, & Lee, Y. (1997). Using active supervision and precorrection to improve transition behaviors in an elementary school. *School Psychology Quarterly, 12,* 344–363.

Colvin, G., Sugai, G., & Patching, W. (1993). Pre-correction: An instructional strategy for managing predictable behavior problems. *Intervention, 28,* 143–150.

DePry, R. L., & Sugai, G. (2002). The effect of active supervision and precorrection on minor behavioral incidents in a sixth grade general education classroom. *Journal of Behavioral Education, 11,* 255–267.

Gottfredson, D. C., Gottfredson, G. D., & Hybl, L. G. (1993). Managing adolescent behavior: A multiyear, multischool study. *American Educational Research Journal, 30*(1), 179–215.

Gresham, F. M., Sugai, G., & Horner, R. H. (2001). Social competence of students with high-incidence disabilities: Conceptual and methodological issues in interpreting outcomes of social skills training. *Exceptional Children, 67,* 331–344.

Gunter, P. L., Denny, R. K., Jack, S. L., Shores, R. E., & Nelson, C. M. (1993). Aversive stimuli in academic interactions between students with serious emotional disturbance and their teachers. *Behavioral Disorders, 19,* 265–274.

Gunter, P. L., Jack, S. L., DePaepe, P., Reed, T. M., & Harrison, J. (1994). Effects of challenging behaviors of students with EBD on teacher instructional behavior. *Preventing School Failure, 38,* 35–46.

Gunter, P. L., Jack, S. L., Shores, R. E., Carrel, D. E., & Flowers, J. (1993). Lag sequential analysis as a tool for functional analysis of student disruptive behavior in classrooms. *Journal of Emotional and Behavioral Disorders, 1,* 138–148.

Jack, S. L., Shores, R. E., Denny, R. K., Gunter, P. L., DeBriere, T., & DePaepe, P. (1996). An analysis of the relationship of teachers' reported use of classroom management strategies on types of classroom interactions. *Journal of Behavioral Education, 6,* 67–87.

Kartub, D. T., Taylor-Greene, S., March, R. E., & Horner, R. H. (2000). Reducing hallway noise: A systems approach. *Journal of Positive Behavioral Interventions, 2,* 179–182.

Langland, S., Lewis-Palmer, T., & Sugai, G. (1998). Teaching respect in the classroom: An instructional approach. *Journal of Behavioral Education, 8,* 245–261.

Latham, G. (1992). Interacting with at-risk children: The positive position. *Principal, 72*(1), 26–30.

Lewis, T. J., Colvin, G., & Sugai, G. (in press). The effects of pre-correction and active supervision on the recess behavior of elementary school students. *School Psychology Quarterly.*

Lewis, T. J., & Garrison-Harrell, L. (1999). Designing setting-specific interventions within school systems of effective behavioral support. *Effective School Practices, 17,* 38–46.

Lewis, T. J., & Sugai, G. (1999). Effective behavior support: A systems approach to proactive school-wide management. *Focus on Exceptional Children, 31*(6), 1–24.

Lewis, T. J., Sugai, G., & Colvin, G. (1998). Reducing problem behavior through a school-wide system of effective behavior support: Investigation of a school-wide social skills training program and contextual interventions. *School Psychology Review, 27,* 446–459.

Lewis-Palmer, T., Sugai, G., & Larson, S. (1999). Using data to guide decisions about program implementation and effectiveness. *Effective School Practices, 17*(4), 47–53.

Mayer, R. G. (1998). Constructive discipline for school personnel. *Education and Treatment of Children, 22,* 36–54.

Mayer, R. G., Butterworth, T., Nafpaktitis, M., & Sulzer-Azaroff, B. (1983). Preventing school vandalism and improving discipline: A three year study. *Journal of Applied Behavior Analysis, 16,* 355–369.

Nelson, J. R. (1996). Designing schools to meet the needs of students who exhibit disruptive behavior. *Journal of Emotional and Behavioral Disorders, 4,* 147–161.

Nelson, J. R., & Colvin, G. (1996). Designing supportive school environments. *Special Services in the Schools, 11*(1/2) 169–186.

Nelson, J. R., Colvin, G., & Smith, D. J. (1996). The effects of setting clear standards on students' social behavior in common areas of the school. *The Journal of At-Risk Issues, Summer/Fall,* 10–17.

Nelson, J. R., Martella, R., & Galand, B. (1998). The effects of teaching school expectations and establishing a consistent consequence on formal office disciplinary actions. *Journal of Emotional and Behavioral Disorders, 6,* 153–161.

O'Neill, R. E., Horner, R. H., Albin, R. W., Storey, K., & Sprague, J. R. (1997). *Functional analysis of problem behavior: A practical assessment guide* (2nd ed.). Pacific Grove, CA: Brooks/Cole.

Paine, S. C., Radicchi, J., Rosellini, L. C., Deutchman, L., & Darch, C. B. (1983). *Structuring your classroom for academic success.* Champaign, IL: Research Press.

Shores, R. E., Jack, S. L., Gunter, P. L., Ellis, D. N., DeBriere, T. J., & Wehby, J. H. (1993). Classroom interactions of children with behavior disorders. *Journal of Emotional and Behavioral Disorders, 1,* 27–39.

Skiba, R. J., & Peterson, R. L. (1999). The dark side of zero tolerance: Can punishment lead to safe schools? *Phi Delta Kappan, 80,* 372–382.

Sprick, R., Sprick, M., & Garrison, M. (1992). *Foundations: Developing positive school-wide discipline policies.* Longmont, CO: Sopris West.

Sugai, G., & Horner, R. (1994). Including students with severe behavior problems in general education settings: Assumptions, challenges, and solutions. In J. Marr, G. Sugai, & G. Tindal (Eds.), *The Oregon Conference Monograph* (Vol. 7; pp. 102–120). Eugene, OR: University of Oregon.

Sugai, G., & Horner, R. H. (1999). Discipline and behavioral support: Preferred processes and practices. *Effective School Practices, 17*(4), 10–22.

Sugai, G., & Horner, R. H. (1999–2000). Including the functional behavioral assessment technology in schools (invited special issue). *Exceptionality, 8,* 145–148.

Sugai, G., Horner, R. H., Dunlap, G. Hieneman, M., Lewis, T. J., Nelson, C. M., Scott, T., Liaupsin, C., Sailor, W., Turnbull, A. P., Turnbull, H. R., III, Wickham, D., Reuf, M., & Wilcox, B. (2000). Applying positive behavioral support and functional behavioral assessment in schools. *Journal of Positive Behavioral Interventions, 2,* 131–143.

Sugai, G., Lewis-Palmer, T., & Hagan-Burke, S. (1999–2000). Overview of the FBA process. *Exceptionalities, 8*(3), 149–160.

Sugai, G., Sprague, J. R., Horner, R. H., & Walker, H. M. (2000). Preventing school violence: The use of office discipline referrals to assess and monitor school-wide discipline interventions. *Journal of Emotional and Behavioral Disorders, 8,* 94–101.

Taylor-Green, S., Brown, D., Nelson L., Longton, J., Gassman, T., Cohen, J., Swartz, J., Horner, R. H., Sugai, G., & Hall, S. (1997). School-wide behavior support: Starting the year off right. *Journal of Behavioral Education, 7,* 99–112.

Tobin, T., Sugai, G., & Colvin, G. (1996). Patterns in middle school discipline records. *Journal of Emotional and Behavioral Disorders, 4,* 82–94.

Todd, A., Horner, R., Sugai, G., & Colvin, G. (1999). Individualizing school-wide discipline for students with chronic problem behaviors: A team approach. *Effective School Practices, 17*(4), 72–82.

Todd, A. W., Horner, R. H., Sugai, G., & Sprague, J. (1999). Effective behavior support: Strengthening school-wide systems through a team-based approach. *Effective School Practices, 17*(4), 23–37.

Walker, H. M., Horner, R. H., Sugai, G., Bullis, M., Sprague, J. R., Bricker, D., & Kaufman, M. J. (1996). Integrated approaches to preventing antisocial behavior patterns among school-age children and youth. *Journal of Emotional and Behavioral Disorders, 4,* 193–256.

Wehby, J. H., Dodge, K. A., Valente, E., & Conduct Problems Prevention Research Group. (1993). School behavior of first grade children identified as at-risk for development of conduct problems. *Behavioral Disorders, 19,* 67–78.

Wehby, J. H., Symons, F. M., & Canale, J. A., (1998). Teaching practices in classrooms for students with emotional and behavioral disorders: Discrepancies between recommendations and observations. *Behavioral Disorders, 24*(1), 51–56.

Wehby, J. H., Symons, F. J., & Shores, R. E. (1995). A descriptive analysis of aggressive behavior in classrooms for children with emotional and behavioral disorders. *Behavioral Disorders, 20,* 87–105.

Wolery, M. R., Bailey, D. P., Jr., & Sugai, G. (1988). *Effective teaching: Principles and procedures of applied behavior analysis with exceptional students.* Boston, MA: Allyn & Bacon.

Zins, J. E., & Ponti, C. R. (1990). Best practices in school-based consultation. In A. Thomas and J. Grimes (Eds.), *Best Practices in School Psychology, II* (pp. 673–694). Washington, DC: National Association of School Psychologists.

Name Index

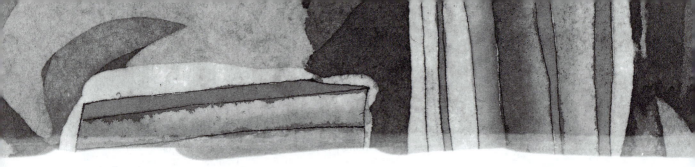

Subject Index